GOD, D[...]

MERIDIAN

Crossing Aesthetics

Werner Hamacher

& David E. Wellbery

Editors

Translated by
Bettina Bergo

Edited and Annotated
by Jacques Rolland

Stanford
University
Press

Stanford
California

GOD, DEATH, AND TIME

Emmanuel Levinas

Support for the translation was provided by the French Ministry of Culture.

Originally published in French in 1993 under the title *Dieu, la mort et le temps* © Editions Grasset & Fasquelle, 1993

Stanford University Press
Stanford, California

Printed in the United States of America on acid-free, archival-quality paper.

Library of Congress Cataloging-in-Publication Data

Lévinas, Emmanuel.
    [Dieu, la mort et le temps. English]
    God, death, and time / Emmanuel Lévinas ; translated by Bettina Bergo.
        p.   cm. — (Meridian)
    Includes bibliographical references.
    ISBN 0-8047-3665-0 (hardcover ; alk. paper) — ISBN 0-8047-3666-9
(pbk. : alk. paper)
    1. Philosophy.   2. Death.   3. Time.   4. God.   I. Title.   II. Meridian
(Stanford, Calif.)
B2430.L483 D5413   2000
194—dc21   00-059523

Original printing 2000

Last figure below indicates year of this printing:
09

Typeset by James P. Brommer
in 10.9/13 Garamond and Lithos display

Contents

Translator's Foreword

The two lecture courses published here—"Death and Time" and "God and Onto-theo-logy"—were edited and annotated by Jacques Rolland, who was a student of Emmanuel Levinas's at the University of Paris, Sorbonne. Under Levinas's direction, Rolland wrote his master's thesis on Dostoevsky (1974). The thesis was later published as *Dostoïevski et la question de l'Autre* (Lagrasse: Editions Verdier, 1983). In the 1980s, he became both friend and companion to Levinas. Rolland has edited and introduced numerous works on and by Levinas. In 1984, the third issue of the journal *Les Cahiers de la nuit surveillée*, entitled *Emmanuel Lévinas*, appeared, edited and introduced by Rolland. In the same year, he coauthored, with Silvano Petrosino, a monograph on Levinas's work entitled *La vérité nomade: Introduction à Emmanuel Lévinas* (Paris: Editions la Découverte). He edited Levinas's first original philosophical work (1932), entitled *De l'évasion* (Montpellier: Fata Morgana, 1982). With Jean Greisch, of the faculty of theology at the Institut Catholique de Paris, Rolland edited the proceedings of the colloquium at Cerisy-la-Salle (1986) devoted to Levinas. It was published under the title *Emmanuel Lévinas: L'éthique comme philosophie première* (Paris: Editions du Cerf, 1993). Most recently, Rolland published a long study of Levinas's philosophy, *Parcours de l'Autrement: Lecture d'Emmanuel Lévinas* (Paris: Presses Universitaires de France, 2000).

In the present volume, Rolland is the author of all notes in his foreword and in the lectures, aside from those notes and portions of notes indicated as mine by square brackets and the abbreviation "—Trans." In general, I have augmented his notes silently (without the use of brackets) only in regard to citations.

English quotations cited from foreign-language editions identified in the notes are my translations. Quotations cited from English editions are the work of those translators unless otherwise indicated.

I wish to extend grateful thanks to Robert Bernasconi, Carolyn Bonacci, The Center for the Humanities of Loyola College, André-Pierre Colombat, Inge Hoffmann, Lisa Hochstein, Claire Mathews-McGinnis, Michael Naas, Robert Gibbs, Adriaan Peperzak, Jean-Michel Rabaté, Gary Shapiro, Marion Wielgosz, and Edith Wyschogrod.

—Bettina Bergo

GOD, DEATH, AND TIME

Foreword

The texts we shall read here reproduce the discourse of two lecture courses taught by Emmanuel Levinas in the academic year 1975–1976. These were the last of his regular teaching duties at the Sorbonne. One of the lectures was given from 10:00 A.M. to 11:00 A.M., the other from 12:00 P.M. to 1:00 P.M., on every Friday. The lectures' proximity in time is like the materialization of their philosophical proximity. Now, a few remarks are in order, several of which will be taken up again and explicated in the Postscript to this volume.

The proximity of the two courses is explained by the fact that, although one chose the intersecting themes of death and time, while the other questioned the "word beyond measure" that is the Name of God, both courses work along the lines of the philosopher's coming to grips with the question that beats at the metaphoric heart of his thought: the interhuman relation, understood as an ethical relationship. It is on the basis of the ethical relationship that the three concepts just named *pose a question* within Levinas's written work and determine the progress of the discourse in these two series of lectures. This amounts to saying that, while they were not written out by Levinas himself, they can and should be considered an integral part of his philosophical work. Let us specify all the same that they belong to the style (in the sense in which one uses the term for a painter)—begun immediately after the publication of *Totality and Infinity* (1961)—that found its most overwhelming philosophical expression in the harsh and intrepid *Otherwise than Being, or Beyond Essence* (1974) and in a few shorter essays most of which were collected in *Of God Who Comes to Mind* (1982).[1] The reader is entitled to know (as Maurice Blanchot would say, a question of methodological probity) that these lectures should be studied in their strict connection with the texts of *this* period.

"These lectures should be studied": let us pause a moment on this point. First, it should be emphasized that, in this edition, we have carefully preserved the actual character of lectures (with references to dates, the recollection of previous lectures, the occasional foreshortening, summaries, and digressions, and, in the case of "God and Onto-theo-logy," the indefatigable recovery of the question itself), because these constitute one of the rare traces of the philosophical teaching of Professor Levinas. But it should not be imagined that this "oral teaching" contains some radical novelty— in the way that we suspect, in Plato, an oral "esoteric" doctrine that is different from the "exoteric" one, which the tradition transmitted to us. No: Levinas's case would be closer to that of Husserl, regarding whom the former considers that the unpublished material contributes nothing *new* in relation to the published works.[2] We should point out straightway, then, that the *same* thinking that was written in the books and essays mentioned above is found here. This is of no small importance, in other words, when one has to do with a thinker so attentive to the question of language and to the marvel of speech.[3] Indeed, this can be surprising when we think of Heidegger, in whom it is difficult, and perhaps ultimately useless, to distinguish between essays and lectures (to recall a title).[4]

In other words, yes: of no small importance—but here, our "other words" are doubly "otherwise." Indeed, we must point out to the reader, before he or she engages in the reading of these pages, what *differentiates* the two courses, which seem so close to each other that they appear at times to enter into a reciprocal competition. Each course poses and re-poses, recovers and repeats the *question of the Other* as a question addressed to *me* in the *face* of the other man: the very heart of Levinas's work. However, the first lecture course does so in order to conjoin two concepts, death and time, whose harshness was dulled at the very moment that they became concepts as philosophy seized hold of them. Now, these concepts came back as first questions with Hegel and especially with Heidegger. As questions, they compelled certain figures to the task of thinking. These thinkers went unrecognized as philosophers by Heideggerians, which is not the case with Levinas. I mean here Kierkegaard, Rosenzweig, Buber, Bergson, and others. This is why the course unfolds in its principal part in the form of a *dialogue* with the philosophical tradition, that is, in the first person, with philosophers welcomed, each one, in his own right and name. This is an exceptional case in Levinas, who, as a professor, sought essentially to teach the history of philosophy, but who, as a writer, worked as if to *imply* this history without "conversing" (to borrow a surprising expression from the second lecture course) with his partners.

The second lecture course tracks a unique concept—*par excellence*! and, for all of philosophy, the highest of all concepts—which Heidegger, once again, showed to have turned thinking from its proper task and likewise from its true home: *God*. God who *is*, *par excellence*, but who is to such a degree that he hides being and the question that being harbors; the *summum ens*, according to the classical or traditional name, which crushes and offends the *esse*, or rather the εἶναι with all its supremacy. Assuredly, Levinas responds. But a question arises: who lost in this game? Was it being —or God? If Heidegger insisted upon proving that the first response was the right one, Levinas will attempt to question the second eventuality. He will do so as a pioneer, and in a certain fashion, for although philosophy has known a few "flashes"[5] in which God glimmered like an enigma, the philosophy of Greek origin was above all given to betraying him and taking him for a foundation. Consequently, the lectures of the second course do not follow a progression in the form of a dialogue or as a conversation, but rather make a sign toward the history of philosophy in the way that Levinas does in his "written teachings." The second course's lectures above all unfold, or seek to articulate in solitude, this *unique* question. This is a face-to-face of the unique before the Unique!

⁓

This likewise explains why the two lecture courses each required a battery of notes of different natures. For the first course, it was necessary essentially to locate and situate the themes of thinkers with whom Levinas converses *ad infinitum* [*à l'infini*].[6] This was necessary in order to give their themes back to them in letter and in name.

As to the second course, it was above all a matter of making explicit certain clusters, turns, stations, and bright points of this patient *exercise in thinking that is questioning*. We must again alert the reader[7] that this questioning represents an *otherwise said* of one of the most adventurous and frightfully difficult essays of Levinas's entire corpus, "God and Philosophy."[8]

A final word is obligatory for those of us who learned from Levinas what a *proper name* means. This work was possible only thanks to a few friends who loaned me their notes and sometimes their memories, and who gave the time required for assistance and advice. They should be thanked here, face to face: Alain David, Harita Valavanidis-Wybrands, Francis Wybrands, Marlène Zarader.

—Jacques Rolland

PART I

Death and Time

Initial Questions

Friday, November 7, 1975

In question in this course is, above all, time—this is a course on the *duration* of time. The word *duration* of time is chosen for several reasons:

—It indicates that we will not be posing, here, the question "What is . . . ?" In the same way, in an unpublished lecture prior to *Being and Time*,[1] Heidegger said that one cannot pose the question "What is time?" because one then immediately posits time as being.

—There is no action in the passivity of time, which is patience itself (this being said as against the intentional approach).

—The word avoids ideas of flux and of flowing, which make us think of a liquid substance and announce the possibility of a measure of time (time measured, or clock time, is not the authentic time). As *temporalization—Zeitigung—*the word "duration" avoids all these misunderstandings and avoids the confusion between what flows *within* time and time itself.

—It is a term that above all would leave to time its own mode.

Within the duration of time—whose signification should perhaps not be referred to the couple "being and nothingness," understood as the ultimate reference of meaning, of everything meaningful and everything thought, of everything human—death is a point from which time takes all its patience; this expectation that escapes its own intentionality *qua* expectation; this "patience and

length of time," as the proverb says, where patience is like the emphasis of passivity. Whence the direction of this course: death understood as the patience of time.

⌒

This search for death within the perspective of time (of time not
considered as a horizon of being, of the ess*a*nce[2] of being) does
not signify a philosophy of *Sein zum Tode* [being-toward-death]. It
is thus differentiated from the thought of Heidegger; this is the
case, whatever the debt of every contemporary thinker might be to
Heidegger, a debt that he often owes to his regret. However, if the
Sein zum Tode, posited as equivalent to being in regard to nothingness, does not exactly seem to posit death within time, this refusal
to treat time and death in relation to being does not reserve us the
facility of a recourse to eternal life. Death: an irreversible (see Jankélévitch's book on death, wherein I know from the first lines that
I shall have to die my own death).[3]

But is that which opens with death nothingness, or the unknown? Can being at the point of death be reduced to the ontological dilemma of being or nothingness? That is the question that is
posed here. For the reduction of death to this dilemma of being or
nothingness is a reverse dogmatism, whatever the feelings of an entire generation suspicious of the positive dogmatism of the immortality of the soul, considered as the sweetest "opium of the people."

⌒

At first, it seems to us that all that we can say or think about
death and dying, and their inevitability, comes to us secondhand.
We know it by hearsay or by empirical knowledge. All that we
know comes to us from the language that names death and dying,
the language that utters propositions: common words, proverbial,
poetic, or religious ones.

This knowledge comes to us from the experience and observation of other men, of their behavior as dying and as mortals aware
of [*connaissant*] their death and forgetful of their death (which
does not here mean a diversion: there is a forgetting of death that
is not a diversion). Is death separable from the relation with the
other [*autrui*]? The *negative* character of death (annihilation) is in-

scribed in hatred or the desire to murder. It is in the relation with the other that we think death in its negativity.

We have this awareness [*connaissance*] through banal or scientific knowledge [*savoir*]. Death is the disappearance in beings of those expressive movements that made them appear as living, those movements that are always *responses*. Death will touch, above all, that autonomy or that expressiveness of movement that can go to the point of masking [*couvrir*] someone within his face. Death is the *no-response* [*sans-réponse*]. Those movements both hide and inform the vegetative movements. Death strips that which is thus covered over and offers it up to medical examination.

Dying, when understood from language and the observation of the other man dying, names a halting of these movements and the reduction of someone to something decomposable—an immobilization. There is not transformation, but annihilation, the end of a being, the stopping of those movements that were so many signs (see *Phædo* 117e–118a on the death of Socrates).[4] The annihilation of a mode of being that dominates all the others (the face), beyond the objective residue of matter, which subsists even if it is decomposed and dispersed. Death appears as the passage from being to no-longer-being, understood as the result of a logical operation: negation.

But at the same time, death is a departure: it is a decease [*décès*]. (In this idea of departure there nevertheless remains negativity.) A departure toward the unknown, a departure without return, a departure "with no forwarding address." Death—as the death of the other [*autrui*]—cannot be separated from this dramatic character; it is emotion *par excellence*, affection or being affected *par excellence*. It is in this sense that we see, in the *Phædo*, at the beginning and the end, the evocation of the death of Socrates. Beside those who find in this death every reason to hope, certain among them (e.g., Apollodorus, "the women") weep more than they should; they weep without measure: as if humanity were not consumed or exhausted by measurement, as if there were an excess in death. It is a simple passage, a simple departure—and yet a source of emotion contrary to every effort at consolation.

My relation with death is not limited to this secondhand knowledge. For Heidegger (see *Being and Time*), it is the certitude *par excellence.* There is an *a priori* of death. Heidegger calls death certain to the point of seeing in this certitude of death the origin of certitude itself, and he will not allow this certitude to come from the experience of the death of others.

It is nonetheless not certain that death can be called a certitude, nor is it certain that death has the meaning of annihilation. *My* relation with death is also made up of the emotional and intellectual repercussions of the knowledge of the death of others. But this relation is disproportionate relative to all secondhand experience. Hence the question: Can the relation with death, and the manner by which death strikes our life, its impact upon the duration of the time that we live, its irruption within time—or its eruption outside of time—which is sensed in fear or in anguish, can this relation still be assimilated to a knowledge and thus to an experience, to a revelation?

Does the impossibility of reducing death to an experience, this truism about the impossibility of an experience of death, and about a noncontact between life and death—do these not signify a being affected, an affection more passive than a trauma? As if there were a passivity beyond shock. And a fission that affects us more than presence, an *a priori* more than *a priori.*⁵ Mortality as the modality of time that must not be reduced to an anticipation, even a passive one; a modality irreducible to an experience, to a comprehension of nothingness. And we must not decide too quickly that only nothingness is dreadful, as in a philosophy wherein man is a being who has to be, who persists in his being, without posing to himself the question of knowing what the dreadful and the dreaded are.

Here, death takes a meaning other than an experience of death. It takes a meaning that comes from the death of another person [*d'autrui*], of what concerns us therein. A death without experience and yet dreadful: does that not mean that the structure of time is not intentional, that it is not made up of the protentions and retentions that are the modes of experience?

What Do We Know of Death?

Friday, November 14, 1975

What do we know of death; what is death? According to experience, it is the stopping of a behavior, the stopping of expressive movements and of physiological movements or processes that are enveloped by these expressive movements and dissimulated by them; all this forming "something" that shows itself, or rather *someone* who shows himself, or does better than show himself: someone who expresses himself. This expression is more than monstration, more than manifestation.

Sickness is already a gap between those expressive movements and the biological ones. It is already a call for medication. Human life is the attiring of physiological movements: it is decency. Human life is a "hiding," a "dressing," that is at the same time a "denuding," since it is an "associating" [*s'associer*]. (There is an emphatic gradation between showing, dressing, associating.) Death is the irremediable gap: the biological movements lose all dependence in relation to signification, to expression. Death is decomposition; it is the no-response [*sans-réponse*].

It is by way of this expressiveness in his behavior—which dresses the biological being and denudes him beyond all nudity: to the point of making of him a face—that someone expresses himself, an other than I, different from me, an other who expresses himself to the point of being nonindifferent to me, that is, of being one who bears me.

Someone who dies: a face that becomes a masque. The expression disappears. The experience of death that is not mine is an "experience" of the death of *someone*, someone who from the outset is beyond biological processes, who is associated with me as someone.

The soul, reified as some-thing, is, phenomenologically, what shows itself in the nonreified face; it shows itself in expression and, in this appearing, has the structure or the glimmer [*la pointe*] of someone. That which Descartes makes a substance, all the while protesting against the image of the pilot in his vessel [*nacelle*], that from which Leibniz makes a monad, that which Plato posits as the soul contemplating the Ideas, that which Spinoza thinks as a mode of thought, is described phenomenologically as a *face*. Without this phenomenology, one is pushed toward a reification of the soul, whereas here a problem other than to be or not to be is posed, a problem prior to that question.

The death of someone is not—despite everything that seemed so at first glance—an empirical facticity (death as empirical facticity whose universality induction alone could suggest); it is not exhausted in this appearing.

Someone who expresses himself in his nudity—the face—is one to the point of appealing to me, of placing himself under my responsibility: Henceforth, I have to respond for him. All the gestures of the other were signs addressed to me. To continue the progression sketched above: to show oneself, to express oneself, to associate oneself, *to be entrusted to me* [*m'être confié*]. The other who expresses himself is entrusted to me (and there is no debt in regard to the other, for what is due is unpayable: one is never free of it). The other individuates me in the responsibility I have for him. The death of the other who dies affects me in my very identity as a responsible "me" [*moi*]; it affects me in my nonsubstantial identity, which is not the simple coherence of various acts of identification, but is made up of an ineffable responsibility. My being affected by the death of the other is precisely that, my relation with his death. It is, in my relation, my deference to someone who no longer responds, already a culpability—the culpability of the survivor.

This relation is reduced to a secondhand experience on the pretext that it does not have the identity, the coincidence of lived experience with itself, and that it is objectified only in external forms. That supposes that the identity of the Same with itself is the source of all meaning. But does not the relation with the other and with his death go back toward another source of meaning? Dying, as the dying of the other [*l'autre*], affects my identity as "I" [*Moi*]; it is meaningful in its rupture with the Same, its rupture of my "I" [*Moi*], its rupture of the Same in my "I" [*Moi*]. It is in this that my relation with the death of another is neither simply secondhand knowledge nor a privileged experience of death.

In *Being and Time*, Heidegger considers death as certitude *par excellence*, as a certain possibility, and he limits its meaning to annihilation. *Gewissheit* [certainty]—that which is proper, or nonalienated in death, that which in death is *eigentlich* [proper, actual]. The *Gewissheit* of death is so much *Gewissheit* that it is the origin of all *Gewissen* [conscience] (see § 52).

The problem we are posing here is the following: does the relationship to the death of the other not deliver its meaning, does it not articulate it by the depth of the affection [*la profondeur de l'affection*], from the dread that is felt before the death of the other? Is it correct to measure this dreaded thing by the *conatus*, that is, by the persevering-in-my-being, by comparing it with the threat that weighs upon my being—that threat having been posited as the sole source of affectivity? For Heidegger, the source of all affectivity is anxiety, which is anxiety for being (fear is subordinated to anxiety; it is a modification of it). Thus the question: Is the dreaded itself derived? The relation with death is thought as an experience of nothingness in time. Here, we are looking for other dimensions of meaning, both for the meaning of time and for the meaning of death.

~

It is not a matter of contesting the negative aspect that is attached to the relation with the death of the other (even hatred is a negation). But the event of death overflows the intention that it seems to fill. And death indicates a meaning that surprises—as if annihilation could introduce us to a meaning that is not limited to nothingness.

Death is an immobilization of the mobility of the face that denies death in advance; it is a struggle between discourse and its
negation (see, in the *Phædo*, the description of the death of Socrates). This is a struggle in which death confirms its negative power
(see Socrates' last words). Death is at once healing and impotence;
an ambiguity that perhaps indicates an other dimension of meaning than that in which death is thought within the alternative to
be / not-to-be. The ambiguity: an enigma.

Death is a departure, a decease, a negativity whose destination
is unknown. Should we not think of death as a question of an indetermination such that we cannot say that it is posed, like a problem, on the basis of its givens? Death, as a departure without return, a question without givens, a pure interrogation mark.

That Socrates, who in the *Phædo* is summoned to affirm the om-
nipotence of being, is the only one perfectly happy, that there intervenes a dramatic event, that the spectacle of death is not bearable—
or is so only for the masculine sensibility—all this underscores the
dramatic character of the death of the other. Death is a scandal, a
crisis, even in the *Phædo*. Can this crisis and this scandal be reduced
to the annihilation that someone undergoes? In the *Phædo*, one
character is missing: Plato. He does not take part therein; he has ab-
stained. This adds a supplementary ambiguity.

Is not death something other than the dialectic of being and
nothingness in the flow of time? Does the end, or negativity, exhaust the death of the other? The end is but a *moment* only of
death, a moment whose other side would be not consciousness or
comprehension but the *question*, and a question distinct from all
those that are presented as problems.

The relation with the death of the other, an external relation,
has contained an interiority (which nevertheless could not be
brought back to experience). Is it otherwise with the relation with
my death? In philosophy, the relation with my death is described
as anxiety and comes back to the comprehension of nothingness.
The structure of comprehension is thus preserved, in touching the
question of the relation with my death. Intentionality preserves
the identity of the Same; it is thinking that thinks according to its

measure, a thinking conceived on the model of the representation of what is given, a noetico-noematic correlation. But being affected [*l'affection*] by death is affectivity, passivity, a being affected by the beyond-measure [*la dé-mesure*], an affection of the present by the nonpresent, more intimate than any intimacy, to the point of fission, an *a posteriori* more ancient than any *a priori*; it is an immemorial diachrony that one can not bring back to experience.

The relation with death, more ancient than any experience, is not the vision of being or nothingness.

Intentionality is not the secret of the human. The human *esse*, or existing, is not a *conatus* but disinterestedness and *adieu*.[1]

Death: a mortality as demanded by the duration of time.

The Death of the Other
[*D'Autrui*] and My Own

Friday, November 21, 1975

The description of the relation with the death of the other and with our own death leads us to some rather singular propositions that we shall have to deepen today.

The relation with the death of the other is not a *knowledge* [*savoir*] about the death of the other, nor the experience of that death in its particular way of annihilating being (if, as is commonly thought, the event of this death is reducible to this annihilation). There is no knowledge of this ex-ceptional relation ("ex-ception" meaning here to grasp and to set outside the series). This annihilation is not phenomenal, nor does it give rise to anything like a coincidence of consciousness with it (yet those are the two dimensions of knowledge). From the death of the other, pure knowledge (i.e., lived experience [*vécu*], coincidence) retains only the external appearances of a *process* (of immobilization) whereby someone, who up until then expressed himself, comes to an end.

The rapport or connection we have with death in its ex-ception —and whatever its signification relative to being and to nothingness might be, death is an exception—which confers upon death its depth, is neither a seeing nor even an aiming [*visée*]. (It is neither to see being, as in Plato, nor to aim at nothingness, as in Heidegger.) A purely emotional rapport, moving us with an emotion that is not made up of the repercussion on our sensibility and our intellect of a previous knowledge. It is an emotion, a movement, a disquietude within the *unknown*.

This emotion does not have, as Husserl had wanted, representation for its basis (Husserl was the first to introduce a meaning into emotion, but he still makes this meaning rest upon knowledge). But neither would it be animated by a specifically axiological intentionality—as [Max] Scheler thinks—which thus preserves for emotion a disclosive opening that is specifically ontological. For Scheler, emotion is oriented from the outset by means of a value, but it preserves an opening, it is still understood as a revelation (of value); it therefore still preserves the ontological structure.

Here, we are concerned with an *affectivity without intentionality* (as Michel Henry clearly noted in his *Essence of Manifestation*).[1] Nevertheless, the emotional state described here differs radically from the inertia of the sensible state of which a sensualist empiricism spoke. Nonintentionality—and yet a static nonstate.[2]

Would not the dis-quiet of emotion be the question that, in the nearness of death, is precisely at the point of being born? An emotion in the sense of a deference toward death; in other words, an emotion as a *question* that does not contain, in the posing of the question, the elements of its own response. A question that attaches to that deeper relation [*rapport*] to the infinite, which is time (time understood as a relation to the infinite). An emotional relation [*rapport*] with the death of the other [*l'autre*]. A fear or a courage, but also, beyond the compassion for and solidarity with the other, responsibility for him in the unknown. But this unknown is not, in its turn, objectified and thematized, aimed at or seen; it is rather a disquietude wherein an interrogation interrogates itself yet is not convertible into a response;[3] a disquietude wherein the response is reduced to the responsibility of the questioning itself [*du questionnant*] or of the one who questions [*du questionneur*].

The other concerns me as a neighbor [*prochain*]. In every death is shown the nearness of the neighbor, and the responsibility of the survivor, in the form of a responsibility that the approach of proximity [*proximité*] moves or agitates [*meut ou émeut*].[4] A disquietude that is not thematization, not intentionality, even if this latter was signitive. This is a disquietude that therefore resists all appearing, all phenomenal aspects, as though emotion passed by way of the question, without encountering the slightest quiddity, toward that acuity of death, and instituted an unknown that is not purely negative but rather in nearness without knowledge. It is as though the question went beyond appearing forms, beyond being and appearing, and, precisely in this passing, could be called profound.

Thus the question of the meaning of the emotional is again posed here, the question that Heidegger taught us to reduce to the confrontation with nothingness in anxiety. This irreducibility of the emotional shows itself even in the Socratic effort made in the *Phædo*, a dialogue that tends to recognize in death the very splendor of being (death there is being stripped of every veil; being such as it is promised to the philosopher and which bursts open in its divinity only with the end of corporeity). Even there, however, the approach of the dying Socrates does not lose its affective resonance, whereas the recognition, in the process of dying, of this announcement of being (Socrates will finally be visible in death) would be the rational discourse of knowledge and theory. This is the whole intent of the *Phædo*: theory is stronger than the anxiety over death. But even in this dialogue there is the *excess* of emotion: Apollodorus weeps more than the others; he weeps beyond measure— and they must send the women away.

What is the meaning of this affectivity and these tears? Perhaps we should not interpret this emotion straightaway as intentionality and reduce it thereby to an opening onto nothingness, or onto being in its connection with nothingness; we should not reduce it to the opening of an ontological dimension. Just as the kinship of affectivity and representation in Husserl has been placed in question, we must ask ourselves whether all affectivity goes back to the anxiety understood as the imminence of nothingness; that is, whether affectivity is awakened only in a being persevering in its being (the *conatus*), and whether the *conatus* is the humanity of man. We should ask ourselves whether the humanity of man is his having-to-be. And this leads inevitably to a discussion with Heidegger.

If emotion is not rooted in anxiety, the ontological meaning of emotion is put back in question and, beyond this, the role of intentionality. It is perhaps not necessary to maintain that intentionality is the ultimate secret of the psyche.

Time is not the limitation of being but its relationship with infinity. Death is not annihilation but the question that is necessary for this relationship with infinity, or time, to be produced.

~

The same problems are posed when one speaks of death as *my* death. The relationship to my own dying does not have the meaning of knowledge or of experience, even if this had only the sense of a presentiment, of prescience. One does not know, one cannot be present at, one's annihilation (inasmuch as death might be annihilation); this is the case not only because of the nothingness that cannot be given as a thematizable event (see Epicurus: "If you are there, then death is not there; if it is there, you are not there"). My relationship with my death is a nonknowledge [*non-savoir*] on dying itself, a nonknowledge that is nevertheless not an absence of relationship. Can we describe this relationship?

What language calls death—what is perceived as the end of someone—would also be an eventuality transferable onto oneself. A transference that is not mechanical [*une mécanique*] but rather belongs to the intrigue or the intrication of My-self [*Moi-même*] and comes to cut the thread of my own duration, or ties a knot in this thread, as though the time in which the "I" [*moi*] endures dragged out in its length.

~

I would open a parenthesis about the comprehension of the time presented here. It concerns the duration of time as a relation with the infinite, with the uncontainable, with the Different. It concerns duration as a relationship with the Different which, for all that, is nonindifferent; a relationship in which diachrony is like the *in* of the other-*in*-the-same—without the Other ever entering into the Same. A deference of the immemorial to the unforeseeable. Time is at once this Other-within-the-Same and that Other who cannot be together with the Same; it [time] cannot be synchronous. Time would thus be a disquieting [*inquiétude*] of the Same by the Other, without the Same ever being able to comprehend or encompass the Other.

~

The acuteness of this transference stems from all the significations of the death of the other and from the context into which
that death is transferred. It is a transference—though one that is
not effected in an indifferent manner but belongs to the intrigue[5]
of the I [*du Moi*], that is, to the identification of the I.[6]

How shall we think about the I in its identity, its uniqueness; or
how shall we think about this uniqueness of the I? Can it be
thought of as a thing identified (the identity of the thing would be
the series of views or intentions that confirm one another, or an
accord of intentions)? Must the I be thought of as identification in
the reflection upon self that assimilates the other to the self, at the
price of no longer being able to distinguish it from the totality
thus formed? Neither of these two solutions is appropriate; a third
one is needed.

The I [*le Moi*]—or "me" [*moi*] in my singularity—is someone
who escapes his concept. The "me" [*moi*] only surfaces in its
uniqueness in responding for the other in a responsibility from
which there is no flight, in a responsibility from which I could not
be free. The "me" [*moi*] is an identity of oneself that would come
about by way of the impossibility of letting oneself be replaced—a
duty beyond all debt—and thus a patience whose passivity no assumption or taking upon oneself could deny.

If the uniqueness of the I [*Moi*] is in this patience—a patience
that must risk itself in the eventuality of nonsense, a patience necessary even before a discovery of arbitrariness—then non-exonerable
patience is possible. There must be an opening onto a dimension
that is a discovery, an opening that ridicules the nobility or the purity of patience that sullies it [*l'entachant*]. If patience has a meaning as inevitable obligation, this meaning becomes sufficiency and
institution if there is not beneath it a glimmer of nonsense. It is
therefore necessary that there be in the egoity of the I [*du Moi*] the
risk of a nonsense, a madness. If this risk were not there, then patience would have a status, it would lose its passivity.

The possibility of a nonsense capable of driving out every enterprise that could enter into the passivity of patience is this deference
to death that is not meaning, is not situatable, not localizable, not
objectifiable—one side of an unthinkable, unsuspectable dimen-

sion. It is a nonknowledge, a nonsense of death, deference to the nonsense of death: here then is what is necessary to the very uniqueness of the I [*Moi*], and to the intrigue of its uniqueness. This is a nonknowledge that translates into experience through my ignorance of the day of my death, an ignorance by virtue of which the "me" [*moi*] writes checks on an empty account, as if he had eternity before him. In this respect, this same ignorance and this carelessness must not be interpreted as a diversion or as falling into decadence.

Instead of letting itself be described in its own event, death concerns us by its nonsense. The point that death seems to mark in our time (i.e., our relationship to the infinite) is a pure question mark: the opening onto that which provides no possibility of a response. An interrogation that is already a modality of the relationship with the beyond of being.

~

The foregoing assertions rest upon a certain number of presuppositions that we must now make explicit:

—If there is no experience of death, the interpretation of death as intentionality must be put in question.

—Affirming the affectivity in relations with the death of the other and with my own death places these relations in the midst of the relationship with the Different, with what lacks a common measure, with what no reminiscence or anticipation could again gather into synchrony.

—We are seeking the connection between death and time in the midst of this relationship with death, where it comes to us like an interrogation before the other, of his beyond-measure.

—The intentionality that, in Husserl, weaves the lacework of time is not the ultimate secret of the psyche.

—The human *esse* is not primordially *conatus* but hostage, a hostage of the other.

—Affectivity does not sink its roots into anxiety in the form of the anxiety about nothingness.

~

All this must be taken up again in a dialogue with Heidegger, in whom the close relationship of death and time is asserted, albeit in another modality.

An Obligatory Passage: Heidegger

Friday, November 28, 1975

Death: a question that disquiets in its restlessness [*sans-repos*] rather than in the problem it poses. Disquietude: what is unrested [*le non-reposé*]. Disquietude is not a modality of intentionality; on the contrary, it is intentionality that is a modality of this not-resting-in-itself of disquietude. The emotion set in motion by this question is not to be interpreted immediately in relation to the couple being/nothingness, contrary to the thinking that sees in man's being the *conatus*, death as a threat for him, and, in anxiety, the source of all affectivity.

Here, I suggest the proposition of a human more human than the *conatus*, one that would be the held-in-awakening [*tenue-en-éveil*] or vigilance (a vigilance that is not vigilance over . . .)—this is an awakening of the for-oneself that was self-sufficient in its identity, an awakening by the unabsorbable alterity of the other [*l'autre*], or an incessant sobering up of the Same intoxicated with itself. This awakening must be considered as an awakening in awakening: awakening as such becomes a state—so an awakening of this awakening is necessary. There is here an iteration of awakening. For this is an awakening by the beyond-measure [*démesure*] or the infinity of the other.

This held-in-awakening, thought concretely and to the point of its own emphasis, is responsibility for another [*autrui*], the responsibility of a hostage [*responsabilité d'otage*]. An awakening that never

22

stops: one does not owe a *debt* to the other. An awakening by the infinite—but an awakening that is produced concretely in the form of an irresistible call to responsibility. Whence the passivity: at no moment may I be tranquilly for-me.

This is a passivity, or patience, that is stretched out in the form of length of time. Time would be a manner of deferring to infinity while never being able to contain or comprehend it. This "while never" would be like the always of time, the duration of time. (Such a passivity, a passivity of the hostage, cannot exist in an organized society or a State, etc.)

An awakening wherein the unknown, wherein the nonsense of death, is the impediment to any settling in to some kind of virtue of patience, and wherein what is dreaded looms up like the disproportion between me and the infinite—like being-before-God, like the to-God [*l'à-Dieu*] itself.

～

These remarks consist in thinking in a certain fashion the relationship between death and time. That relationship has been defended by Heidegger, in another spirit, albeit with an extreme rigor and vigorousness. We must first study the context in which the question is posed: paragraphs 1 to 44 of *Being and Time*. (Death is less at issue in the final works of Heidegger.) This first part of the work introduces the question that this philosopher renewed, that of the fundamental ontology that turns on the *verbal* signification of "being." By way of this, Heidegger reawakens the verbal sonority of being in its difference from beings (beings we understand as the substantive meaning of "being," that which one can show and thematize; in grammatical terms, the noun, the substantive).[1]

～

Now, the verb "to be" is comprehended by men before any explicit ontology. It is comprehended preontologically, and thus without a full understanding, but, on the contrary, with the subsistence of questions. In the preontological comprehension of being, there is the question itself of being, which is therefore a question possessing a pre-response. One must therefore approach the meaning of being starting from man, who is a being that comprehends being and questions, indeed questions himself about, being. But to pose a question about being is not to pose a banal question about the constitution of some being or entity. This interrogation is not a psychological particularity, but is, on the contrary, essential to man (though not in the sense of the Spinozistic essential attribute). This question would be essential as the very manner of being of man. The essential attribute of man consists in being in a certain manner.

The manner by which man is, by which he follows his calling as a being, follows his train of being [*mène son train d'être*]—that is his being in the verbal sense of the term, which consists precisely in questioning oneself about the meaning of the verb "to be." Such questioning is not representation; rather, it is following his train of being [*mener son train d'être*], it is having-to-be [*avoir-à-être*]: this is not to mistake oneself for the being [*l'être*] that is to be understood, but to grasp its possibilities.

Being and its signification have such importance to man that his own affair lies therein. The relationship between what is in question and the questioning itself is a unique relationship; it is the very fact of having an affair of one's own, mineness [*mienneté*], Jemeinigkeit. The closeness of the relation between the questioning and what is in question allows (for the first time, with such a rigor, the I [*Moi*] is "deduced" from ontology, "deduced," that is, from being) the personal to be "deduced" from the ontological. See § 9: *Dasein* has a *Jemeinigkeit*, and, because it has a *Jemeinigkeit*, it is *I* [*Ich*]. This same fact of mineness [*mienneté*] measures the manner of being concerned by being, which concretely signifies the able-to-be [*le pouvoir-être*].[2]

Because man has, as his own affair (in the sense of the *Sache*, though the word is not found in *Being and Time*), being to do, being to fulfill, to carry on according to its train of being, his essence consists in having-to-be. He will thus be in his own questioning; he is going to question. It is necessary that there be a distance between his being and the being that he grasps: man will thus be an ec-sistence.

Man is the being for whom—in his being—his very being is at

stake; he is the being who has to grasp his being. Therefore he is designated not as *Daseiende* but as *Dasein.* To comprehend being is to have to be. Thus his being and the being to comprehend are almost the same being (see the *Letter on Humanism*).[3]

This mineness, this having to fulfill one's being, or having it before oneself as a possibility to grasp, a possibility to exist, must be described. To describe this existence is to describe the self-questioning-about-being. Or, inversely, to describe the humanity of man on the basis of his existence, from his *Dasein,* is precisely to describe the interrogation of man concerning being.

The expression "*Dasein* is a being for whom, in his being, his own being is at stake" was seductive in *Being and Time,* where it signified the *conatus.* But in reality the *conatus* is deduced from the degree of his being strictly bound to being itself. There is no existentialism here. Here, man is interesting because he has been strictly bound or obligated to being [*astreint à l'être*], and his strict obligation to being is his questioning. The *conatus* measures his obedience to being, the wholeness of this to-be-in-service-to-being, which is in man's charge (*Letter on Humanism*).[4] The affair of being is to such a degree his own that the meaning of being is *his affair.*

Man is thus *Da* [There], because this manner of having being in his charge is not an intellectual affair but man's entire concreteness. The *Da* is the manner of being-there in the world, which is to question about being. The search for the signification of being does not come about in the same manner as in Aristotle. Like Aristotle (see *Metaphysics* A, 2),[5] Heidegger speaks of astonishment or wonder, but for Aristotle wonder is nothing other than the consciousness of one's own ignorance: knowledge comes from my wanting to know. There is in Aristotle a complete separation between *Sorge* [care] and questioning, a complete disinterestedness of knowledge. This is not at all the case in Heidegger.

Being and Time can be read as making explicit—with a view to answering the question of fundamental ontology—the *Da* of *Dasein* as the being who is preoccupied with being and must be enlightened in advance in order to pose the question of being. From there comes the analytic of *Dasein.* In reality, the fact that man's

Dasein makes being into his affair, his question, the fact that he has questioning in his charge, is what is proper to being: it is proper to being to put itself in question. The analytic of *Dasein* is thus already a step taken within the description of being. *Being and Time* is not a preparation for ontology but already a step within ontology itself.

The first characteristic of being is to be already in question. It is itself to be finite, in question, and contested. To be in question is to be in such a way as always to have to be, and this, thanks to a being who himself has to be. To be in question is to be in such a way that there would always be a being who has to make being his own [*un étant qui a à se le rendre propre*], one, that is, who must *sich zu ereignen* [appropriate being to himself, make it his own]. To be in question is to be *Ereignis* [event][6] (this was not perceived in France in the 1930s, because *eigentlich* was translated by "authentic").[7] The question is then to know whether to be [*l'être*], in the verbal sense of the term, is not in effect to let oneself be appropriated [*se laisser approprier*], or to be an event and so give rise in this way to the human dimension [*l'humain*] and the personal (see § 9, in which all the modes of *Dasein* are *eigentlich*, proper to oneself, including those that are called *uneigentlich*).[8]

In *Being and Time*, Heidegger makes clear what is meant concretely by the being-there [*être-là*] in which being [*l'être*] is comprehended, apprehended, appropriated. This phenomenological analysis leads to the formula: to be-there is to be in the world in the sense of being alongside of things for which one must care; from this comes care. And from this, the *existentialia* [*existentiaux*]. Care has the structure of the question *how*, and not that of the question *what*. The *existentialia* are brought together in a unique expression: to be already out ahead of oneself in the world (i.e., to be alongside of things). There lies the question: Are these *existentialia* a totality; do they form something whole, something original or primordial?

~

The expression "to be already out ahead of oneself as being in the world" contains the temporal expressions "already," "out ahead of," and "alongside of."[9] Here there is an attempt to describe temporality without bringing in the flow of instants, or the time that flows. There is a concern to look for a primordial time that would not be defined as a flowing river.

In an unpublished lecture prior to *Being and Time*,[10] Heidegger noted the impossibility of posing the question "What is time?" If one poses this question, one already answers: it is a being. In place of that question is substituted this other one: *Who* is time? Taking Aristotle up again ("time is the number of movement"),[11] Heidegger observed that we accede to time by measuring it; that is, our primitive access to time is had on the basis of the clock. With the temporal expressions "already," "alongside of," "out ahead of," there is an attempt to accede to time otherwise than on the basis of what measures it. Heidegger will deduce measurable time starting from an original or primordial time.

The Analytic of *Dasein*

Friday, December 5, 1975

It might be asked what the relation is between the remarks coming to light in this course and the studies made by the sciences.

The concepts of nature and of natural science, outside their elaboration within science itself, proceed from a metascience, from an intelligibility and a meaningfulness [*signifiance*][1] that signifies within concrete human and interhuman relations. Science never works without our hearing the echoes of that infrastructure of intelligibility or significance, that is, without this horizon of meaning, which we must now make clear.

If it is a matter of life and death translated objectively, then it is fitting to set forth these horizons of meaning, both in the relationship of man and death, and in the impact of death upon human time—in the impact, that is, of death in its ever-open possibility, its necessity, which cannot be averted but whose hour remains unknown. This is to recognize that codetermination, and to recognize that the human dimension [*l'humain*] does not simply make universal reason incarnate or individuated but signifies its own intrigue. It signifies a rupture in which the adventure of being [*la geste d'être*] takes on meaning,[2] where perhaps it dissolves itself in meaning; a rupture without which objectivity threatens to dissimulate the original sense [*l'objectif menace de subreption*] (it threatens a "slippage of meaning," in Husserl's terms).

"To dissolve in meaning": the upsurge of the human dimension

[*l'humain*] is perhaps a rupture in the epic of being through the relationship of the one to the other (i.e., the domain of ethics),
which would be not a stage above being but the gratuity in which
the *conatus*, or the perseverance in being, is dis-solved [*dé-fait*].

~

To be more specific:
—Time must be considered in its dimension of awaiting or anticipation, without any anticipating aiming; it must thus be considered as having engulfed its intentionality of awaiting, in an
awaiting that is patience or pure passivity, a pure undergoing without a taking upon oneself (contrary to the suffering in which there
is a taking charge of). This is a non–taking upon oneself or a nonassumption of what is equivalent to no content. A nonassumption
of the infinite, a disquietude: here, that is a relation without the
willing [*vouloir*] of intentionality, which would be a willing proportionate to itself. There would thus be a deference whose effect
one could never obtain. The *"never"* of patience would be the *always* of time.

—A deference in disquietude and, thus, an awakening, and an
awakening as awakening for the neighbor in responsibility for
him. That means a responsibility from which one does not slip
away: the fact of being irreplaceable in responsibility for the other
defines me, as me and as a unique me [*moi*]. That is an awakening in which awakening is not complacent in its state of awakening, and does not fall asleep standing up.

—Because a phenomenology of naturalist concepts is necessary
(if only to be able to work and to take notes), we shall now turn
toward the phenomenology Heidegger elaborates.

~

The preceding session aimed at showing the meaning of the analytic of *Dasein* for the problem of ontology. It is not simply a pro-
pædeutic. Being is in question in *Dasein*, and to be in question is,
as it were, the *status* of being as a verb, the manner by which its
epic is made, its epic or adventure [*sa geste*]. To be in question is
essential to this ess*a*nce.[3] The *Da* [there] of *Dasein*, which is at
once a question but also already a comprehension of being as verb,

is a foundation without a ground and has been elaborated in the structure of care.

Human existence (or the *Da-sein*) is readily described in its *Da* (being-in-the-world) by three structures: *being-out-ahead-of-oneself* (the project), *being-always-already-in-the-world* (facticity), being in the world as *being-alongside-of* (alongside of things, alongside of what is encountered within the world).

Therein lies the structure of care, in which one finds a temporal reference described solely on the basis of relations within *Dasein*.

> project—future
> Time always already—past
> close to—present

(This structure is presented by Heidegger as *co-originary*, as arising from the same *Ursprung* [source], from the same impulse [*prime-saut*]. A paradoxical simultaneity of diachrony.)

The question of being, equivalent to the comprehension of being, is not a disinterested knowledge like that of which Aristotle speaks in his *Metaphysics* A, 2 (i.e., a disinterestedness worthy of the gods). The analytic of *Dasein* is not an arbitrary approach to the verbal sense of the word "to be" by a humanity come from who-knows-where, and curious to know. This anthropology reveals the exact way in which the adventure of being carries on, as an adventure that has not the security of an event grounded on the earth or on some principle imposed by itself, whether absolute or divine (note that the word "absolute" appears nowhere in *Being and Time*). But it is precisely a question of an adventure that is the stage upon which being plays, an adventure carried out as if delivered over to the risks entailed by this manner of being placed in question within *Dasein*, whose proper affair is being, proper to the point of requiring *mineness* (as the possibility of the "mine" and of all "having"). This adventure of being is like an adventure within an adventure (precariousness). Being here gives itself in an extreme generosity, in an extreme gratuity or disinterestedness. One notes that there are many Christian virtues in the "pre-Socratic" being (generosity, modesty, humility, etc.), and Heidegger's teaching would have it that these structures or these virtues have a root in being itself. *The only question is the following*: do not these ethical significations *presuppose* the human dimension [*l'humain*] in the sense of (that which is) the *rupture* with being?

The structure of care designates the comprehension of being in the *Da* as always referred back to the encounter with things, and comprehending on the basis of those things. This corresponds in Heidegger to everyday life in all its banality, in its banal style of life extending out in the succession of days and nights, of "works and days," and filled with occupations and distractions (life as an interminable series of dinner parties, said Pushkin). This mode of existence is taken for the very reality of life. This manner of being, this daily life is a possibility that, for Heidegger, is not foreign to mineness, to one's own affair, or to authenticity (and therefore to comprehension and questioning). It derives from mineness; it refers back to it; and it seems to render unrecognizable that first leap (the impulse [*primesaut*]) or *Ursprung* of existence toward the affair of being that is the *question*.

In *Being and Time*, the analysis is carried out on the basis of everyday life, that is, on the basis of that existence that is not-mine, although derived from what is properly mine. Can the co-originarity of the structures of care be found again in something that is not the simultaneity of the everyday?

If the everyday assumes for itself the privilege of signifying *Dasein*, it no longer permits us to comprehend the structure of the project, of the out-ahead-of-oneself, which describes *Dasein* as the task of being, as a possibility having to be seized. In everyday time, the unity of the "me" [*du moi*] appears only when the time of each life has flowed by: *Dasein* is total only in its necrology: "Changed by eternity into his true Self,"[4] totality would be fulfilled at the very moment in which the person ceases to be a person. Heidegger writes in this regard, "To care, such as it forms the totality of *Dasein*'s structural whole, what is manifestly repugnant—in conformity with its ontological sense—is a possible being-whole of this being."[5]

Does not the primary moment of care, namely, being-out-ahead-of-oneself, signify that *Dasein* is in-view-of (in view of itself)? As long as it relates to its end, it relates *to its being able to be*; even when, still existing, it has nothing before it, its being remains determined by the out-ahead-of-itself. Even despair, the without-hope, is but a mode proper to being with regard to its possibilities. Even being ready for anything, without distance relative to its future, without illusions, still harbors an out-ahead-of-itself.

In the description of care, totality is excluded: "Thus, this structural moment of care indicates unequivocally that there is yet in *Dasein* a *surplus*, something that, as an able-to-be by itself [*pouvoir être de lui-même*], has not yet become effective."[6] There is then, in the structure of care, a permanent nonclosure of *Dasein*. Its non-totality signifies the "outside" of *Dasein*. The disappearance of the distance, of *this* distance, amounts to the disappearance of *Dasein*. In the structure of *Dasein*, it is impossible to grasp the whole; for a being that is always in the possible, it is impossible to be a whole.

But Heidegger wonders whether he has not treated *Dasein* here on the model of what is present-to-hand, or on exhibit (*Vorhandenes*), that is, of purely present reality. Now, what is in question is *Dasein*. What does it mean, *for Dasein*, to be a whole?

In *Dasein* such as it is, something is lacking, something is still needful [*en manque*], and this, by a lack that belongs to being itself, and this lack is death. It is therefore through a certain relationship to death that time will be possible, a time relative to which the question of the possibility of the whole is posed.

～

Two questions come up simultaneously:
—What does "authentic" time mean?
—Is the whole possible?
The following lecture shall have to examine these two questions: How shall we think of *Dasein* as a whole? Can this lead us to think of an authentic time?

Dasein and Death

Friday, December 12, 1975

There is a current image of time within which death appears as the *end* of the duration of a being in the uninterrupted flow of time. Death is then the destruction of a thing. The contribution of Heidegger—for whom the unequivocal sense of an end remains attached to death—will consist in rethinking time itself on the basis of this annihilation and, thus, in substituting philosophical concepts for the common concepts of death and time. This is why the connection between these notions in Heidegger was presented here. There is a necessary passage through a reading of Heidegger, even if death did not seem to us to come down to annihilation, nor to the presentation of pure being as in the *Phædo*. Death seems to summon a difficult or impossible thought—a thought or a dis-quiet—to the question without givens, in the modality of an exclusion that makes us think of an excluded third [*un-tiers-exclu*][1] (outside the alternative "being or nothingness"). We must nevertheless hold fast to this impossible thought or dis-quiet, which we will have to approach as a question without givens, and which we shall have to bear.

For Heidegger, the problem of anthropology is not primordial. Heidegger is not interested in the signification of human existing for itself. The human dimension [*l'humain*] does not come up in his thought except insofar as being is in question in the epic of being. *Sein* [Being] is in question in man, and man is necessary because being is in question. Man is a modality of being. *Dasein* is the very fact that being is in question.

The way in which Heidegger goes toward death is entirely dictated by the ontological preoccupation. The meaning of man's death is dictated by this preoccupation of being in its *epos*.[2] Consequently, for Heidegger, we must be sure that the analysis of being-there, carried out as an analysis of the question in which being is in question, develops *esse* or being in its proper sense, according to its proper meaning and not according to a derived deformation of some kind ("proper," which is translated by "authentic," that is, by a word that hides what is in "proper," viz., *eigentlich*).

Where to find a criterion for this originality, for this "authenticity," if not in the very approval of the question of being by the being-there? A proper meaning in the appropriation, in what Heidegger will later call the *Ereignis*.[3] There where the affair of being is imposed on being-there to the point of its making this affair its own—to the point where someone says, in the first person: this affair is my own [*mienne*]. Thus the proper arises from its impulse [*primesaut*] as mineness wherein, by dint of having this questioning as its own, this affair of being in questioning becomes the questioning of the me [*de moi*]. (The *Ereignis* of "Time and Being"[4] is already in *Being and Time*.) That the taking charge of this question of being contains the end, that death might thus be what can come to pass as most mine—this will be the Heideggerian analysis later on. In the emergence of the proper, death is already announced.

This appropriation, this *Ereignis*, this to-being in which appropriation itself arises as originary, in which appropriation is originated, and arises in its impulse; this appropriation in which the relationship to being concerns *Dasein* as properly its own [*en tant que sienne propre*]—that is where *Dasein* gathers itself in its proper meaning. It is there that the distinction between the proper and the derivative becomes meaningful.

Now, in sections 1 to 44 of *Being and Time*, the entire analysis of the *Da* (as the questioning of being that is a comprehension) *qua* care was carried out on the basis of the forms of being that this mineness presupposes. It is in the everyday that the *Da* was analyzed. Being-there had thus shown itself not in its appropriation but in its alienation, fleeing its task of being and thus adrift, growing distant from its undeniable attachment to the task of being.

Can the being-there thus described ever be called back to its meaning of being? Conversely, would not *Dasein*—gathered into a whole (if it could gather itself in this way)—lose its structure of having-to-be, its being-out-ahead-of-itself? And would it not thereby lose its very existence (its having-to-be) only to be exposed like something on exhibit, or present-at-hand (according to Maldiney's translation of *Vorhandenheit*)?[5] Gathered together, having come to its end and its goals, would not the *esse* of *Dasein*—once the hours of its life have been traversed—be dead, would it not be close to a thing and so, exhibited behind glass, exposed, like a portrait in a museum?

In *Dasein*, inasmuch as it is, something is always lacking: precisely that which it can be and become. To this lack belongs the end itself; but the end of being-in-the-world is death. It is a matter of unfolding for once the question of *Dasein*'s being-able-to-be-a-whole, while the end of being-in-the-world is death. It is by way of a certain relationship to death that *Dasein* will be a whole.

From there comes the question: Can being at the end still be thought as being at a distance from oneself? Can there be a signification of being-there as a whole beyond the biography? Is a person as a whole possible?

Not unless time, as a relationship to death, could be considered otherwise than as a pure and simple flow or a flood of instants. We can get out of the aporia only by rethinking the notion of time.

The question: "In what way can *Dasein* be grasped as a totality and as properly carrying on its course?"—which is intended in *Being and Time*'s system to elaborate being as a placing in question —has led us to a temporality or a duration of time in which ipseity,[6] as a whole, is not destroyed by the fact of its temporal history, in which this totality does not signify the totality of a thing without temporal life. (This is the very problem of what a person is. Whether the person is defined as biography or as a substance present at its biography—both these solutions are rejected here.)

It happens that this ipseity of *Dasein*, established from the appropriation of the affair of being by the being-there in man, is authentic in the appropriation of a possibility in which this appropriation is its most proper, its most inalienable, to the point of being inevitable: death. Time will be precisely, as out-ahead-of-oneself, that appropriation or that confrontation with death in which the ipseity of *Dasein* is whole. In this way, *Dasein* would be proper, or properly thought—the care for being that, in its being for which it feels care, is destined for death. Consequently, it is at once anxious for being and before being [*pour l'être et devant l'être*] (that nothingness that causes fear is also the nothingness that one wants). This is an anxiety at once for and before: this *for which* [*pour quoi*] one is anxious is simultaneously that *before which* [*devant quoi*] one is anxious—contrary to fear, where I have fear *of* the *dog* and fear *for me* (see § 30).[7]

Thus the totality of the human being and of its own being-there is sought without any intervention by another, solely in *Dasein* as being-in-the-world. The meaning of death is from the beginning interpreted as the *end* of being-in-the-world, as annihilation. The enigma is erased from the phenomenon.[8] The temporality or duration of time, without being identified with the common interpretation (as a flux), is interpreted as being-out-ahead-of-oneself, as being unto-being or being to-being [*être à-être*], which is also a question *qua* pre-comprehension: a question with a given [*avec donnée*]. Through and through, then, ontology, the comprehension of being and nothingness, remains the source of all meaning. In no way is the infinite (which perhaps brings thinking closer to diachrony, to patience and length of time) ever suggested by this analysis. Since Kant, philosophy has been finitude without infinity.

~

It is not possible to fail to read the end and annihilation in the phenomenon of death. But this end does not coincide with the destruction of an inanimate object or a living being of some kind, or with the erosion of a stone or the evaporation of a body of water, where there always remains some material after the destruction of the configuration, and where the destruction itself is placed between a before and an afterward that belong, along with the destruction, to the same time line, the same appearing, the same world. Does the end that is death coincide with the destruction of a form or a mechanism—or are we disquieted by a surplus of meaning or lack thereof, when man's death is in question? Man's death, on the basis of which is perhaps understood every living being's death (there too could lie something like a surplus or lack of meaning in relation to annihilation).

There is here an end that always has the ambiguity of a departure without return, a decease, but also of a scandal ("Is it possible that he is dead?") of no-response [de non-réponse] and of my responsibility. This is a departure to which I can assign no place of welcome; an exclusion that is other than negation—the same exclusion that excludes the contradiction "being and nothingness"—having the form of the excluded third [tiers-exclu] (but in no way a world to aim at): the very rise of the question, which can in no way be deduced from the modalities of being, and which is par excellence a question without response, and one from which every question borrows its interrogative mode [modalité d'interrogation].

We must confine ourselves to this and bear thoughtfully this question that is not posed as a problem, this para-doxical question; we must be obstinate in this questioning as we speak of death and of time and describe, where such a state of paradox is possible, all its meanings that are founded on no information about the beyond.

This is the infinite—which no finite can draw from itself, but which the finite thinks.

Does the time of our life, which death grasps, borrow its meaning in the first place from this emotion (anxiety), or does this emotion come from this question without the possibility of a response? We have to bear this question, which asks whether it is through its own nothingness that this end marks our time and whether this anxiety is the true emotion of death; whether time borrows its meaning as duration from this end or whether this interrogation comes from the unknown that is without a response.

The Death and Totality of *Dasein*

Friday, December 19, 1975

We have examined the phenomenon of death, behind which death crouches like a question with no givens, and which is irreducible to any doxic form of the Kantian categories. This is beyond or beside the position of the question to which one must confine oneself in order to speak of death and to think about the time in which this impossibility can be. This is a form that borrows nothing from some information [*renseignement*] about the beyond; it is, rather, the basis from which "information about the beyond" could itself take on meaning. Time must be understood in its duration and its diachrony as deference to the unknown.

~

Heidegger wonders whether the experience of being-there as a totality might be given through the death of the other man. Such a death has the advantage of being given to me, whereas my own death is the suppression of the experience I could have of it. Yet this attempt to approach death in the other man runs up against the same difficulties as those encountered in regard to my own death. The death of the other is an effective final event [*achèvenement*] and cannot provide access to the experience of the totality of *Dasein qua Dasein* (everything unfolds here as though experience were the deepest thing that could happen to us).

Although an impasse, this detour via the death of the other nevertheless has a positive aspect for the investigation: in this detour, it is as though we thought we found the experience of death in the experience of something that happens to everyone. *But we thereby miss death itself.* We thereby fail to see in death our ownmost possibility; death would not be fastened to each of us like his most proper possibility. Death thus shows itself as a possibility without any possible substitution. One can, no doubt, "für einen Anderen in den Tod gehen" [go to one's death for another], but nevertheless, one cannot "dem Anderen sein Sterben abnehmen" [take from the other his own death].[1] In dying, the ontological structure that is mineness, *Jemeinigkeit*, reveals itself.

(Sympathy and compassion, to suffer for the other or to "die a thousand deaths" for the other [*l'autre*], have as their condition of possibility a more radical substitution for an other [*autrui*]. This would be a responsibility for another in bearing his misfortune or his end *as if one were guilty of causing it.* This is the ultimate nearness. *To survive as a guilty one.* In this sense, the sacrifice for another [*autrui*] would create an other relation with the death of the other: a responsibility that would perhaps answer the question of why we can die. In the guiltiness of the survivor, the death of the other [*l'autre*] is my affair. *My* death is my *part* in the death of the other, and in my death I die the death that is my fault. The death of the other is not only a moment of the mineness of my ontological function.)

In fact, it is in relation to my own *Dasein* that death can be thought of as a concept that does not betray its existential sense. Heidegger delimits the notion of being-there by starting from a group of derived notions (the end and the totality), in order to show how the end can be thought of in the very order of *Dasein*, and not as the *Vorhandenes*. That is, how the end can be thought in its mode of being-there, how such an ending can constitute a whole, or how that whole can be gathered.

1. *Dasein* contains a distance relative to itself (an *Ausstand*, an "outstanding debt" in the sense of money withdrawn).

2. Its being-at-the-end, its coming-to-the-end, seems no longer to be there (the loss of its structure of *Dasein*).

3. The result of this analysis: to come to the end is the most

proper, the most untransferable, and the most inalienable possibility of *Dasein*.

The originality of Heidegger consists in placing in question the idea of being-out-ahead-of-oneself as an outstanding debt (in the sense in which one has money out). The gathering of the being that is *Dasein*, over the course of its being, is not done by an adjunction of pieces that are, or were, together. *Dasein* is in such a way that its "not-yet" belongs to it, and yet is not yet. This is not in the manner of money that is "elsewhere," or "outside," or "withdrawn." Nor is it in the manner of the quarter moon that the moon is "missing" (in fact, it is not missing; it is not apprehended).

Ought we to think of this on the model of organic development, of the maturity that belongs to the fruit? Heidegger does not dispute the resemblance: the fruit is going to ripen; it is not yet ripe since it is green; and yet maturity already belongs to it. What constitutes the nontotality of *Dasein* is a not-yet that *Dasein* has to be, like maturity for the fruit. But death is not maturity. The fulfillment of the fruit in becoming itself [*du fruit en devenir*] is not the death that surpasses its fulfillment. In dying, *Dasein* has not exhausted all its possibilities the way the fruit has done in ripening. When *Dasein* dies, *its* possibilities are *taken away* from it. To finish is not to be fulfilled. Death as our end does not necessarily await a certain number of years.[2]

In what sense, then, shall we take death as the end of *Dasein*? The end of death can be understood neither as a completion, nor as a disappearance, nor as the cessation of the rain that ceases, nor as the finishing of the finished work, nor in the sense of a debt that is paid back. For *Dasein*, the end is not the final point of a being but a way of assuming or taking on the end in one's very being. It is a possibility that *Dasein* grasps (*übernimmt*),[3] not a seizing [*rapt*]. "Der Tod is eine Weise zu sein, die das Dasein übernimmt, sobald es ist": "Death is a form of being that *Dasein* assumes from the moment that it is."[4] It is not in an as-yet-unfulfilled future, according to a time that stretches out in a series of days and nights, minutes or seconds, that death must be thought; it is on the contrary on the basis of the to-being [*l'à-être*] of existence that the to-death [*l'à-mort*] that is *Dasein* must be grasped. "Sobald ein Mensch zum Leben kommt, sogleich ist er alt genug zu sterben": "As soon as a person comes into life, he is then old enough to die."[5] To have to be is to have to die. Death is not somewhere in time, but time is, in its origin, *zu sein* [*to be*], that is to say, *zu sterben* [*to die*].

If death completes *Dasein*, *Eigentlichkeit* [what is one's most proper] and the totality go together. We can see here, in ridding ourselves of any reified notions, the coincidence of the total and the proper. Death is a mode of being, and it is on the basis of this mode of being that the not-yet arises.

Being-Toward-Death as the Origin of Time

Friday, January 9, 1976

Death as an end, but equally as a question, is the focus of our research. What is to be determined is how the manner of this questioning contrasts with the positivity of experience, with the phenomenality of appearing, with comprehension and the grasp of the given—and this, not only in my mind but in every manifestation that confirms the positive quality of all positivity. The question is the way in which belief, or *doxa*, to which the universe is referred, is reversed in a radical fashion; it is the way in which this *doxa* reverses itself into a question. This is a question that would be not a modality of judgment but, beyond judgment, something that is not another judgment, something that is a question without the posing of a problem. A question in which the turning [*la version*] toward the other is effected (every question is a request or a prayer). A turning toward the other in which theoretical or doxic thinking itself is contained, to the degree that it questions itself (is not the dialogue of the soul with itself possible by virtue of another's questioning, even if in its operation theoretical thought does not take account of this dimension?). This would be a turning toward the other not in order to collaborate with him, a turning that, in its questioning, does not pose the prior question of existence (for the question is not preceded by existence).

The death signified by the end could not measure the entire significance of death without becoming responsibility for another—by

42

which one becomes oneself in reality: one becomes oneself through this untransferable, undelegatable responsibility. It is for the death of the other that I am responsible to the point of including myself in his death. This is perhaps shown in a more acceptable proposition: "I am responsible for the other in that he is mortal." The death of the other: therein lies the first death.

Time will have to be presented on the basis of this relationship, from this deference to the death of the other and this questioning that is a relationship to the infinite. We must pass beyond Heidegger, who sought an experience of death and for whom death's end is asserted to be nothingness, without anything penetrating from beyond the nothingness in the manner in which death's nothingness is demonstrated in *Dasein*.

Heidegger wants to grasp being-there, that is, man, or the fact that being is in question. He wants to grasp being-there in its totality and not in just one of its aspects (especially not in the aspect in which *Dasein* is the loss of self in the everyday). He wants to grasp it in the aspect by which it is in possession of itself, in which it is most properly itself, *eigentlich*. And this possession of self will be shown to be being-toward-death [*être-pour-la-mort*] *or* being-to-death [*être-à-la-mort*] (in the sense that one loves to the point of madness, which means to love in a way that implies going all the way to unreason).

To die, for *Dasein*, is not to reach the final point of one's being but to be close to the end at every moment of one's being. Death is not a moment of one's being. It is not a moment, but a manner of being of which *Dasein* takes charge as soon as it is, such that the expression "to have to be" also signifies "to have to die." It is not in an unfulfilled future that death must be thought; on the contrary, it is on the basis of this to-be [*à-être*], which is also to-death [*à-mort*], that time must be thought in an originary way. Just as *Dasein*, as long as it is, is always a "not yet," it is also always its end. It is its end, or it is *at* its end: that is the significance of the transitivity of the verb "to be" (the transitivity of the verb "to be" is Heidegger's greatest discovery).

Time is the mortal being's mode of being, so that the analysis of being-toward-death[1] will provide us with the origin of a new conception of time. Time as the future of being-toward-death, a future defined exclusively by the unique relationship of being-to-death as being outside oneself, which is also being whole, or being properly oneself.

The finishing that we must understand by death means not that *Dasein* is at its end but that this being is in the mode of being-toward-the-end, and that what constitutes an event in this being [*Dasein*] is to go to its end. The energy or the very power of being is already the power of its end. There is a new and irreducible relationship here: it is irreducible to a distance in regard to what remains outside of and distinct from a ripening.

What does being-toward-death mean, as distinct from ripening? In an originary sense, the future is the imminence of death. The relation with death is thought on the basis of the formal structure of care, which is the proper mode of being-there (of the being who is in having to be its being). This manner of being is expressed by three structures: being-out-ahead; always-already-in-the-world (facticity); close-to-things (in which the world is forgotten). How can these three structures be united in the *Sein zum Tode* [being-toward-death]?

To be for the end is a not-yet; but this not-yet is the not-yet toward which being-there is referred in *welcoming* it as imminence. Being-there does not represent this not-yet, it does not consider it; neither is this welcoming an awaiting. It somewhat resembles Husserlian protention, but with the dimension of a threat. Heidegger speaks here of a power: I am capable of an imminent power [*je peux un pouvoir imminent*]. Now, death is a possibility of which *Dasein* must itself take charge, and which is untransferable. I here have a power that is my own, proper to me. (For Heidegger, the word "power" is also applied to death.) With death, *Dasein* protends [*se pro-tend*] toward the imminence of its ownmost possibility. In being-toward-death, the imminent possibility concerns the being-in-the-world itself that is threatened—but threatened by this being-in-the-world and to-death. The power that is the mode according to which imminence concerns *Dasein* is the possibility—

or the eventuality—of no longer being there. To be toward death is, for *Dasein*, to be out ahead of oneself. Herein lies a possibility of which each *Dasein* is capable, on its own account.

This extreme and unsurpassable possibility is the imminence of nonbeing: death is the possibility of the radical impossibility of being-there. Thus its imminence is itself privileged, and this, in the manner by which I am capable of this imminence: it is to be capable of a possibility [*pouvoir une possibilité*] marked by its untransferable, exclusive, and unsurpassable character. The relationship to death, as possibility, is an exceptional *to-* [*à*], an exceptional *toward-*, privileged.

Now such a relationship is possible only through the structure of *Dasein*, which has to be its being, that is, which is on the basis of this out-ahead-of-oneself. To-be-out-ahead-of-oneself is concrete in being-toward-death. In the same way, facticity and being-close-to-things are contained in being-toward-death. In its ipseity, implicit in mineness, *Dasein* is only possible as mortal. An immortal person is a contradiction in terms.

Death, Anxiety, and Fear

Friday, January 16, 1976

Time and death: these themes are subordinated to the search for the signification of the being of beings, a search that itself does not come from the curiosity of the explorer, but is a search essential to man, characteristic of his essence, his *esse*. Being *qua* being is already to-be-in-question. This essence in question is equivalent to being-there as the humanity of man, who is a being whose being is equivalent to the essence in question. This placing in question is also a pre-comprehension of being; it is effectuated in the form of a taking charge: a taking charge within *Dasein* and a charge imposed in the most incontestable way—to the point of becoming properly my own. This superlative thus takes the meaning of mineness, in such a way that being *qua* being-in-question is the affair of ipseity. This taking charge is the mode of the human being's to-be, which unfolds as being-there, as being-the-there, and this unfolds as being-in-the-world, which itself unfolds as care, where care is broken into a triple structure: being-out-ahead-of-oneself (ec-sistence) as already-in-the-world (facticity), alongside of things (dispersion or dereliction among things).

It is from there that Heidegger seeks to discover the totality or integrity of these diverse moments set forth by his analysis. And it is in the concern to think together the structures of *Dasein* that we again find notions like time and death. Is not the totality of the human being its life from its birth to its death? Is it not therefore the time its life fills, and is not the time that its life fills the sum of instants elapsed? Is death—which marks the end of time—the totality and being proper to *Dasein*? Or are we not here using vulgar concepts (elaborated in an inauthentic mode and not in the proper mode of *Dasein*)?

We have shown that dying, understood as the end or term of a series of temporal units, does not apply to the strictly existentiell structures of being-there, and it even contradicts them.[1] In dying understood this way, being-there is already interpreted as being part of a reality presented as "on display" and in conformity with the mode of being of an entity within the world. From this comes the attempt to rethink death, the end of *Dasein*, in terms of its existential structure. Death is not, then, the ending of a duration made up of days and nights but an ever open *possibility*. This ever open possibility is the most proper possibility, exclusive in regard to an other, isolating, and extreme or unsurpassable as a possibility. "The most proper" designates its tie with mineness, which leads from to-be [*à-être*] to ipseity. If we think this to the end, mineness is mortality: alone the I [*Moi*] dies, and only the mortal is an I [*Moi*].

This "most proper" possibility is not a thing that happens to *Dasein* "on some occasion." It is a possibility to which *Dasein* is *always already* compelled. This always already is attested to by a *Stimmung* [mood]: to-be-delivered-to-death already belongs to being-in-the-world without *Dasein* having a distinct consciousness of it. This past that is already past is attested to in *anxiety*.

Anxiety is an emotion, and emotion in Heidegger always has two intentionalities: an *of* and a *for*. I have fear *of* the dog and I have fear *for* me. Now, in anxiety, the two aspects coincide. Anxiety is the anxiety *of* death *for* a being that is precisely being-toward-death. The able-to-be is in danger of death, but the able-to-be is precisely what threatens.

This emotion is not the fear of finishing life; it is the opening of the fact that *Dasein*, as thrown into being, exists toward the end. *Dasein* has to be, but to-have-to-be is also to-have-to-die. Thus facticity is again discovered. But we again find the moment of the fall [*déchéance*]: the ignorance or unawareness of death that character-

izes everyday life is a mode of being-toward-death, a flight that attests to a relationship with this anxiety. *Dasein* in fact dies, inasmuch as it exists, but in the mode of flight, of the fall. One flees
death in holding close to things and in interpreting oneself on the
basis of things from everyday life.

Heidegger thus shows the originary determination of being-there
by being-toward-death. He pushes his analysis farther by starting
from the everyday being that is a flight before death and that is
also, thereby, a true recognition of death. This flight is more properly a being-toward-death than the way in which one calms oneself
in order to think about death.

How does being-toward-death show itself in the everyday? The
oneself [*soi-même*] has not disappeared in flight, for the being-there
would itself have disappeared, but it is in the loss of self (which is
again a way of being a self, of being a mineness): in *das Man* [the
they].[2] This is a They that is not possible without the reference to
mineness, for it is a modification of it.

The question is consequently taken up with greater breadth: is
the They, in which the proper becomes the improper, still being-
toward-death? Heidegger answers that to flee, to hide death from
oneself, is a deficient mode implying the positivity of a being-
toward-death. The They is characterized by the fact that it *chats*,
and its idle talk (*Gerede*) is an interpretation of this being-toward-
death that is a fleeing-death, a distraction. There is a special affectivity that characterizes this flight: anxiety reduced to fear. Anxiety
becomes fear. Death becomes *a case* of death. One dies, but no one
in particular dies. The others die, but it is an event in the world
(for Heidegger, the death of an other is also an event in the world).
Death is something that can come to pass [*peut se produire*] but
that, for the moment, has not yet come. One dies, but not I, not
just now. This is the equivocal language in which dying, in its
mineness, becomes a neutral public event, a news item. The They
effaces the character of death as ever possible by giving it the effective reality of an object. We console ourselves as if we could escape
death. Public life does not want to let itself be troubled by death,
which it considers a lack of tact. "The They forbids the courage of

the anxiety of death to come to light," writes Heidegger: "Das Man lässt den Mut zu Angst vor dem Tode nicht aufkommen."[3]

The *Stimmung* [mood, tonality] of the affectivity of everydayness is fear before the event. The They, in its flight before death, speaks of the necessity and certainty of death, but this certainty is purely empirical, whereas the certainty of the authentic relationship to death is *a priori*; it is a certainty in whose regard the empirical certainty is a flight. Death is a possibility that is absolutely certain. It is the possibility that makes all possibility possible.

Time Considered on
the Basis of Death

Friday, January 23, 1976

Death is the reversal of appearing [*l'apparaître*]. Contrary to what appears, death is like a return of being in itself, where that which beckoned turns back into itself, and can no longer respond. It is a movement opposed to phenomenology. But is death itself to be thought of as an end, the end of being in the absolute sense of its annihilation, the end of its manifestation? Or should it be thought of as a question with no positive determination, a question in which nothing refers to a *doxa* of any sort, a *doxa* of which the question would be a modification?

Death is the phenomenon of the end, all the while being the end of the phenomenon. It strikes our thought and makes it precisely a questioning, whether this be in its future (if we privilege our own death as in Heidegger) or in the present. As a phenomenon of the end, death concerns our thought; it concerns our life, which is thought, that is, our life as manifestation manifesting itself to itself, a temporal or diachronic manifestation.

The problem consists in asking ourselves what this end is for the temporality of manifestation, what death is for time. What is the very mortality of life? Such is the true problem of our inquiry, the meaning of death for time.

For Heidegger, death signifies *my* death in the sense of my *annihilation*. For him, the inquiry into the relationship between death and time is motivated by the effort to assure oneself that, in the analytic of *Dasein* in which being is in question, being-there is grasped and described in its authenticity or its integrity. Because death marks from the start the end of being-there, it is through death itself that being-there—or man, who, in the form of a being, is the event of that being-there—is the totality of what it is, or is properly there.

Starting from there, Heidegger shows that dying is not what marks some final instant of *Dasein* but what characterizes the very way in which man is his being. From there comes the notion of being-toward-death, which signifies being in regard to the possibility of no-longer-being-there, this being-in-regard-to indicating not some contemplation of the end adding itself to the being that I am. To-be-for-death is to relate to death by the very being that I am.

Therein lies an existential relationship to the possibility of dying. An irreducible or privileged relationship, which Heidegger describes on the basis of the privileged character of this possibility of dying as a possibility for our power, a possibility to seize. This possibility is:

—the most proper, or ownmost possibility; a possibility in which the proper as such is produced;

—an untransferable possibility; a possibility that consequently is "me" [*moi*], or ipseity;

—an isolating possibility, since it is a possibility that, as my ownmost, cuts all my ties with other men;

—an extreme possibility that surpasses all others and next to which all the others grow pale; a possibility by which *Dasein* sets itself off from all other possibilities, which then become insignificant.

The power that is capable of such a possibility reunites the structures of *Dasein*, made explicit as *care*. To-be-out-ahead-of-oneself is precisely to-be-projected-toward-this-possibility-of-no-longer-being-in-the-world. But on the other hand, care is facticity; it is the fact of being-already-in-the-world without having chosen this. Finally, this being-to-death is already a fall, already being-alongside-of-things in everydayness where there is consolation and diversion from death, where death is viewed as an event coming to pass within the world (as the death of the other).

It is on the basis of this avoidance that Heidegger conducts a new approach in order to clarify another trait of being-toward-the-end [*l'être-à-la-fin*]: the certainty of death. This certainty is described from the everydayness that avoids the certainty.

Among the modes of everyday being there is above all chitchat, idle talk. This idle talk sums up the attitude in regard to death: one dies, sometime, but not just now. There is thus indeed a certainty of death, but it is as if calmed in its gravity by that adjournment. Such is the ambiguity of idle talk, in which certainty is not the authentic certainty of death. For certainty is a mode of truth that is itself a discovery, a disclosure, wherein the disclosed is not authentically disclosed unless *Dasein* is open to itself. Now in everyday life, *Dasein* is precisely not open to itself. Certainty signifies first a certain comportment of *Dasein.* Everyday *Dasein* covers up its ownmost possibility—it is therefore in nontruth. Its certainty of death is inadequate; it is covered up. Death is an event in the world; the certainty relative to it comes out of experience; it coincides with the fact that the others pass away.

Does *Dasein* escape the certainty of death in the mode of the fall? Does its discourse allow it to escape certainty? It avoids death —and it is this fact of avoiding that is the true relation to death. It is to the degree that it is compelled to flee death that it attests to the certainty of death. *It is its flight before death that is an attestation of death.*

It is thus that we come to a complete characterization of death. Death is certain, and that means that it is always possible, possible at each moment, but in this way its "when" is indeterminate. Such will be the complete concept of death: the most proper possibility, an unsurpassable possibility, isolating, certain, indeterminate.

What remains to be shown is the authentic way to be-for-death. It must be shown that the power or capacity for the possibility of death is not a banal power, or a power like the others, in that it realizes nothing. What does the relation to such a possibility signify? It is a matter of maintaining this possibility *as* a possibility; one must maintain it without transforming it into a reality. The relation with every other possibility is characterized by the realization of this possibility. The relation with this exceptional possibility is characterized by *Vorlaufen*, by anticipation. The anticipation of this imminence consists in maintaining this possibility. The possibility of dying is not realized (and it realizes nothing). Death is not the moment of death but the fact of relating to the possible as possible. This is a privileged relation to the possible that does not end in its realization; this unique possibility of relating to the possible as possible is being-toward-death. "Death, as a possibility, gives nothing to *Dasein* to 'realize,' nor anything that it could itself *be* as actual."[1]

If existence is a comportment with regard to the possibility of existence, and if it is total in its existence with regard to this possibility, then it cannot but be toward- or for-death. If being is to-being, being is being-toward-death.[2] To-be-out-ahead-of-oneself is precisely to-be-toward-death (if being-toward-death is abolished, then being-out-ahead-of-oneself is suppressed at the same time, and *Dasein* is no longer a totality). This, then, is how man is considered in his totality, how *Dasein* is at every moment whole: in its relationship to death.

~

In this description we see how time was, throughout these analyses, deduced from its length of time—within measurable and measured time. We see how measurable time is not the original time, how there is a priority of the relationship with the future as a relationship with a possibility and not as a reality: the concrete manner in which such an idea is thought is therefore the analysis of death. It is through death that there is time and there is *Dasein*.

Inside Heidegger: Bergson

Friday, January 30, 1976

Death as annihilation marks being-there. It would imply, as its referent, a time similar to a span that extends out infinitely prior to birth and after death. This time counts, and we count it in everyday life: it is everydayness itself. This time is the dimension in which being unfolds. It would be the production of the ess*a*nce of being. For Heidegger, death as annihilation marks being-there in such a way that everyday time would be a consequence of being-there. The ultimacy of the ultimate moment of death in everyday time proceeds from mortality. There is therefore a more profound, or originary, time behind linear time, which is understood only on the basis of the mortality that is comprehended as the capacity for a possible incurred *as possible*, that is, without the assumption of this possible making it lose its contingency as possible.

Being-there is the way in which to-being (*Zu-sein*)[1] is expressed, and this to-be is a structure that states that being in general is in question and is pre-comprehended. Now, to-be is to be in regard to my being [*à-être, c'est être en étant à l'égard de mon être*] as in regard to a possible, or as not-yet-being. This not-yet is not the not-yet of linear time. This not-yet is like being with regard to a possible as possible. That is being-to-death [*être-à-la-mort*]. To approach death is therefore not to approach realization but to allow this possible to stand out better as the most properly possible. To die is not a realization but the nothingness of all reality. Therein lies a relationship unique in its kind, where to-be is to-dying.

It is in exposing oneself to one's most proper possibility, in the power to die, that meaning is projected—the same meaning toward which every project is aimed: the future, or what is to-come [*l'à-venir*]. In this way, without recourse to quantitative notions of time, the future and an originary notion of time are sketched out, and one more properly time than was everyday time.

As in Bergson, the idea that there are various levels of time is affirmed here. The entire Western tradition approaches time through measurement (time is the number of movement, says Aristotle). For Bergson, linear time is a spatialization of time in view of acting upon matter, which is the work of intelligence. Originary time he calls *duration*; this is a becoming in which each instant is heavy with all of the past and pregnant with the whole future. Duration is experienced by a descent into self. Each instant is there; nothing is definitive since each instant remakes the past.

For Heidegger, originary time, or the time of the being-there that is fulfilled in the human, describes the finitude of being-there. It is fulfilled in anxiety and dispersed in the everyday. For Heidegger, infinite time is deduced from original finitude. For Bergson, finitude and unsurpassable death are not inscribed in duration. Death is inscribed in the degradation of energy. Death is the characteristic of matter, intelligence, and action; it is inscribed in what is, for Heidegger, *Vorhandenheit* [on exhibit, present-at-hand].[2] For Bergson, on the contrary, life is duration, the vital impulse, and these must be thought together with creative freedom. "All the living beings hold together, and all yield to the same tremendous push. The animal takes its stand on the plant, man bestrides animality, and the whole of humanity, in space and in time, is one immense army galloping beside and before and behind each of us in an overwhelming charge able to beat down every resistance and clear the most formidable obstacles, *perhaps even death*."[3]

Nothingness is a false idea, and death is not identical to nothingness. The human being is thus a way of not being-to-death.

But the vital impulse is not the ultimate signification of the time of Bergsonian duration. In *Two Sources of Morality and Religion*, the duration that *Creative Evolution* considered as vital impulse becomes interhuman life.[4] Duration becomes the fact that a man can appeal to the interiority of the other man. Such is the role of the saint and the hero beyond that of matter, the same hero and saint who lead to an open religion in which death no longer has a meaning.

This sympathy of time is not a drama of being *qua* being; not because it is a question of a philosophy of becoming but because the to-be does not exhaust the meaning of duration. For Heidegger, on the contrary, being is a matter or an affair; it is a *Sache*. The way in which being is with regard to its own nothingness is the oneself [*soi-même*]. The "to-" [*à-*] of to-be [*à-être*] is comprehended on the basis of its being. So questioning is a modality of its adventure of being [*sa geste d'être*].

The Radical Question:
Kant Against Heidegger

Friday, February 6, 1976

In order to be thought radically, must death and time have their ultimate reference in ontology, that is, in a thinking about being as being? It was so for Heidegger. In his work, death and time are thought as modes of being as being. Death is the end of being-in-the-world, and as that end, it is interpreted on the basis of man's being-toward-death, which is a pre-comprehension of the being essentially in question in man. Death as the end of being-in-the-world characterizes death as anxiety. It is a matter of taking on this death in anxiety, in the form of courage and not as pure passivity. A death where being-to-death is sketched out as having-to-be, as being its being [*étant son être*] in the not-yet. There is no other epic than the epic of being. To be is to-be-in-question; to-be-in-question is to-be; to-be or unto-being is to-be-there; to-be-there is to-be-in-the-world as being-to-death, to project oneself into the possible and, in projecting oneself toward the possible, to-be-in-one's-totality-as-being-there—and not as what is on exhibit or present-at-hand (*Vorhandenes*).

From this came a characterization of time, that is, of the originary time of which our everyday time is but a fall or—to use a word that does not confer value on this—a drifting. To take death on in anxiety as the possible is what is originally to-come, or future [*à-venir*] (which is itself to-be); a future engaged in a past because anxiety is an affectivity containing the always already, and the al-

ready-there. The entire structure of time is drawn from the relationship to death, which is a modality of being.

The very ipseity of being-there is understood on the basis of its
own being, which equals its own nothingness. Ipseity is drawn from
its own finitude. It is a modality of being. (Not only: I am in being;
but: the modalities of man are the modalities of being.) Everything
human [*tout l'humain*] is reduced to ontology. *Dasein*'s privilege resides in the fact that it exists ontologically. All that is man, all his
modalities, are adverbs: not properties but manners of being. The
humanity of man comes down to being (see in this regard Heidegger's *Letter on Humanism*, where to be a man is to be in service of
being, to be part of its adventure, to be the shepherd or guardian of
being). Man's humanity is referred to the concern about death in its
fullest sense. Man's time is this sense of being-to-death.

Here a radical question has to be posed. Is meaning always an
event of being? To be—is this the significance of meaning? Should
we say that humanity, taken simply as a meaningful order, that reason, as meaning or rationality or intelligibility, or as spirit, and that
philosophy, taken as man's expression—are all reducible to ontology? The question mark of every question comes from the question: What does being signify? (This, Heidegger asserts; there is no
other question for him, even if this question immediately became
anxiety about death.) Is everything that comes into play in being,
itself being? (Through this question we contest the first pages of
Being and Time.) Does everything that is examined in man come
down to the question: What is it to be? *Or indeed*, is there not a
more interrogative question behind this question, such that death,
despite its certitude, would not be reduced to the question, or the
alternative between to be and not to be? Does death come down
only to tying the knot of the intrigue of being? Does death not
have its eminent meaning in the death of others, where it signifies
"by way of" an event that cannot be reduced to its being? In this
being that we are, do "things" not come to pass [*se produit-il pas
des "choses"*] in which our being does not count as first? And if humanity is not exhausted in the service of being, then does not my
responsibility for another (in its emphatic sense: my responsibility

for the death of another, my responsibility as a survivor) rise up behind the question: What is it to be? Does it not arise behind the
anxiety over my own death? And would time then not call for a
different interpretation of the projection toward the future?

We must now study a few aspects of the history of philosophy in
which meanings are attested that ontology does not exhaust, meanings that can, on the contrary, place ontology in question in its pretense to be the encompassing adventure of humanity. Heidegger
accustomed us to seek in the history of philosophy the very history
of being. His entire work consists in bringing metaphysics back to
the history of being. But whatever the place of the epic of being,
does not the history of philosophy indicate another disquietude? Is
the beyond-being inscribed in the epic of being [*la geste d'être*]?
Does the transcendence of being relative to beings (a transcendence
whose meaning Heidegger awakened) permit us to think it completely? In philosophy, has not the disquietude of God other meanings than the forgetting of being and the errancy of onto-theo-logy?
Is the God of onto-theo-logy—who is perhaps dead—the only
God; are there not other meanings of the word "God"? (That is
what the "believers" would think—those, at least, who are presented and who present themselves under this term!—in thinking a
faith *more thoughtful* than onto-theo-logy, a faith *more awakened,
more sobered up.*)

To reduce every philosophical effort to the error or errancy of
onto-theo-logy is only one possible reading of the history of
philosophy.[1]

Kantian philosophy was thus reduced by Heidegger, who insisted above all on the *Critique of Pure Reason*, to the first radical
exhibition of the finitude of being. But of the four questions posed
in philosophy, according to Kant (What may I know? What must
I do? What am I entitled to hope? What is man?), the second
seems to surpass the first with all the breadth of the last two. The
question *What may I know?* leads to finitude, but *What must I do?*
and *What am I entitled to hope?* go farther and, in any case, elsewhere than toward finitude. These questions are not reducible to

the comprehension of being; they concern the duty and salvation of man.

In the second question, if we comprehend it formally, there is no reference to being. That meaning might signify without reference to being, without recourse to being, without a comprehension of being given is, moreover, the great contribution of the Transcendental Dialectic in the *Critique of Pure Reason*.

Among the conditions of the constitution of a phenomenon (i.e., to be given), there figures, beside space and time, the synthetic activity of understanding according to categories. The categories are constitutive of the given: what we can know is being that is given, and for which the categories are constitutive. But in order that there be something given, it is also necessary to appeal to the *whole* of reality, to the whole that is a transcendental ideal that is never given, which never receives the predicate "being," and relative to which the objects given by experience are thought of as entirely determined.

This transcendental ideal is a meaningful and necessary notion, but one that we would be wrong to think of as being. To think of it as being is to prove the existence of God, which is dialectical, that is, aberrant. The transcendental ideal is thought *in concreto*, but Kant refuses it being, since he is guided by the prototype of being that is the phenomenon. In this sense, Reason has ideas that go beyond being.

This position of the transcendental ideal, which bears out the limited character of the givenness of any valid sense, is contradicted by practical Reason. Moving to the practical plane, Kant puts finitude back in question. There is a mode of practical signification that remains—beside the theoretical access to being—an access to an irrecusable meaning. It remains an access to a signification in which what is after-death can be thought of not as an extension after death of the time that came before death but rather as a signification in which the after-death has its own motivations. In Kant, the practical is totally independent in relation to the cognitive access to being. So the death included in the finitude of being becomes a *problem*. Time reveals itself to be a relative concept.

There is the problem of the reconciliation of morality and happiness, as though this problem had its own meaning, whatever the ontological truths of the *Critique of Pure Reason* might be. Kant thus shows the existence, in thought, of meanings that have a sense of their own, without being reduced to the epic of being.

I am free in my respect for the moral law, although theoretically I belong to the world of necessity. God and the immortality of the soul are demanded by Reason in order that the accord between virtue and happiness be thinkable. This accord demands—independently of the ontological adventure and *against* everything ontology teaches us—an *afterward* [*un après*]. Therein lies a motivation proper, in the midst of being as it unfolds. Kant certainly does not think that we must think of an extension of time beyond limited time; he does not want a "prolongation of life." But there is a *hope*, a world accessible to a hope; there is a motivation proper to a hope that signifies. In an existence determined by death, in this epic of being, there are things that do not enter into the epic, significations that cannot be reduced to being. This hope cannot have a theoretical response, but it is a motivation proper. This hope occurs in time and, in time, goes beyond time.

Kant's practical philosophy thus offers a response to the second and third questions, which cannot be reduced to the terms in which being and the given are in play and in which the given appears. This response is not reducible to the terms of the first question. (This does not mean that Kant manages to demonstrate the existence of God and the immortality of the soul.)

The practical philosophy of Kant shows that the Heideggerian reduction is not obligatory. It shows that there might be, in the history of philosophy, a signification other than that of finitude.[2]

A Reading of Kant (Continued)

Friday, February 13, 1976

Heideggerian thought appears to stand out in all its brilliance in the analysis of being-toward-death and the description of originary temporality. Death and time have, as their ultimate reference, the question of the meaning of being, of being as being, or of ontology. Temporality is ec-stasis toward the future, and this is the first ec-stasis. This ec-stasis toward the future amounts to exposing oneself to death in anticipating it; such a disposition toward death is an exposure to a possibility as possibility; and this disposition toward the possibility is being-out-ahead-of-itself. Being-out-ahead-of-itself is being-there, which is to-be [*Zu-sein*], which is to pre-comprehend or question oneself about the meaning of being, which is to be in question, which is to be [*sein*]. Such is the path of *Being and Time*.

Therefore, the entire human adventure is reduced to being as being. Everything that could have a meaning, every project, every comprehension, is reduced to this being, and death is the ultimate, the certain, the ownmost and unsurpassable possibility—or again, time goes back (speculatively) to the epic of being as being, which is being-to-death. To this epic can be traced the dimension of time and even that of intemporality or of the ideal (in Husserl, eternal ideality is already an omni-temporality). There is no eternity; eternity is, like linear time, a modality of finite time; it is derived from originary time. The person in his uniqueness and ipseity, which is authenticity (the ownmost or proper) itself, is traced back to this epic of being [*la geste d'être*].

To state the radical problem is to ask whether the humanity of man, whether meaning, is reducible to the intrigue of being as being. Is meaning this event of being? Does every intrigue that is tied up in being merely cause the epic or adventure of being [*la geste d'être*] to unfold, merely write the epic of being (see Trakl's explication: to comprehend the poem is to go back to the thinking of being)?[1] This is a radical question; it is *the* radical question, for it concerns the first claims of *Being and Time*.

This reduction of every question to being can be seen both in Heidegger's struggle against and his irony in regard to every philosophy of value. It is not a matter here of discovering or restoring values; rather, beyond the pressure toward values, something can show itself to thought. It is for this reason that we read Kant last week. It was not to find in him a proof of the existence of God liable to calm our anxiety before death, but to show, in the heart of the *finite* being of subjectivity and the phenomenon (the *Critique of Pure Reason* is a philosophy of finitude), that there is a rational hope, an *a priori* hope. It is not to some will to survive that Kant gives satisfaction, but to a wholly other conjunction of meaning. An *a priori* hope, that is, one inherent in finite reason. Thus a hope just as sensible and as rational as mortality. This meaning could not refute the mortality that shows itself in being as being (i.e., finite being), but neither does it simply rank the hope of immortality among the derivatives of being-toward-death and therefore of the originary temporality of being-there. There is here a wholly other motivation, a rational motivation.

This orientation does not refute being-toward-death, which is, according to Heidegger, the presupposition of finitude. There lies the great force of Kant's practical philosophy: the possibility of thinking a beyond of time by way of hope, but obviously not a beyond that would prolong time, not a beyond that *is* (and would be). But neither an everyday derivative of originary time. Rather, a rational hope, as though in finite time there opened another dimension of originarity that was not a denial inflicted on finite time but something that had a meaning other than finite *or* infinite time. The meaning of this hope in despair does not undo the nothingness of death; it is a lending to death of a meaning other than that which it draws from the nothingness of being. It is not to a need to survive that this hope answers.

It is as if another relationship with the infinite signified this hope, where death and its nothingness are the ultimate intensity and where they are necessary to this relationship. It is as if, in the human dimension, and behind the *Sein zum Tode* [being-toward-death], an intrigue were woven of hope for immortality that was not measured by the length of time or by perpetuity, and which consequently had in this always [*toujours*] a temporality *other* than that of being-to-death. This intrigue is called "hope," without having the usual sense of the term, which signifies an awaiting in time. It is a hope that resists every knowledge [*connaissance*], every gnosis. A relationship relative to which time and death have another meaning.

~

Alongside the theoretical access to the being of the phenomenon, which is had only in the time and space of the finite being, and which gives us access only to the phenomenon bound by the categories but not to the noumenon, Kant examines human existence or reasonable subjectivity in the implications of moral action —implications that can be clarified without becoming the object of any knowledge of being.

Moral action is characterized by its universal maxim, a determination of the will that, acting in conformity with the law, acts freely. This freedom goes back to Reason, to the universality of the maxim. Moral action in its freedom signifies independence vis-à-vis all divinity and every beyond (Kant describes the divine *on the basis of free action*): we are *internally* bound by the moral obligation of duty, says Kant. God is not necessary to the moral act. On the contrary, it is on the basis of the moral act that one can describe God. God becomes necessary if, beyond the moral act, we desire *happiness*.

Hope would come from the rational character of a virtue that accords with happiness. Happiness is acceptable only if it accords with what makes one worthy of being happy; and, for its part, morality by itself is not the Sovereign Good, either. Therefore, neither happiness alone nor virtue alone—both of these injure Reason. In order that the Good be perfect, it is necessary that he who has not behaved in a way that would make him unworthy of happiness might hope to participate in happiness. In the "other life," after death (in an otherwise than living, an otherwise than being), we find a hope for the accord between virtue and happiness, which is possible only through a God. We must behave as if the soul were immortal and as if God existed. This is a hope against all knowledge [*savoir*], but nevertheless a rational hope. To allow the existence of God and the immortality of the soul is demanded by Reason, but the supreme Good can only be *hoped for*.

The important point here is that hope does not refer, like an awaiting, to something that must come about. Awaiting is an access to what can be contained in some knowledge. Here, hope is something other than a prescience, something other than the desire to survive oneself (for Kant, death is the limit of what can be known). But this hope is also not a subjective nostalgia. It designates a domain that is more than a human behavior and less than being. But one may ask oneself this question: Is hope—as more than some human behavior and less than being—not also *more* than being?

Time is not prolonged after death such as it was, going toward death. Knowledge [*connaissance*] is always proportionate to what it knows. The relationship with something beyond-measure [*démesuré*] is hope. Hope must thus be analyzed as this very temporality itself. A hope in the form of a relationship with a more than being, which shall never be proved to exist or be signified as what is correlative of some domain of knowledge [*d'un savoir*]. On that basis, a subjectivity might be thought that can be in relation with what cannot be realized—and yet not with the romantic unrealizable: with an order above, or beyond, being.

～

We shall retain from Kantianism a meaning that is not dictated by a relationship with being. It is not accidental that this reference comes from a morality, which, to be sure, is said to be rational on account of the universality of the maxim. It is not accidental that this way of thinking about a meaning beyond being is the corollary of an ethics.

How to Think Nothingness?

Friday, February 20, 1976

The Kantian postulates do not postulate a time after time. Rational hope is not for those who, in time, await events that would come to fill hope's void. For Husserl, intuition fills a signitive aim, as though, one day, what is hoped for would have to make itself known. For Kant, that is impossible: time is the form of sensibility and belongs to the understanding's constitution of phenomenal objectivity. If rational hope were to be fulfilled, if it had to make itself known at a certain moment, that would mean that immortality would have a temporal fulfillment, known in the manner of the phenomenon. But such a contact with the absolute is excluded by the *Critique of Pure Reason*. The rational hope is a hope that cannot be compared with hope in time.

The postulates of the immortality of the soul and of the existence of God define a hope that Kant does not deduce from a subjective inclination of the feeling, thinking being. They do not result from a "pathological" desire (in the Kantian sense). Kant does not deduce hope from the *conatus essendi*; he does not deduce it from the ontological adventure, as though—in spirit, in Reason— there were something other than the fact, for the being, of being. We find in him a rational hope for the reconciliation between virtue and happiness, a hope that transcends, but does so otherwise than within the dimension of time, as though human rationality were not exhausted in holding to its being (as for the Heideggerian

Dasein, whose being is at stake in its being), nor even in serving being (being the "guardian" of being). Here, the perseverance in being is found to be in the service of a rationality, of a reason demanding a reconciliation between virtue and happiness. Neither happiness nor virtue nor duty signifies an attachment of the being to its being, nor are they defined by this attachment of the being to its being. This is a rational hope that is like an extra-ordinary projection of meaning within a domain (which is not a temporal ecstasis outside time and given being) of *pure nothingness.*

(Note: This is so, unless the temporal ecstasis that we take for an extension or adventure of being {as we have seen with Heidegger's anticipation of the experienced possibility of the impossibility [death] itself contained in everyday temporality} were other than this. Unless time, understood as the horizon of being or the dimension in which we are, were a relation not with what comes to pass but *with what cannot come to pass*, and this, not because our awaiting it would be vain but *because what is awaited is too great for the awaiting*, and time's length is a relation that holds more than it can hold. Hope, become an awaiting and length of time, is already a relation {in a nonnegative sense}, and a welcoming of a surplus. Eugen Fink, who shows the importance of this rational hope, says that it is more than some sort of behavior, but *less* than being.[1] Thus, for Fink, being remains the ultimate notion, and one cannot speak of a *beyond being*, for that is mythology.)

⁓

Rational hope is projected nontemporally into the domain of pure nothingness, which it is impossible to mistake [*méconnaître*] in the lived experience of being-toward-death (in affectivity, in anxiety, it is impossible to efface the negative character of death), but which it is also impossible to know, to equal, and to contain. This is a domain in which the relation is in no sense an adequation. A nothingness impossible to think. When one thinks it, it is immediately necessary to unsay it [*le dédire*], that is, to signify it as a noema that is thinkable only "in quotation marks."

One cannot fail to acknowledge the nothingness of death, but one cannot know [*connaître*] it, either. This is so, even if this non-failure to acknowledge [*non-méconnaissance*] does not yet measure what death, in its nothingness, puts in question *other than our being*. Even if it does not yet measure the negativity of death, as more negative than nothingness, as vertigo and risk experienced in the "less than nothing." A negativity that is neither thought nor even felt; a pure nothingness that it is impossible not to acknowledge, and whose *inaccessibility* has virtually characterized Western thought from Aristotle to Bergson.

Thus Bergson proceeds, in *Creative Evolution*, to a critique of the idea of nothingness:

> The idea of absolute nothingness, in the sense of an annihilation of everything, is a self-destructive idea, a pseudo-idea, a mere word. If suppressing a thing consists in replacing it by another, if thinking the absence of one thing is possible only by the more or less explicit representation of the presence of some other thing, if, in short, annihilation signifies before anything else substitution, the idea of an "annihilation of everything" is as absurd as that of a square circle.[2]

As for death, it is in Bergson a degradation of energy: entropy (as in nineteenth-century physics). It is matter come to a state of perfect equilibrium, without a difference in potentials. It is impossible to think nothingness.

For Heidegger, on the other hand, there is an access to nothingness, a nonintellectual access: it is the access to death in anxiety. The refutation of the idea of nothingness is refuted by Heidegger: *nothingness is accessible in the anxiety that is the experience of it.*

Phenomenology seems to make possible the thinking of nothingness thanks to the idea of intentionality as an access to something other than oneself, and an access that can be had in a nontheoretical manner (thus, in sentiments, actions, etc., which are all irreducible to serene representation). Thus, in Scheler, emotions are an access to value. For Heidegger, manual activity is a revelation of the tool *qua* tool (all of technology has a revelatory function for Heidegger; it is a way of discovering or revealing); just as, in him, sentiments are modes of implication in being (to be in the world is to be *affected* there). It is sentiment that measures my being-in-the-world. In the same way, anxiety, which has no object, has the non-object as its object: nothingness. Heidegger's description of death thus reveals a possibility, the possibility of nonpossibility. Nothingness is *thinkable* in death. What fascinates Heidegger about death is the possibility he finds in it of thinking nothingness.

But can the ideas of thought and experience be applied to these ways of acceding to nothingness? We speak of thought when there is a position of a subject, whereas the vertigo of the question escapes the thinking of death, and makes death escape thought. Is to think simply to live, even if life is intentional life? Does the intentionality of life not retain, at bottom, a *representation* (or a thetic *doxa*), as it does in Husserl? The place that Husserlian phenomenology gave to nonrepresentational intentionality promised a significance that did not proceed from knowing, but the promise was not kept. Affective, practical intentionality, that of pleasure or desire, are shown as definite intentional stances, and every position or stance hides a doxic thesis expressible in a predicative proposition: "*Every act, or every act-correlate, envelops a 'logical' factor that is implicit or explicit.*"[3] Every act is ontological, and every thought *qua* thought is correlative of meaning. But has nothingness ever been thought in a thinking by which it should have been *equaled*?

This impossibility of thinking nothingness goes back to Aristotle. For him, it is impossible to think annihilation with the acuteness with which it announces itself in anxiety. For Aristotle, where becoming is movement, it is impossible to think the change that is death. The *metabolē* is the turning of being into nothingness, and Aristotle seems in this sense to acknowledge the possibility of thinking being and nothingness separately. But in his analyses, corruption, or the passage to nothingness, is always thought of in connection with generation. Generation and corruption, distinguished from alteration to be sure, are structured in the same manner. It is as if Aristotle would not allow himself to think nothingness for itself.

Thus nothingness appears, in Aristotle, as a moment of essence, as the negativity proper to being, whose essence is finite. *Not-yet-*

to-be or *no-longer*-to-be will be negative for Aristotle. Temporal nothingness is thinkable to the extent that the *present* is the measure of being. Nothingness is what is old, used, and corrupted by time, but it is then as if embraced and encumbered and carried by being (just as Bergson thought).

In death, as pure nothingness, as foundationlessness—which we feel more dramatically, with the acuteness of that nothingness that is greater in death than in the idea of the nothingness of being (in the *there is*, which wounds less than disappearance does)—we arrive at something that European philosophy has not thought.

We understand corruption, transformation, dissolution. We understand that shapes or forms pass into and out of being, while something subsists. Death contrasts with all that; it is inconceivable, refractory to thought, and yet unexceptionable and undeniable. It is not a phenomenon; hardly thematizable, unthinkable—the irrational begins there. Even in anxiety, even through anxiety, death remains unthought. To have experienced anxiety does not allow one to *think* it.

Nothingness has defied Western thought.

Hegel's Response:
The *Science of Logic*

Friday, February 27, 1976

The nothingness of death is undeniable, but the relationship to death as nothingness is, in any case, a negativity radically other than the negativity thought by Greek philosophy and particularly by Aristotle. In thinking of change all the way to the *metabolē*, one might think that one has isolated the nothingness of being. Actually, in Aristotle, even the *metabolē* preserves the style of alteration, where being subsists in nothingness in such a way that nothingness is not thought as a pure nothing [*néant pur*].

What is knowable and natural to thought is nothingness as *dissolution*; annihilation as *decomposition* in which something subsists even if the forms of things pass away. *Relative* disappearance shows itself without difficulties. Thus, in the two Aristotelian models of the passage from nothingness into being (childbirth and fabrication), *phusis* and material are presupposed. Childbirth is a becoming and not a leap from nothingness to being (the seed was there).

Now, a nothingness like that of death, rigorously thought, *is pregnant with nothing at all*. It is an absolutely indeterminate nothingness that alludes to no being, and it is not a chaos aspiring to form: death is the death of someone, and the having-been of someone is carried not by the one dying but by the survivor.

In Aristotle, being is maintained within nothingness, as potential being. It is always a question of the manner by which one being becomes another. Now, the ontic origin and perishing that a being undergoes are very different from the origin and annihilation of *essance*.[1] Everything unfolds in death as though man were not a simple being that perishes, but one who offered us the very event of finishing or perishing—even if this event occurred in its ambiguity as the unknown.

In the death of another, in his face that is exposition to death, it is not the passage from one quiddity to another that is announced; in death is *the very event of passing* (our language says, moreover, "he has passed" ["il passe"]) with its own acuteness that is its scandal (each death is the first death). We should think of all the murder there is in death: every death is a murder, is premature, and there is the responsibility of the survivor.

Aristotle does not think nothingness in this way. For him, that does not "demolish" the world; the world remains.

~

How is it in Hegel? In order to know this, it is necessary to read the beginning of the *Greater Logic* (book 1, the chapter "With What Must the Science Begin?").[2]

One would say, at first glance, that it is impossible here to think the nothingness of death in all its purity. After having reviewed the different entities (*Seiende*) that philosophy placed at the beginning (water, *noûs*, etc.), Hegel says that the beginning cannot first be thought of as determinate. We must take the beginning in indetermination and in its immediacy. The beginning of philosophy thus becomes a philosophy of the beginning. Thinking will then determine and realize what the determination implies: to determine the various predicates that one might add to this indeterminate beginning.

We must begin, then, with pure being, empty and indeterminate being. What is necessary to the beginning is a nothingness that must become something. "As yet there is nothing and there is to become something. The beginning is not pure nothing, but a nothing from which something is to proceed; therefore being, too, is already contained in the beginning," writes Hegel.[3] Thus, the model of the beginning—though it presents itself as empty and pure—is again the beginning within the world: it is something that begins, a something, and not the beginning of being in general. In the beginning, there is already being. This beginning is the unity of being and nothingness, or a nonbeing that is at once being and nonbeing.

We are thus right away in a situation similar to that which Aristotle contemplated: there is a nothingness, but a nothingness that awaits being, that wants being, that will pass into being. One may therefore wonder whether, in this way, one is not supposing entities as already there. One may wonder whether the beginning is not, thus, the beginning of some thing, the beginning of *that which* begins. This is a beginning that lacks the determinacy of water, as in Thales, but one that has the structure of a something [*du quelque chose*].

The beginning is not yet, but it is going to be. It thus contains that being that grows distant from nonbeing or supersedes it (*aufhebt*) as its opposite.[4] Nothingness and being are here distinguished like that from which the beginning departs and that toward which it aims. The beginning contains both states distinguished from each other; it is their nondifferentiated unity.

But have we not here confused a becoming that is growth with a becoming that is absolute in the sense of an absolute emergence? In these descriptions, is there not a confusion between the relative and the absolute becoming? Would Hegel have been fooled?—as if Hegel could be fooled by something!

Hegel's thought is, in fact, much more radical than this. The absolute beginning is a notion belonging to common sense. When one thinks, one sees that being and nothingness are not separable; one sees that they are identical, and that their unity is becoming.

For Aristotle, the presupposition is that all intelligible meaning must go back to the unmoved mover. It is in this resting of being that all becoming culminates; there is therefore no sense in speaking of absolute nothingness. In Aristotle, we must go back from movement in things to the unmoved mover, whereas Hegel introduces movement *into being itself* and delivers being entirely to movement. "There is not a single proposition in Heraclitus that I have not taken up in my *Logic*," as he will say in this respect.[5]

The difference between absolute emergence and relative emergence is in fact the crude comprehension of being by opinion. Not only does Hegel consciously reject it, he turns it over: what seems to us a relative becoming is precisely the emergence, the origin—which is to say that *becoming is the absolute*, and, consequently, one cannot think before this.

If the beginning must be thought, it is first necessary to bear its emptiness and its indeterminacy. This is a most difficult asceticism, for we are accustomed to beginning where being is strongest and fullest. But what must be uttered about being is, at the beginning, only an empty word, nothing but "being" ["*être*"]. This emptiness is thus the very beginning of philosophy. Being is the first thing that is thought by a thinking that is reasonable.

Yet how must we think it? Therein lies the most important thing to be said.

The philosophical tradition separated being and nonbeing. For Plato and Aristotle, the Eleatic distinction is not valid in the world of becoming: here, there is no pure nothingness. But the distinction is nevertheless maintained: things are "between the two," between being and nothingness. Is it then possible to *think* nothingness? Hegel will set aside every mystical approach to nothingness; nothingness, for him, is going to be *thought*. And to think nothingness is to assert the identity of being and nothingness.

Pure being, indeterminate and without content, is empty; there is nothing to see in it, nothing to intuit. It is therefore "only this pure intuiting itself."[6] There is in pure being, then, nothing to think. Pure being is in fact nothing, neither more nor less than nothing. Pure being is like nothingness. Consequently, being and nothingness have the same structure, they are identical.

But how can the indeterminate be identical to itself? In effect, it is always a content that is identical to itself. In reality, the proposition "pure being is pure nothingness" works on a special level of identity: it is an identity that is speculative, that consists in *becoming* [*consiste à être devenir*]. Being and nothingness are identical in becoming. The coincidence of opposites is not a factual given but is produced as becoming. The simultaneity of opposites is becoming. It is not here a matter of an ordinary becoming; rather, all thinking is in this becoming, and one cannot think outside of it.

> *Pure being and pure nothing are, therefore, the same.* What is the truth is neither being nor nothing, but that being does not pass over—but has passed over into nothing, and nothing into being.

Nicht übergeht—sondern übergegangen ist: ALWAYS ALREADY—we have thought being in nothingness, but being is already becoming.[7]

> But it is equally true that they are not undistinguished from each other, that, on the contrary, they are not the same, that they are absolutely distinct, and yet that they are unseparated and inseparable and that each immediately *vanishes in its opposite.* Their truth is, therefore, this movement of the immediate vanishing of the one in the other: *becoming,* a movement in which both are distinguished, but by a difference which has equally immediately resolved itself.[8]

Becoming is thus the difference *and* identity of being and nothingness.

Genesis and corruption return into something that encompasses them. In the absolute, nothing is radically new; nothing subsists that is not handed over to annihilation. The absolute has emptiness not outside itself but in itself. Nothingness runs through being.

One might wonder whether that reaches the level of death, that is, whether what is outside-the-circuit in death—in the death that man knows—finds a place adequate to it in this absolute. The question is in fact posed by Fink.[9]

Reading Hegel's *Science of Logic* (Continued)

Friday, March 5, 1976

The nothingness of death isolated from the process of being, the nothingness of death that is not a moment of this process, the undeniable annihilation of death—whatever the unknown to which it is attached—appears without common measure with the nothingness about which Aristotle and Hegel, in his *Logic*, are speaking.

"Pure being and pure nothingness are the same," as we read last time. To the degree that they are identical, the truth is not their state of in-differentiation (they are different inasmuch as identical), but the fact that they are not the same, that they are absolutely different; and yet they are just as absolutely un-separated and inseparable, and immediately each one disappears into its contrary. Their truth is therefore that movement of immediate disappearing, the one into the other: their truth is becoming. One cannot think being and nothingness without becoming. "Their truth is, therefore, this movement of the immediate vanishing of the one in the other: *becoming*, a movement in which both are distinguished, but by [the mediation of] a difference[1] which has equally immediately resolved itself." *Becoming is therefore the unity of this difference, which is the greatest possible one, but which has already been the most complete identity.* To think that being comes from nothingness and that there would be an absolute becoming there, or to think that being goes into nothingness as separated and separable nothingness, is a thought insufficiently thought. There is no separable nothingness.

In Hegel's "Remark 1: The Opposition of Being and Nothing in Ordinary Thinking,"[2] he writes: *"Nothing* is usually opposed to *something*; but the being of something is already determinate and is distinguished from another *something*; and so therefore the nothing which is opposed to the something is also the nothing of a particular something, a determinate nothing. *Here, however, nothing is to be taken in its indeterminate simplicity."*[3] If we nevertheless considered it more appropriate to oppose to being not nothingness as the nothingness of something, but *nonbeing,* then the result would still be the same, for "in non-being the relation to *being* is contained."[4] It is both of these two, being and the negation of being. "There is therefore no pure nothing, but nothing such that it is already in becoming."[5]

Hegel will then show the progress toward this speculative thinking on the identity of being and nothingness. When Parmenides inaugurates philosophy, he begins with the absolute distinction between being and nonbeing. For Hegel, this is still an abstract thought: Parmenides saw that the beginning is being, but he did not see that nonbeing in some way is. "Buddhism," in its turn, places nothingness at the beginning. "The deep-thinking Heraclitus brought forward the higher, total concept of *becoming* and said: *being as little is, as nothing is (das Sein ist so wenig als das Nichts),* or, everything *flows,* which means, everything is *becoming."*[6]

For Hegel, this unity of being and nothingness is a biblical thought, which for him means a Christian thought. "Later, especially Christian, metaphysics whilst rejecting the proposition that out of nothing comes nothing, asserted a transition from nothing into being; although it understood this proposition synthetically or merely imaginatively, yet even in the most imperfect union there is contained a point in which being and nothing coincide and their distinction vanishes."[7] Thus, creation *ex nihilo* would conform to the speculative proposition, the only reservation being that it is still representative, still abstract.

Now this being/nothingness identity is a speculative proposition, a thought of Reason and not that of the understanding that separates things. We cannot justify this identity by definitions:

every definition already presupposes the speculative; every definition is an analysis, a separation, and presupposes the thought of the nonseparable.

We cannot name any difference between being and nothingness; it is impossible to find a difference because, were there one, being would be something other than pure being: there would be a specification here. The difference therefore does not turn on what they are in themselves. The difference appears here as that which embraces them: it is in becoming that the difference exists, and becoming is only possible by reason of this distinction.

But is death equivalent to this nothingness tied to being? Becoming is the phenomenal world, the manifestation of being. Now, death is outside this process: it is a total nothingness, a nothingness that is not necessary to the appearing of being. A nothingness that is obtained not by pure abstraction but as a kind of seizure. In death, one does not make an abstraction of being—it is of us that an abstraction is made.

Death, such is it is appears, concerns and frightens and causes anxiety in the death of an other, is an annihilation that does not find its place in the logic of being and nothingness. It is an annihilation that is a scandal and to which moral notions such as responsibility do not come to be simply added on.

Yet is there not in the *Phenomenology of Spirit* another notion of death? That is what we shall see next time.

From the *Science of Logic* to the *Phenomenology*

Friday, March 12, 1976

Ours is a questioning about the possibility of responding by way of thought, of being, of world, and of positivity to the undeniable end, the end of being and the annihilation inscribed in the death of another, and imminent in my own time; an annihilation inscribed in death in all the ambiguity of nothingness and the unknown. This is a questioning that is not a simple modality of the theoretical expression of belief, of *doxa*, in which we accede to being, to the world, and to positivity.

In the thinking of being, this nothingness is thought, but it is not the pure nothingness, the annihilation, and the unknown that is death; rather it is a moment of the thinking of being. Do not certain passages in the *Phenomenology of Spirit* treat death in a way that better accounts—not for the constitution of becoming or of the thinking of becoming—but for the *end* of becoming and for the whole scandal that is this end, which is expressed in the affective register (anxiety in Heidegger) and which shall be stated here in moral terms (responsibility for the death of another, the scandal of every new death)? It is that we must search not for a positive thought for death but rather for a responsibility according to the measure or the beyond-measure of death. We must search for a response that is not a response but responsibility, that is not of the same measure as a world but belongs to the beyond-measure of the infinite.

Today we will proceed to a reading of one of the famous pages of the *Phenomenology,* where death is not simply a moment playing its role in the thinking of being. The passage is found in volume 2, on page 14 and the following, in Jean Hyppolite's translation.[1] We should first situate this passage.

It is at the heart of the singular consciousness that Hegel discovers a relation necessary to other singular consciousnesses. The *I think* is only possible if, at the same time as I am in my thought, I am in relation with other thoughts. Each singular consciousness is at the same time for itself and for another. It can be for itself only to the extent to which it is for another. Each one demands recognition by the other to be itself, but it must also recognize the other, because the recognition by the other holds only if the other is himself recognized. Therein resides the surpassing of immediacy (for Hegel, all thinking is a thinking between consciousnesses; it is immediate when it ignores this relationship between consciousnesses; the immediate is the *cogito* all alone).

What Hegel calls Spirit is when this reciprocal recognition of consciousnesses is maintained and transcended (*aufgehoben*) in these relations and conflicts. That is the universal and nonimmediate consciousness. But this universal consciousness is first of all immediate; Spirit is thus like a sort of nature [*comme une nature*] before being opposed to itself. Hegel calls this stage of Spirit's immediacy *substance.* Spirit is substance, and it has before itself a progression whereby it must become a *subject.*[2]

It is substance insofar as it makes its own history, develops itself "insofar as its spiritual content is engendered by itself." It will become a subject, become the Knowledge that Spirit has of itself, that is, absolute thought or the living truth that knows itself. From the Spirit that simply *is,* it will become the Self-Knowledge of that Spirit.

The problem of the relation with death will be posed, for Hegel, at the level of this immediate Spirit, of this Spirit as substance (a people that has not yet put itself in question, that has not yet encountered other peoples). The immediate Spirit is a historical given. The oneself [*soi-même*] adheres immediately to its action. There is no place where the Self [*le Soi*] denies and opposes itself to its being. Concretely, that means that there is an ethical nature (ἦθος [ethos] means custom).

For Hegel, there is in this substance, in its immediate state, something like a scission between the universality of laws and the singularity of the substance that must itself be understood as a relation between singular consciousnesses. Hegel calls this the scission of this ethical state into human law and divine law.[3]

Human law corresponds to the laws of the city, of the State, and consequently this ethical substance according to human law consists in living the social and political life. What, then, would be the other side of this existence? It is the *family*, which goes back to the obscure origins of all things. Thus the masculine element represents human law and the feminine element the divine law, which is also the law of the home.

The law of the city is public; everyone knows the law, which moreover expresses the will of all. In this human law, man posits himself; he is the very position of self as a self, its style of self [*sa manière de soi*]. Man contemplates himself in the public law and opposes himself to the obscurity from which he detached himself. In the law, in broad daylight, he reflects himself.

But there is also the law of the family. These two laws are other than and complementary to each other. The divine law is immediate substance; it is not an operation of thought. It is the being of these men, which has not yet been reflected and which renounces the human law that has detached itself from it.

The State is the dominant order of a people that maintains itself by labor in times of peace and by combat in wartime. Individuals can become aware of their being for self [*leur être pour soi*] within the State, because the awareness the State has of itself is a force from which everyone benefits, since everyone has been recognized by this law. Nonetheless, being recognized in this way, the units inside the State, that is, the families, can in this atmosphere of security separate themselves from the Whole; that is, they can become abstract. It is war that will call back those individuals detached from the Whole. Without war, individuals would return to the state of pure and simple nature, to the immediate, to the absolutely abstract. War, on the contrary, gives them anew the consciousness of their dependency; at the level of the community, war is necessary:

> In order not to let them become rooted and set in this isolation, thereby breaking up the whole and letting the communal spirit evaporate, government has from time to time to shake them to their core, by war. By this means the government upsets their established order, and violates their right to independence [Hyppolite: *l'être-pour-soi*], while the individuals who, absorbed in their own way of life, break loose from the whole and strive after the inviolable independence and security of the person, are made to feel in the task laid on them their lord and master, death.[4]

Here death appears as the absolute Master.

Spirit exists as the individuality of a community, and not in an abstract form. Negation is here present in a double form. On the one hand, the community as a particular people is a determinate people (and every determination is a negation). On the other hand, there is the second negation that is individuality. And war is that negativity that surmounts nature or the possibility for families to fall back into nature. War checks the relapsing of families into natural being-there far from the ethical being-there.

The State is legislation; it is the action of several in view of a common goal. To the State is opposed the divine law, the family bonded in blood and the relation of the difference of the sexes. The divine law is different from the State because it proceeds from that which is common, whereas the State, by way of the universal law, tends toward what is common. On the basis of this natural unity, from this blood-unity, Hegel expresses this by relating the family to the gods of the Earth (the mysticism of blood and ground in the family!). The State proceeds from Reason conscious of itself and raising itself to the universal. The family, on the other hand, is something natural; it is the substratum of life from which the human law detaches itself. But family is also the immediate nature *of Spirit*, and thus it is not a pure nature; it has an ethical principle. It becomes moral in relation to the *Penates*, to the protective spirits of the household.

What then can the ethical spirit of the family signify? The family's morality is other than that of the State. This morality is in the State and has many of the State's virtues: it raises children, prepares citizens for the State, and in this sense it is for the disappearance of the family. But there exists an ethics proper to the family that, on the basis of its terrestrial morality, relates to the subterranean world and consists in *burying the dead.*

It is here that the relationship with death is inscribed, or more precisely, with the dead *one.*

Hegel first gives a negative definition of the ethical principle proper to the family: "In the first place, because the ethical principle is intrinsically universal, the ethical connection between the members of the family is not that of feeling, or the relationship of love."[5] It is not love, not education, not a contingent service rendered by one family member to another that can furnish the ethical principle proper to the family. It is necessary that there be a relationship with a singularity, and in order for this to be ethical, the content of this relationship must be a universality. "The ethical action can therefore only be related to the *whole* individual, or the singular being *qua* universal."[6]

Hegel thus gives the solution:

> The deed, then, which embraces the entire existence of the blood-relation, does not concern the citizen, for he does not belong to the family, nor the individual who is to become a citizen and *will cease* to count as *this particular individual*; it has as its object and content *this* particular individual who belongs to the family, but is taken as a universal essence, freed from his sensuous, i.e. individual, reality. The deed no longer concerns the *living* but the *dead*, the individual who, after a long succession of separate disconnected experiences, concentrates himself into a single completed shape, and has raised himself out of the disquiet of the accidents of life into the peace of simple universality.[7]

One who has a universal essence without being a citizen is the deceased. There is virtue proper to the family in its relationship to the shadows. The duty with regard to the dead is that of burying them, and it is this that makes up the virtue proper to the family. The act of burial is a relationship with the deceased, and not with the cadaver.

Reading Hegel's *Phenomenology* (Continued)

Friday, March 19, 1976

For Hegel, the relationship with death and with the deceased, outside any reference to being and nothingness, is a necessary moment in the logic of the *Phenomenology of Spirit*, that is, of the movement, or the becoming, or the history wherein consciousness attains its full possession of self, wherein its freedom is an absolute thought. This is history not in the empirical sense of the history of the formation of thought, but history coming to pass as history, by way of the articulations necessary to its evolution, in which it becomes Absolute or concrete thought (of what is not separated from anything). At one of these stages, that where we can speak of immediate spirit, this consciousness is produced as an ethical nature, a nature having the content or the *ethos* of the law. This is a stage in which consciousness is not the experience of this Spirit, but immediate Spirit, that is, where Spirit is substance or nature. In this substance, as the immediacy of nature, a scission develops between the universality of laws and the singularity of substance, between the city and the family.

At this stage where the human law is public, what does the divine law or the law of the family consist in as *law*? If the family is an *ethical* substance, if it is not pure nature, in what does its ethic consist? (It is significant that for Hegel, ethics is always universal. The person is always thought of by virtue of the universality of law. On this point Hegel is a Kantian. The person as individual is not Spirit and has no ethic. Here, in our present inquiry, the person is an individual other, and every universal must begin from there. However, in German idealism, the person is the universal.)

The family is the natural community, and yet there is a universality in the family itself. Where is the ethical element peculiar to the family? It will be necessary to invent an exceptional notion in order to speak of the ethics of the family.

There must be a singularity that could also be universal. From this comes Hegel's response, which we saw last time: "This action no longer concerns the living, but the deceased." Death is here understood as a return into self [*recueillement*], as a gathering into oneself. Here is a universality of the person who has fulfilled his destiny: it is an essence. Everything is fulfilled, everything is consummated when one is dead.

The relationship with the deceased and with the universality of death has its decisive trait in burial. There is, in death, something that corresponds to the concept necessary to ethics. The family cannot acknowledge that, with death, he who had been a consciousness is now submitted to matter, that matter has become the master of a being that was formed, that was a self-consciousness. One does not want this conscious being to be given over to matter, for the ultimate being of man, the ultimate fact of man, does not belong to nature. The family accomplishes an act of piety in regard to one who had been active: the appearance of nature's domination over the one who had been conscious must be rendered invisible.

The blood-relationship supplements, then, the abstract natural process by adding to it the movement of consciousness, interrupting the work of nature and rescuing the blood-relation from destruction; or better, because destruction is necessary, the passage of the blood-relation into mere being, it takes on itself the act of destruction. Through this it comes about that the *dead*, the universal *being*, becomes a being that has returned into itself, a *being-for-self*, or, the powerless, simply isolated individual has been raised to *universal individuality*. The dead individual, by having liberated his *being* from his action or his negative unity, is the empty singular, merely a *passive being-for-another*, at the mercy of every lower irrational individuality and to the forces of abstract material elements, all of which are now more powerful than himself: the former on account of the life they possess, the latter on account of their negative nature. The family keeps away from the dead this dishonoring of him by unconscious appetites and abstract entities, and puts its own action in their place, and weds the blood-relation to the bosom of the earth, to the elemental imperishable individuality. The family thereby makes him a member of a community which prevails over and holds under control the forces of particular material elements and the lower forms of life, which sought to unloose themselves against him and to destroy him.[1]

Thus the blood relatives effect a destruction of death and bring about a sort of return, as though there were a fulfillment, as though beneath terrestrial being there were a subsoil to which one returned and from which one came (cf. in this regard the biblical term for dying, "to sleep with one's ancestors"). In death, there is the idea of a return to a maternal element, to a level situated *beneath* the phenomenological sphere.

The living remove the dishonor of anonymous decomposition by way of the honor of the funeral rites. In this way, they transform the deceased into a living memory. In the act of burial there is an exceptional relationship of the living with the dead. The burial rite is a deliberate relationship of the living with death, through their relationship with the deceased. Here, death is thought and not simply described. It is a necessary moment in the conceptual progress of thought itself, and in this sense it is thought.

We must wonder whether there is not, in these descriptions, a supplementary element—already stemming from the fact that the region of death is identified with the earth—just as there is also something unfounded in the description, that is, the relationship of death and of blood. As for the enigma of death, which the *Logic* reduced to the nothingness that was already thought with being, Hegel comes closer to it here, but he speaks of it on the basis of the behavior of the survivor—although one could not take a less reifying approach to death than Hegel does here, since it is neither a thing nor a person, but a *shadow*.

～

We can now turn to Hegel's chapter on religion; a religion that, in the development of the *Phenomenology*, represents the penultimate figure of the progress of Spirit, and that is divided into natural religion, aesthetic religion, and revealed religion.

Death is of central importance to religion. In aesthetic religion, tragedy is not simply a literary genre but a certain manner in which consciousness thinks or comprehends itself. Here, Hegel sees in death a subterranean destiny that causes beings to arise that are delivered up to a knowledge that is false, a pure appearing that is but an appearance. And it is the return of destiny that is the tragedy where death plays the role of the subterranean.

~

In Hegel, the way in which death points to the obscure and veiled ground introduces the world of appearance into thought (Plato's Cave is here one moment of this thought). Again it is burial that remains the symbolic act by which those related through blood freely protect the deceased in returning to him what was in him and was him, even on the eve of his death: ipseity. In the thought expressed in aesthetic religion, death is not only nothingness but a return to the ground. Is it legitimate to interpret death in this way? It can no doubt be *felt* or *sensed* in this way, as the biblical expression cited earlier attests. In the same vein, Eugen Fink quotes the words of a Japanese man condemned to death: "I go to the gallows without pain and without trembling, for I see the smiling face of my mother."[2]

But in this composition of the idea of ground, or final ground, this ground of being and death, there is a certain phenomenal model that seems to remain in Hegel. Likewise in the second aspect of this return: to be taken under the protection of one's blood relatives. There again, a supplementary step is made when the return to the elements is interpreted as a return to the ground of being.

The Scandal of Death:
From Hegel to Fink

Friday, April 9, 1976

In the nothingness of death in Hegel and Aristotle, a nothingness that is already a beginning, as all ends are (e.g., definition and determination), it is as though being followed its train of being in a circular fashion. Corruption is the correlate of generation, just as generation is that of corruption. In the being of beings, death is not understood.

For Hegel, on the one hand, nothingness is always already being (this proposition has a speculative meaning, it only has meaning as speculative); on the other hand, in immediate Spirit, death is the return to the elemental quality of blood or of earth, which death has rejoined. The deceased returns into the simple being of the elements, but he is also torn from them by the conscious gesture of the survivor who fulfills—in honor of him who was conscious and is no longer so—the act of burial that tears him from natural being-there. The funeral transforms the deceased into a living memory; the living thus have a relationship with the deceased and are determined in their turn by his memory.

In the same spirit in the chapter on religion, Hegel identifies the reign of death with that of destiny. The relation with death is glimpsed in tragedy, which is not simply a literary genre but the site at which this meaning is played out. What is real is destined for destruction by the very knowledge it has of reality: knowledge is ambiguous and leads the hero to his undoing.

Is it legitimate to interpret death as the return to the depths? Are the depths of the same measure as death? How shall these depths, this *Urgrund* of things, be thought? Is Hegel not drawing from a symbol a meaning that does not escape the model of the world? Everything seems to be modeled on the relation of the living to the dead. There is the earth, where the blood relatives carry out the burial; the earth is something particular in reality (Hegel calls this the elemental individual). But at the same time the earth is not a particular thing but an element, in which there is something other than things. The latter are constituted of solids, liquids, and so on. They hide their elemental quality, as opposed to that order that cannot, in its turn, be called a thing. The earth is neither the work site nor the field nor the mountain; it refers to a fundamental *where*, to a stable ground by which precisely the earth is defined. From there comes the temptation to take the ground of things for the ground of being. Burial is interpreted as the return to the ground, and the ground of the earth as the ground of being. Moreover, the family in itself is considered as what unites prior to the separation. The relation of the family to its members is the same as the relation of the earth to that from which it is made: the blood relatives are other among themselves, but at the same time they are not others since they are of the same bloodline. Thus there is a passage from the phenomenal order to the nonphenomenal order of the earth, that is, a passage from the bottom of things to the bottom of being.

In this way, death is thought in the world as a moment of the grasping of self by self. Hegel always focuses on death in an interpretation of the behavior of the survivor. As a moment in the appearing of the world, death is intelligible.

∼

In Fink,[1] the difficulty in speaking of death is presented as its very *intelligibility*. We must receive death in silence, although philosophy may state the reason for this silence. We know death, but we cannot think it; we know it without being able to think it. It is in this sense that death is a veritable rupture and in this sense also that it must be received in silence.

In Fink, as in Heidegger, intelligibility coincides with what can be said, with the fable, with what may be recounted. Language [*le langage*] is brought forth through the comprehension of being, which is human existence. Language belongs to being and is intelligibility as being-in-the-world. Philosophy is a self-comprehension [*est auto-compréhension*] of presence in the world, which is action upon the world and a way of comprehending.

Fink classifies the different manners of being in the world. Thus, there are:

—labor, economy;

—war, struggle, will to power, affirmation of self as substantiality;

—eros, which is presented as a relationship with the world, the other being here understood on the basis of the world;

—play.

These activities are the comprehension of being, and comprehension is a mode of being. Comprehension is in language [*la langue*], and language [*la langue*] can recount comprehension according to its modes (labor, war, love, play), which are behaviors in and toward being.

Can death be said without its nothingness being converted into a structure in-the-world? Does death not imply a rupture with the comprehension of being? Is death only a particular case of annihilation in-the-world? Each death is a scandal, a *first* death; there is no genus for death, says Fink, no approach possible to the notion in general.

The comprehension of being is subsumed under the structure of the being that it comprehends, as though this structure were itself a being. *Dasein* is a being, a substantive. Man *qua* comprehension of being falls under the categories of that comprehension. Man finds that he is a being, a reasonable animal.

From that comes the tendency to treat death as a fact concerning a being (Aristotle, Hegel), whereas the scarcely thinkable specificity of death concerns the very comprehension of being. Death is the end of what makes the thinkable thinkable, and it is in this sense that it is unthinkable. One can no longer even say that death is nothingness, for nothingness and being concern comprehension.

Philosophy, the comprehension of being, protests against reification and emphasizes what man is not and what constitutes his dignity. But in reality, in the various modes of the comprehension of being, there is, in the being [*l'étant*], already an inhabitation of being [*l'être*]. It is in the world that we come into the world, and in the world that we go out of the world. In the world, we are always already subsumed under the worldly. There is no liberation.

The tendency to withdraw into subjectivity by way of a negative anthropology, a search for a transcendental concept of man, a quest for a thinking prior to being—this is not a simple error or a simple errancy, but is instead as inevitable as the discovery of being prior to thought [*le pensé*].

The problem of death is incomprehensible when it concerns man not as a being subject to annihilation but as the very comprehension of being. This end finds no model in intelligibility.

Another Thinking of Death:
Starting from Bloch

Friday, April 23, 1976

We are considering death as a negation of the human being. The human being, in Aristotle, Hegel, and Heidegger, was considered in reference to the world, a term back to which the notion of being and ontology brings us. We have ended up at a nonequivalence between nothingness and a notion of death developed on the basis of ontology. In this ontology, the world appeared as the very site of meaning, and nothingness was thought in its kinship with being.

In Fink, death is the end of the comprehension of being—the end of nothingness alternating with being—and must not be too quickly merged with the negation of negation that gives us being. We must wonder whether we do not here find ourselves in a dimension of meaning in which a beyond being and nothingness is thought; we must even wonder whether another dimension of thought takes on meaning here, a dimension that is not the silence that Fink suggests.

In the Heideggerian analysis of death, one is struck by the reduction of death to being-toward-death, to the structure of *Dasein*—that is, once again to subjectivity in its origin, as the true relationship with being on the basis of which the other man is understood. In this way, if we exaggerate somewhat, we might say that, for Heidegger (who would, no doubt, not say this), the fear of being an assassin does not manage to surpass the fear of dying. To be-to-death is to-be-to-*my*-death. There is a total equivalence between death and nothingness and a reduction of affectivity to the emotion of anxiety, on the basis of which originary time is understood. This originary time is a mode of being of the finite being. Temporality is defined by the relationship with nothingness. Consequently, the deepest desire is the desire to be, and death is always premature. Death is not proportionate to my desire to be; my being cannot cover my desire to be: the coverage is too short. In the formalism of the pure *conatus*, existence is the supreme prize. There is but one value, and it is that of being; a purely formal value, in which the Heideggerian denial of values is rooted.

~

Here I propose to leave this study of death as a moment of ontology, the study of death as nothingness, and of the temporality that hinges on the anxiety of nothingness, to come to a thought in which meaning would certainly still be attached to the world but in which the meaning of the world is profoundly tied to other men. This is what comes about in a philosophy in which the preoccupation with the social animates the entirety of knowledge and culture, and wherein ontological terminology is tied to the other. This is what comes about, for example, in a religious or social thought.

While remaining the end and annihilation of the individual, while being interpreted as an ineluctable, natural necessity, death is not the source of all sense and nonsense. Its very emotion does not amount to an anxiety of being toward the eventuality of one's not-being, and time does not go back to being-toward-death. That time, in its very ad-vent or future, does not go back to finitude stretched toward being-toward-death but rather might have another signification, and that there might be another eventuality in the analysis of death—this is what I would like to address here through the philosophy of Ernst Bloch.

Throughout the entire history of philosophy, time is a sign of nonbeing, of nonvalue, to which eternity is opposed. For Heidegger, there is no eternity, but the tragic character of finite existence remains, and time has no other meaning than to-be-toward-death. In time, there is an essential disappointment. For social philosophy, there is at least a temporality that draws its meaning from beyond this nothingness, if only by way of the idea of progress. It is thus with Bloch that these possibilities appear in the analyses of death and time.

Bloch's mature texts, like those of his youth, justify humanism. "As real and non-formal, humanism is set back on its feet," he writes. "The human dimension receives its place in a democracy really made possible, just as democracy represents the first humanly habitable site." The human dimension is here absolutely dominant. "Marxism well practiced, stripped of its dangerous cousins, is *humanity in action*." It constitutes the ineluctable march of humanity toward its *Heimat* [homeland], where being is rejoined in the human being-at-home [*le chez-soi humain*]. This march is ineluctable insofar as it is the march of being, and insofar as it is inscribed in the essence of being, which is here thought in its human finality.[1]

What incites this revolutionary movement is the meaning of human misery. What led those to socialism who had no need for it? Perhaps the soul, perhaps the conscience that throbs in the silence of those who are sated. Thus, for Bloch, the spectacle of misery, the frustration of the neighbor, and the rigorously ethical discourse engendered thereby, rejoin the ontological discourse. The fulfillment of man is the fulfillment of being in its truth.

Never, perhaps, has a body of ideas presented such a surface, where ethics and ontology—standing in opposition as long as the world is incomplete—are in superimposition without our knowing which writing carries the other. How does Bloch think this solidarity between what being and the world are on the one hand, and humanity on the other, this same humanity that is inseparable in its ultimate constitution from human solidarity?

Like Michel Henry,[2] Bloch understands Marxism as a *philosophy* in the line of the *Phenomenology of Spirit*, where labor attains its categorical dignity. Likewise, for Bloch, no priority of action could come to be substituted for the search for truth. Without the intervention of some sort of voluntarism, the truth of being is conditioned by labor, action is a part of the manifestation of being. This is only possible if one has elaborated a new notion of being's intelligibility—and it is this notion that, prior to politics or economics, would constitute the specifically *Marxian* contribution to philosophy.[3]

The intelligibility of being would coincide with its completion as uncompleted [*achèvement d'inachevé*]. It is a potentiality having to pass into act, and the act is humanity. But that by which the possible is determined is not an operation of spirit. The act is labor. Nothing is accessible, nothing shows itself without being determined by the intervention of the corporeal labor of humanity.

The world is not completed because work is not completed. And as long as the world is not completed, as long as there is non-human matter, man is in the obscurity that is his share of facticity. Consequently, labor is always alienating: man is always opposed to the world before this completion in which being shall become the "at-home," or the *Heimat*.

Man's work is nevertheless the transcendental condition of truth. To produce is at once *to make* and *to present being in its truth*. This producing is *praxis*. There is nothing purely theoretical that is not already labor. The appearance of sensation already supposes work. It is, therefore, as a worker that man is subjectivity. Consequently, man is not a region of being but a moment of its effectuation as being. The truth of being is therefore the actualization of potentiality or history.

Time is then neither a projection of being toward its end, as in Heidegger, nor a mobile image of the immobile eternity, as in Plato. It is the time of fulfillment, a complete determination that is the actualization of all potentiality, of all the obscurity of the factual in which stands the subjectivity of man alienated in his technical activities. He is the actualization of the incomplete. The fact that there is a Master and a Slave is this same incompletion.

Thus, social evil is a fault in being, and progress is the progress of being itself, its fulfillment. What is not yet is not, and is nowhere. The future [*avenir*] is the not-yet-come [*le non-advenu*]; it is not virtually real, and it does not preexist.[4] Time is thus taken seriously. The drive toward the future is a relation with *utopia* and not a march toward a predetermined end of history in the present, which is obscure.

Time is pure hope. It is even the birthplace of hope. This is hope for a completed world in which man and his labor shall not be merchandise. A hope and a utopia without which the activity that fulfills being—that is, humanity—could neither begin, nor continue in the long patience of its science and effort.

For Bloch, this hope is inscribed in culture or, more precisely, in an entire side of culture that escapes the damnation of the incomplete and alienated world. This philosophy, which is presented as an interpretation of dialectical materialism, pays an extreme attention to all the forms of human works; it proceeds to a refined hermeneutic of the universal culture that vibrates in sympathy [*qui vibre par sympathie*]. In culture, the completed world is *glimpsed*, despite the class struggle or as a source of courage in that struggle.

A Reading of Bloch (Continued)

Friday, April 30, 1976

The philosophy handed down to us rests upon a certain number of identifications:

—the identity of human death and the nothingness of the philosophers (death is a moment of becoming);

—the identity of philosophy and ontology (being is the privileged site to which all meaningful thought refers);

—the identity of being and world;

—the identity of man and *Dasein* (i.e., the comprehension of man on the basis of the world, with dying understood as no-longer-being-in-the-world);

—the original identity between death in general [*la mort*] and *my* death (according to which responsibility for the death of another is derived; it should be emphasized, however, that in Plato, committing an injustice is worse than undergoing one);

—the identity of the affectivity wherein the relationship with death is established, and the anxiety engendered in its purity by the injury death causes to my desire to be;

—the identification of originary time and being-toward-death, of time and finitude;

—the identification of human finitude and human perfection.

In religious and social thought, a number of these equivalences have been shaken, even though the identity of philosophy and ontology and the primacy of the world in all intelligibility are maintained. (It is necessary to see; all understanding is showing; language is apophantic or predicative—it shows; language gets ensconced in that which it expresses.)

In Marxism such as Bloch interprets it, being and the world have meaning only as subordinated to man's liberation, to his emancipation or salvation. There is an ethical structure to this ontology! The ethico-ontological ambiguity is presented in such a way that concern for the human dimension no longer is a simple human science but commands all intelligibility and all meaning.

Death in its concretion cannot be reduced to the pure negation of being. If something can be saved, death loses its sting (we must not hide from ourselves the danger of this "preacher's" language, which can be hypocrisy). As for time, it is seen in a different way than that which draws from it the meaning of death understood as the end of being. In Bloch, the time of work is taken seriously, as is the time of the future understood as what has not yet come to pass, as what has not come about in any way, not even in the form of a project. The world in history is unfinished; being is not yet. The end is utopia. *Praxis* is possible not by way of the end of history but by way of the utopian hope for that end. The present and the human "me" [*moi humain*] in this history contain a zone of obscurity that is illumined by utopia.

Hope [*l'espérance*] is necessary to history. It is inscribed, for Bloch, in culture, which is a moment of being that escapes the damnation of the unfinished. In hope [*espérance*], there is an anticipation; we are in the world as though the world were finished. This hope does not signify the necessity of what will be produced; it is utopia. Neither is it a matter of an absolute Knowledge but, to use an expression that is not found in Bloch, of an absolute habitation. *Heimat* signifies being-there.

This utopia "short-circuits" time, but it is at the same time an agent of the human dimension and of work. This short-circuiting of time is the condition of the revolutionary consciousness. The utopianism of hope [*d'espoir*] is the temporization of time, the patience of the concept. Time, as the hope of utopia, is no longer the time that is thought of on the basis of death. Here, the first ecstasis is utopia, not death. And yet there is an analogy between Bloch's utopianism and the contemporary philosophies that see in the future the very meaning of time.

For Bergson, duration is freedom for the future. The future is open; one can therefore put in question the definitive quality of the past, which can receive at any time a new meaning (note the break with the time of the *Timæus*). In *Two Sources of Morality and Religion*, duration has a certain kinship with the relationship to the neighbor. Here we find a time full of spring, the principle of life that becomes the time of social existence, and generosity for the neighbor.

In Heidegger, there is another philosophy of time, thought on the basis of the ecstasis of the future. Time owes its originality, as a temporalization that starts from the future, to the finitude of human existence destined to being. Being-toward-death is what is most proper to man; it is anxiety, wherein the imminence of nothingness comes about, that is the most authentic mode of human being.

The nothingness of utopia is not the nothingness of death. For Bloch, it is not death that opens the authentic future; on the contrary, it is in the authentic future that death must be understood.

This is the utopian future as the hope of realizing what is not yet. It is the hope of a human subject who is still a stranger to himself, still a *Dass-sein*, that is, a pure fact of being, the pure fact that he is, the facticity of man in the historical world. It is the hope of a historical subject separated from the world in its facticity, invisible to himself, at a distance from the site where he would be able to be, himself, *Dasein*. Here is the subjectivity of a subject that does not amount to a tension over itself, or to the concern for being—a subjectivity that is like a dedication to a world to come.

For Bloch, the anxiety of death comes from the fact of dying without finishing one's work [*œuvre*], one's being. It is in an unfinished world that we have the impression of not finishing our work. Bloch does not want to ignore the obscure core of subjectivity in its singularity, to which nature is opposed. He reproaches Bergson and the philosophies of the *élan vital* for having neglected that singularity of subjectivity. The work of man is historical, but it is not proportionate to utopia. There is failure in every life, and the melancholy of this failure is its way of abiding in unfinished being. This is a melancholy that does not derive from anxiety. On the contrary, the anxiety of death would be a mode of this melancholy of the unfulfilled (which is not a wounding of one's pride). The fear of dying is the fear of leaving a work unfinished, and thus of not having lived.

However, there is the possibility of instants of true inhabiting, the hope of a few moments in which "a place is left for the consciousness of the glory of utopia in man."[1] That instant wherein the light of utopia penetrates into the obscurity of subjectivity, Bloch calls *astonishment*. Thus, in *Traces*, the astonishment that it *rains*, an astonishment that is not confused with the wonder "that there are beings."[2]

A Reading of Bloch: Toward a Conclusion

Friday, May 7, 1976

The subject, in the darkness of the pure fact of being, works for a world to come and for a better world. His work is therefore historical. In the immediate future, the utopia succeeds only partially; it is therefore always a failure, and the melancholy resulting from this failure is the way in which man reconciles himself with his historical evolution [*son devenir historique*]. This is a melancholy that does not derive from anxiety, as in Heidegger's case. On the contrary, for Bloch, it is the anxiety of death that would be a modality of melancholy. The fear of dying is the fear of leaving a work unfinished.

Bloch shows that the concern about the true future might not be merely agitation—it might not be mere diversion—by evoking those privileged moments in which the darkness of the subject (as a *Dass-sein*) is shot through by a ray of light coming from the utopian future. There, "a place is left for the consciousness of the glory of utopia in man," says Bloch, who calls this "penetration" *astonishment.*[1] Culture itself must be interpreted as hope (there is no "Cultural Revolution" in Bloch!).

Astonishment or wonder stems not from the quiddity of what astonishes but from a certain moment. What is able to provoke it is found not only in highly significant relations but also in the way in which a leaf is stirred by the wind, in the beauty of a melody, the face of a young girl, a child's smile, a word. It is then that as-

tonishment comes in, which is a question and a response, the hope
for a home and for *Dasein*, where the *Da* might be fully realized,
and not simply *Dass-sein*.

To evoke this moment of astonishment, Bloch refers to Knut
Hamsun (i.e., the astonishment of "it rains"), as he cites Tolstoy
(*Anna Karenina* and *War and Peace*). In *War and Peace*, we find
such a moment when Prince André, wounded on the battlefield of
Austerlitz, contemplates the *high* sky that is neither blue nor gray,
but only high. And Tolstoy, who insists on the *height* of this sky,
writes, "Looking Napoleon in the eyes, Prince André dreamed of
the vanity of grandeur, of the vanity of life whose meaning no one
could understand, *and of the still greater vanity of death, whose meaning no living being could penetrate and explain.*"[2] Here, death loses
its meaning; it is vain relative to this accord with being that Prince
André feels.

Astonishment is a question that is not the posing of a question
and in which there is also a response. It is a question by virtue of
the obscurity of the subject, and a response by virtue of the full-
ness of hope. Bloch thus describes this astonishment with the
term *home*, which is an anticipation of the world perfected, in
which the obscurity of singularity disappears.

Bloch also describes astonishment with the term "leisure," op-
posing this leisure of pure disposition to that which the unfinished or capitalist world offers, which is either the emptiness of
time ("sad Sundays") or the continuation of exploitation (holidays
as the rejuvenation of the labor force). This leisure is one in which
the strangeness of being disappears in the question, one in which
being is entirely mine. It is mine to such a degree that what
comes to pass in the world is my affair. This is where the expression *tua res agitur* [your interest is at stake] takes on its strongest
sense. The intensity of this "your" is stronger than any possession
or any property.

Therein lies the way of personal being in a perfected and successful world, without melancholy; and this is what takes the sting
from death. The me [*moi*] is a "me" [*moi*] in the brightness of a
world to which man is no longer opposed. Death cannot touch

man then, for humanity has already left the individual. There only, a being who is happiness would reign.

The constitution of a site[3] of human habitation and the event of being as being are the same event, the same *Ereignis* of self-appropriation; it is the appearing of the possessive aspect of the *tua res agitur*. In this appearing of being come to its end, there is an end to the opposition between man and being, and an end of facticity. The transformation of the world that is in formation, the same world in which man introduces forms into matter through *praxis*, is an objective process so intimately, or authentically, or properly tied to that *praxis* that objectivity exalts in a possessive pronoun; it becomes possessive, the possessive pronoun of the *tua res agitur*. Perhaps the original site of the possessive is located here, rather than being located in the possession of things.

On the basis of the *tua res agitur*, the identity of the "me" [*moi*] is identified. Consequently, the old Epicurean principle is justified: when death is there, *you* are not there. Indeed, for Bloch, there is not yet a *you*. In the humanized world, man is not touched by death. Everything is actualized, everything is accomplished, everything is outside. In this way fulfillment resolves the problem of death—without suppressing it, however.

From this vision, three things should be kept in mind:

—The possibility for man to get his identity from somewhere other than the perseverance in his being, to which Heidegger accustomed us; that is, from elsewhere than this *conatus* where death strikes its blow to the highest of all attachments, the attachment to being. Here, on the contrary, man is not primarily preoccupied with his being.

—The subordination of being and the world to the ethical order, to the human order, and to completion (the end of exploitation). This is the case even if, in order to speak of this completion, Bloch speaks the language of being and ontology.

—The way in which Bloch detaches time from the idea of nothingness so as to attach it to the utopian completion. Time, here, is not pure destruction—quite the contrary.

∿

There is in all this an invitation to think death on the basis of time, and no longer time on the basis of death. This takes nothing away from the ineluctable character of death, but it does not leave it the privilege of being the source of all meaning. In Heidegger, at least in *Being and Time*, everything that is a forgetting of death is inauthentic or improper, and the denial itself of death in distraction refers back to death. Here, on the contrary, the meaning of death does not begin in death. This invites us to think of death as a moment of death's *signification*, which is a meaning that overflows death. We must note carefully that "to overflow death" in no sense means surpassing or reducing it; it means that this overflowing has its signification, too. Expressions like "love is stronger than death" (in fact, the Song of Songs says precisely: "Love, as strong as death") have their meaning.

We should notice also those expressions of Vladimir Jankélévitch in his book *Death*: "Death is stronger than thought; thought is stronger than death."[4] And "Love, Freedom, and God are stronger than death. And vice versa!"[5] Jankélévitch also writes:

> Death and consciousness each have, the one and the other, the last word, which (this comes to the same thing) is each time but the second to last. Consciousness prevails over death just as death prevails over consciousness. Thinking is conscious of the total suppression, but it succumbs to that suppression, which it thinks, and which nevertheless suppresses it. Or, reciprocally: thinking succumbs to suppression, and yet it thinks it. . . . The thinking reed knows he will die; and we add immediately, and he dies all the same. But here we are back at our point of departure: he dies, but he knows that he dies.[6]

Jankélévitch again cites Ionesco (*Exit the King*)—"If you are madly in love, if you love intensely, if you love absolutely, death withdraws"[7]—before going on to note, "This is why Diotima, in the *Banquet*, says that love is άθανασίας ἔρως, a desire for immortality."[8]

Do these reciprocal negations stop at their reciprocity, or do they have a meaning that should consequently be specified? Is not death—though it is the strongest—necessary to the time whose course it seems to halt? The love that is stronger than death—a privileged formulation.

We come to the same challenge to the subordination of time to being-toward-death in recalling Bloch's audacity in interpreting otherwise than as anxiety for my being the affectivity in which death is announced. In Heidegger, death is signaled in the consciousness of the end of my being. It is in relation to my being, which is having-to-be, that anxiety would be understood. For his part, Bloch tends to find in the anxiety over dying a threat other than that which concerns being. It is as if within being were produced what is higher or better than being. The event of being is for Heidegger the ultimate event. Here, the event of being is subordinated to a completion in which man finds his home. Being, in a certain sense, contains more or better or something other than being; for Bloch, this is the completion of the world, its quality as a home, which is attained in the perfected world. In its primordial aim, anxiety would be the melancholy of a work uncompleted. What counts above all for Bloch, and what must be kept in mind here, is that such an emotion could dominate the ineluctability of death, that death might not be marked solely by the threat that weighs upon my being, and that death does not exhaust its meaning in being the sign of nothingness.

Thus we come back to the love "as strong as death." It is not a matter of a force that could repel the death inscribed in my being. However, it is not my nonbeing that causes anxiety, but that of the loved one or of the other, more beloved than my being. What we call, by a somewhat corrupted term, love, is *par excellence* the fact that the death of the other affects me more than my own. The love of the other is the emotion of the other's death. It is my receiving the other—and not the anxiety of death awaiting me—that is the reference to death.

We encounter death in the face of the other.

Thinking About Death
on the Basis of Time

Friday, May 14, 1976

To think death on the basis of time rather than time on the basis of death, as Heidegger does, is one of the exhortations drawn from our glimpse of Bloch's utopianism. Another such is to start from the questioning, in this utopianism, of the meaning given to the emotion that greets death (i.e., the melancholy of a work in check). This thinking invites us to emphasize the question raised by death in the nearness of the neighbor, a question that paradoxically is my responsibility for his death. Death opens to the face of an *Other* [*d'Autrui*], which expresses the command "thou shalt not kill." We shall have to attempt to start from murder as suggesting the complete meaning of death.

We thus find again the traits already suggested in the phenomenology of death. That is, the end inscribed in death and the question beyond every doxic mode; an original question, one without the posing of a question; a question without a thesis; a pure question that raises itself; a question that is the pure raising of a question. From this comes the question that we propose here. Can one seek the meaning of death on the basis of time? Does this meaning not show itself in the diachrony of time, understood as a relationship to the other? Can one understand time as a relationship with the Other, rather than seeing in it the relationship with the end?

A preliminary question comes up. Is there an understanding of time when the temporal—as what becomes or evolves—is pledged to reason? How to lend a meaning to time, when for philosophy identity is the identity of the Same, when intelligibility thrives in the Same, when it thrives on being in its stability as the Same, when it thrives on assimilating the Other into the Same—when every alteration is senseless, when understanding assimilates the Other into the Same?

In thinking of what the rationality of becoming is for Hegel, we can assert that the Same maintains its privilege as rational despite the force of negativity attached to the subject and his role. There is a possibility of thinking the identity of the identical and the nonidentical, in which a rationality of the same persists. Everything that does not coincide with oneself, everything that is still becoming, then passes as purely subjective and romantic. Disquiet, searching, desire, and the question in its call as a question, the question as a prayer addressed to the other: all this receives ill esteem among the positive values; all this is interpreted as a decline of these positive values and as indigent knowledge. We would like to suggest, here, that one might think these ill-esteemed privations according to other criteria.

Yet these privations, and temporal becoming itself, refer in our customary intellectualism to the stability and the fulfillment of what is present to itself, of what has come to term. The term would be the living present, a stability apt to present itself and to be represented, apt to hold together in a presence, and thereby to be taken in hand. Whence comes the fractioning of time into instants, identical atoms, points or pinpoints, pure "where's" and pure "when's" that are like birth and extenuation in some pure density. A reference to the consistent or the substantial.

From this comes the confusion between time and being that lasts in time.

Husserl—who brings ultimate intelligibility back to temporality—brings the ideas in all their eternity (eternity understood here as omni-temporality) back to temporality; Husserl, who finds the genesis of all beings and all meaning in the living present, describes this immanent temporality as a *flux* or a current of sensible qualities. Here there is a tacit presupposing of the composition of time as a series of instants. Time is the form of qualities that flow by as they are altered, a flux of quiddities identifiable through their order in time. Even if time is the form of these qualities, does the form itself not reconstitute time's identity? The form recalls identity, the status of the identity of the contents. A form made up of qualities, of sensations that are interpreted as quiddities, givens, elements of knowledge and appearing discernible by their order in time. The instants go by as though they were things. They flow past, but they are retained or "protained."

The category of the Same, which dominates these descriptions, is not put in question. Becoming is a constellation of identical points. The other remains another same, identical to himself, discernible from without by way of his place in this order. The comprehension of time would reside in the relationship between a term identical to itself and presence. Every alteration of the identical would find its identity anew in this copresence governed by retention and protention. This possibility of the synchrony of terms is the very criterion of their meaning; to the difference between the terms it assures the stability of an instant, in which time and the real continue to be confused. The identity of the term that refers only to itself is thereby assured.

The disquiet and nonrest of time are abated in this analysis. The possibility of representation and of copresence is the possibility of presence, which is the possibility of the term in an order (whether beginning or end); it is thus the possibility of the very notion of the original and the ultimate, of the term referring only to itself. A rationality of rest, or repose, and of positivity, that is, of being.

The ultimate metaphor of time would be the flux, the flowing by of a liquid—a metaphor drawn from the world of objects, although it is supposed to grasp the source of all objectivity. Is time not presupposed, then, as the support of every moment?

One might suppose that the flow of the current, the flowing by of things, and movement itself were metaphors borrowed from the stream of consciousness, and that taken literally the flux can only be predicated of the time that is not to be confused with the contents that endure. Perhaps it is there that we find the Bergsonian idea of the duration that precedes the content of what endures. But can we lend this idea to Husserl, for whom time is always thought on the basis of the content? To the question "Does not the flow of time suppose another time?" Husserl responds in the negative. The flow would be originally the mark of the description of consciousness.

The Heideggerian deduction of the ecstasis of time on the basis of being-to-death, which anticipates itself without this self-anticipating being borrowed from anything fluvial, is speculatively more satisfying than any image of a river.

But are we compelled to start from the image of a flux or a flowing, in order to comprehend a time that would be irreducible to the identity of the Same? Can the nonrest of time, that by which time contrasts with the identity of the Same, signify otherwise than according to the continuous mobility that the privileged metaphor of the flux suggests? To answer this question, we must ask ourselves whether the Same and the Other owe their meaning simply to a distinction of quality or of quiddity, that is, to the given in time and to the discernible? To put it differently, do the nonrest or the disquiet of time not signify, prior to any terminology or recourse to terms appealing to no images of rivers or flux, a disquieting of the Same by the Other, which takes nothing from the discernible and the qualitative? This would suggest a disquietude that would be identified as indiscernible, or that would not be identified by any quality. To be identified thus, to be identified without being identified, is to identify oneself as "me" [*moi*]; it is to identify oneself internally without thematizing oneself and without appearing. It is to be identified without appearing and prior to taking on a name.

This is what we glimpse in phenomena such as searching and its becoming [*le devenir en elle*], which can signify in me a relation with that which is not said to be absent by default but rather which, as unqualifiable, could neither coincide with anything, nor form a present with anything, nor lodge itself in a representation or in a present. No present would have capacities equal to the unqualifiable, which is wholly other than a term, wholly other than a content. Because it is infinite, this unqualifiable would not be assumable—one could not take charge of it.

Time and all temporal phenomena (searching, questioning, desire, etc.) are always analyzed by default. Is it not possible, in these
phenomena, to think of their emptiness and their incompletion as
a step beyond contents, a mode of relationship with the noncontainable, with the infinite that one could not say is a term?

The relationship with the infinite is an untenable question; it is
unrepresentable and without a punctuality that would let it be designated; it is outside of the compass of comprehension in which
the successive is synchronized. Infinity, nevertheless, does not exclude searching, that is, its absence is not a pure absence. Searching would be not the nonrelation with the different but the relation
with the singular, a relation of difference in nonindifference excluding any common measure, whether this were ultimacy, community, or copresence. A relation would nevertheless remain, and
this would be diachrony itself. It would be for us to think of time
as the very relation with the Infinite [*l'Infini*]. The search or the
question would be not a deficiency of some possession but, from
the outset, a relationship with what is beyond possession, with the
ungraspable wherein thought would tear itself apart.

Always. Always would tear itself apart. Always, explaining the
how of this tearing apart. The always of time would be engendered
by that disproportion between desire and what is desired, and this
desire itself would be a rupture of intentional consciousness in its
noetico-noematic equality.

A searching as a questioning, and a questioning arising prior to
every question about the given. *Infinity in the finite*. A fission or
a putting in question of the one who questions. That would be
temporality.

What does this *in* signify? It signifies the putting in question of
me [*moi*] by the other [*l'autre*] that takes the form of an appeal to
my responsibility, that confers on me an identity. A questioning in
which the conscious subject is liberated from himself, in which it
is split apart [*scindé*] but by excess, by transcendence: there we find
the disquietude of time as awakening. This disturbance by the
other puts into question the identity in which the essence of being
is defined. This fission of the Same by the untenable Other at the

heart of myself, where disquiet disturbs the heart at rest, and is not reducible to some intellection of terms—this disquiet at the heart of the rest that is not yet reduced to identity points, burning and shining in their identity, and suggesting by that rest an eternity older than any disquietude—this is awakening, this is temporality.

It is necessary to think in an ethical manner this tearing of the Same by the Other. The return, or recurrence, of this identification of the Same amounts to undergoing every passion to the point of passive languishing [*pâtir*], that is, of suffering an assignation without possible evasion, without escaping into representation in order to outwit its urgency. To be in the accusative before any nominative form. Inner identity signifies precisely the impossibility of holding oneself at rest. It is ethical from the first.

Time, rather than the current of contents of consciousness, is the turning of the Same toward the Other. This is turning toward the other who, as other, would jealously preserve temporal diachrony in this unassimilable turning to representation. Like the immemorial at the site of the origin, it is the infinite that is the teleology of time. This turning toward the Other responds, according to a multiple intrigue, for the other, my neighbor. It is a nontransferable responsibility whose urgency identifies me as irreplaceable and unique.

The always of time, the impossibility of the identification of I [*Moi*] and the Other, the impossible synthesis of I and the Other. Diachrony. Diastole or dilation. The impossibility of settling on the same terrain, of com-posing in the world, the impossibility in the form of a slippage of the earth beneath my feet.

The "incessant" quality of this difference. Diachrony. The patience of this impossibility, and patience as the length of time; patience or passivity, a patience that is not brought back to the anamnesis that gathers time anew. This is an irrecoverable lapse of time that emphasizes the powerlessness of memory over the diachrony of time. A powerlessness of memory over the lapse of time in the image of the flux, a powerlessness that emphasizes the diachrony of time.

The difference does not differ like a logical distinction, but as nonindifference, as desire for the noncontainable, a desire for infinity. Against all good logic and ontology, we find the reality of the impossible in which the Infinite, which places me in question, is like a more in the less.

Nonindifference, or desire, as a "tendency" distinct from erotic tendencies. The erotic is like impatience in this patience, like impatience itself. This is a turning of the Same and not the intentionality that is a correlation that is absorbed in its correlate, not a correlation that is synchronized with the graspable or the given. The turning turns itself toward ... , but does so otherwise.

For the Infinite, that which encompasses would be insufficient.

To Conclude: Questioning Again

Friday, May 21, 1976

What we have attempted to do is to think of time independently of the death to which the passive synthesis of aging leads us,
to describe time independently of death or the nothingness of the
end that death signifies. We have attempted to think death as a
function of time, without seeing in death the very project of time.
To think the meaning of death—not to render it inoffensive, nor
to justify it, nor to promise eternal life, but to try to show the
meaning death accords to the human adventure, that is, to the essance of being or to the beyond of ess*a*nce.[1] We have tried to think
of time all the while acknowledging in death a difference relative to
the nothingness that comes out of the simple negation of being.

Death is not of the world. It is always a scandal and, in this sense,
always transcendent in regard to the world. The nothingness that
comes out of negation always remains tied to the intentional gesture of negation, and thus keeps the trace of being that this gesture
refuses, repels, and repudiates. Against this, death raises a question
that is not posed, that turns out not to be a modality of consciousness; a question that is without a given [*sans donnée*]. Every act of
consciousness, as knowledge, is belief and position or *doxa*. The
question that the nothingness of death raises is a pure question
mark. A question mark entirely alone, yet marking also a demand
(every question is a demand, a prayer). The question that the nothingness of death raises is not a doxic modification of some sort; it

belongs to a layer of the psyche that is deeper than consciousness; it belongs to an event in which the event is broken off—and it is there that we must go to search for time.

The possibility of posing a question to oneself, the famous dialogue of the soul with itself, would never be possible unless the relationship with the Other [*Autrui*] and the question mark of his face had come about.

~

The previous lecture showed that time lasts like a psychic mode without a *doxa*. It lasts as a duration that is in no sense knowledge, one that endures without regard for the consciousness one might have of duration—a consciousness that itself lasts (the consciousness of duration is the duration of consciousness). The preceding lecture pointed out that such a duration might nonetheless have a meaning, and even a religious meaning, the meaning of a deference to the Infinite.

To set forth the signification of this duration, we must seek it without holding ourselves to the mobile image of immobile eternity, or to the idea of a flux, or to being-toward-death and the time considered on the basis of the play of being and nothingness. We must think rationality and meaning without having to hold onto the model of fulfillment (Husserl), where an entire history of Reason ends, and according to which the *meaningful* is the fully *possessed*, that which gives itself, fills and satisfies, and is equal to what one expects of it, what can be held and contained [*tenu et contenu*], and which is a result.

That is a rationality of the graspable, comprehensible result, relative to which duration disturbs us by its not-yet, by what is unfulfilled. An ideal of the meaningful for a consciousness attached to the unshakable terrain of the world, that is, to the earth under the vault of the sky. The same rationality of a thought thinking to its own measure, on its own scale, and relative to which every search, every desire, every question is a becoming, constituting a not-yet and a lack; for this rationality, searching, desiring, and questioning are the nonsatisfying; they represent impoverished knowledge [*d'indigentes connaissances*].

Do searching, desiring, and questioning signify only the absence of a response, that is, an insufficiency of identity—or would they be thoughts of that which *exceeds* thought? And we must wonder, moreover, whether we are here entitled to use the demonstrative pronoun *that* [*ce*], which indicates a content proportionate to its thought, a correlate of thought—and whether this relationship of thought to the beyond-measure can still be called thought.

Is the time beyond consciousness not the modality of the psyche in which the ontological event is undone, in which, contrary to every ontological event, what cannot be contained, what is totally other—or God—affects the Same within time? In speaking of "affection," we want to state together the impossibility of the Other entering into the Same (an impossibility of the seen, the aimed-at), while wondering whether this impossibility of entering *into* nevertheless does not amount to a way of being concerned according to a passivity more passive than any passivity, that is, according to a nonassumable passivity. We wonder whether this affection does not mean to endure patiently, to endure with a patience whose *temporal duration*—which is a relationship unique in its genre—would be the name.

If it were in the finite, the Infinite or the Other would be assimilated, if only by its own reflection. Yet the duration of time would be that relationship that no pre-position could make finite or define [*finir ou définir*]. It is impossible to *receive* time's blow; it is more like receiving the blow, or force, of time and waiting still; it is to receive without receiving, without taking upon oneself, to endure that which still remains outside in its transcendence, and yet to be affected by it. This is to await, in its transcendence, that which is not a *that* [*ce*], a term, or something awaited. It is an awaiting without something being awaited.

A patient awaiting. The patience and endurance of the beyond-measure, to-God [*à-Dieu*]; time as to-God.[2] An awaiting without an awaited object, this would be a waiting for that which cannot be a term and which always refers from the Other to an Other [*de l'Autre à Autrui*].[3] The always of duration: a length [*longueur*] of time that is not the lengthiness [*longueur*] of the river that flows by. Time as a relationship of deference to what cannot be represented and which, thus, cannot be expressed as *this*, but which is not indifferent. Nonindifference is a way of being disquieted, disquieted in a passivity with no taking charge.

This nonindifference or disquiet is, as a result, infinitely more than representation, possession, contact, and response—it is more than being. The consciousness in which knowledge, responses, and results would be a psyche *insufficient* for the demand. To the Infinite would be suited thoughts that are desires and questions. Time would thus be the bursting of the *more* of the Infinite in the *less*, which Descartes called the idea of the Infinite. Time would thus amount to the way of "being" of the Infinite. This way is a way of enduring the Infinite: it is patience.

It is necessary, here, to think the Other-in-the-Same as a first category, and do so in thinking the *in* otherwise than as a presence. The Other is not another Same; the *in* does not signify an assimilation. It is rather a situation where the Other disturbs the Same and where the Same desires the Other and awaits it.[4] The Same is not at rest; the identity of the Same is not that to which all its meaning is reduced. The Same containing more than it can contain—that is Desire, searching, patience, and the length of time.

~

How does death take on a meaning in time as patience, or suffering of the Other by the Same, which is a patience that becomes the length of time? What concrete signification does this patience, this disturbance, this trauma, or this diachrony of patience take? The temporality of time is, in effect, ambiguous. The duration of time can show itself as a continuity in a synopsia[5] in which an internalization of time is produced (this is not a human failing: it is a matter of an essential ambiguity in this patience we are describing, that is, of an impatience with this patience within this very patience). Time loses its diachrony to gather itself into the continuity of memory and aspiration; it offers itself up to the unity of transcendental apperception in order to be constituted as the unity of a flux, a unity of a person in an inhabited world. Thus, for Husserl, time will be thought of as a process of immanence.

~

So, does the trauma of the other [*l'autre*] not come from *another person* [*d'autrui*]? Is the nothingness of death not the very nudity of the neighbor's face? "You shall not commit murder" is the nudity of the face. Is the nearness of the neighbor not my responsibility for his death? If that is so, then my relationship with the Infinite would be inverted into that responsibility. Death, in the face of the other man, is the mode according to which the alterity that affects the Same causes its identity as the Same to burst open in the form of a question that arises in it.

This question—the question of death—is unto itself its own response: it is my responsibility for the death of the other. The passage to the ethical level is what constitutes the response to this question. The turning of the Same toward the Infinite, which is neither aiming nor vision, is the *question*, a question that is also a response, but in no way a dialogue of the soul with itself. A question, a prayer—is this not prior to dialogue? The question contains the response as ethical responsibility, as an impossible escape.

However, this relationship with the Other in the question that the mortality of another poses can lose its transcendence through the customs that organize it, thereby becoming continuity in society where another and I belong to the same social body. The for-the-other is thus produced reasonably, as a meaningful activity. Consequently, the substantiality of the subject is reborn from its ashes. But does subjectivity not become frozen in this way?

Passivity is therefore possible only if a pure madness may be suspected to lie at the very heart of the meaning that signifies in the codified devotion to the other. This absurdity is my mortality, my dying for nothing, which keeps my responsibility from becoming the assimilation of the other within a behavior. My mortality, my being condemned to death, my time at the point of death, and my death are not the possibility of impossibility but a pure being seized; this constitutes the absurdity that makes possible the gratuity of my responsibility for another.

The relationship with the Infinite is the responsibility of a mortal being for a mortal being. As in the biblical passage (Genesis 18:23ff.) where Abraham intercedes for Sodom. Abraham is frightened by the death of others, and he takes the responsibility to intercede. It is then that he says, "I am, myself, ashes and dust."

PART II

God and Onto-theo-logy

Beginning with Heidegger

Friday, November 7, 1975

The theme of this course, "God and Onto-theo-logy," is Heideggerian in origin. It appears especially in Heidegger's readings of Hegel (in particular, in "The Onto-Theological Constitution of Metaphysics").[1] We shall therefore begin here with Heidegger. But we will make only a first approach, that is, with remarks that it will be necessary thereafter to unsay.

In Heidegger, the theme of the onto-theo-logical character of metaphysics goes together with the characterization of a certain *epoch*. Now, an epoch signifies not a space of time but rather a certain way for being to show itself. It is by means of this "certain way" that time is divided up, and that history runs its course.[2] The epoch in question here (that of onto-theo-logy) embraces all of philosophy.

That epoch is something noncontingent. It is not the result of some human decline, but rather reflects a certain process, a certain history of being itself (which is the ultimate of all questioning and the ultimate in meaningfulness). Nevertheless, it is not necessary in the way in which the result of a deduction would be; it is not logically, or mechanically, or dialectically necessary.

In the delimitation of this epoch, there is a pejorative nuance. Heidegger's problem is not to turn backwards, and yet there is in his critique something pejorative: like the recalling of missed possibilities, or of what went unsaid or unthought, in this epoch.

And there is a sort of exhaustion of this epoch, an exhaustion that leaves, once again, a chance:³ the possibility of resuming [*renouer*] —but this time in a mature fashion—this unsaid and this unthought.

⁓

I will recall here some fundamental motifs of Heidegger's thought:

1. The most extraordinary thing that Heidegger brings us is a new *sonority* of the verb "to be": precisely its *verbal* sonority. To be: not what is, but the verb, the "act" of being. (In German, the difference is easily drawn between *Sein* [to be] and *Seiendes* [beings], and the latter word does not have in German the foreign sonority that the French *étant* [a being] carries, such that Heidegger's first French translators had to set it between quotation marks.) This contribution is what is unforgettable in the work of Heidegger. It has, as its consequence:

2. *The radical distinction between being and beings*, the famous *ontological difference*. There is a radical difference between the verbal resonance of the word "being" and its resonance as a noun. It is the difference *par excellence*. It is Difference. Every difference supposes a certain community; between being and beings, however, there is nothing in common. (This is proposed here as a statement [*dit*] to be unstated [*dé-dire*].)

3. *Language*. This is the site of this difference; it is here, in language, that being is lodged. Language is the house of being.⁴

4. *The forgetting of the difference*. This difference has been forgotten, and that forgetting constitutes Western thought.

This forgetting is in no way the result of some psychological deficiency of man: it is founded in being, it is an event of being itself. Being itself has made itself, or let itself be forgotten; it has veiled itself—and it is that veiling that gives rise to the (human) forgetting of being. Forgetting is *an epoch of being*.⁵

Western thought consists in understanding being only as the *foundation of beings*. (All philosophy has been merely the language of being; it is the modality according to which being can be said, for there is a silent language of being to which man responds.)

Now there is an *epic* or *adventure* of being [*une geste d'être*], a *reign* of being. In German, one uses the verb *wesen. Das Sein west*: being does its business of being [*métier d'être*] (whereas the entity is —*ist*). Being *west*, it does its work [*métier*], carries out its reign of being, or follows its train of being [*il mène son train d'être*]. One can thus indeed say that the entity is founded in being. But this already entails a certain interpretation of being, and already a veiling. In speaking of being as foundation, one does not utter being in its truth, in its own epic [*sa propre geste*]—which shall have to be found again, in the thinking of being.

For Heidegger, the comprehension of being in its truth was immediately covered over by its function as the universal foundation of beings, by a supreme being, a founder, by God. The thinking of being, being in its truth, becomes knowledge [*savoir*] or comprehension of God: theo-logy. The European philosophy of being becomes theology.

See, for example, Heidegger's reading of Aristotle: the problem posed by Aristotle is indeed that of being *qua* being (of being in its verbal quality), but being is immediately approached in the form of a foundation of beings, and, finally, it comes to be named God. From that moment on, philosophy becomes theology. Hence the title cited earlier: "The Onto-Theological Constitution of Metaphysics."

It is a question, however, not of a pure and simple deviation but of a certain comprehension of being (on the basis of beings): never, in effect, would anything have been thought if we did not think the being (of beings). In the epoch of metaphysics, nevertheless, we think being as a foundation, that is, we think metaphysically. Hence Heidegger's way of working, his rereading of metaphysics to discover, in it, its unsaid. A certain destruction (or deconstruction) of metaphysics is therefore necessary. Nevertheless, Heidegger opposes his way of *conversing* with philosophy to Hegel's manner of doing so: Hegel reads philosophy as a progress; the central concept of his reading is the *Aufhebung*, a word that we can in fact translate, with Derrida, by *relève*[6] (whether we think of the relief of a sentinel, or of the changing of the guard, etc., that which *auf-*

gehoben ist is at once rejected, preserved, and raised up). In Heidegger, it is a matter not of a *relève* but of a *step backward.*

5. The same movement that substitutes onto-theo-logy for the thinking of being leads, in a series of successive forgettings, to science, which pays attention only to beings, which subordinates them to itself, which wants to conquer and dispose of them, and which seeks power over beings. This movement thus leads to the will to power (which is a certain comprehension of being, the manner by which, in our epoch, being is or does its business of being); it opens onto technology. The end of metaphysics, the crisis of the technical world, which leads to the death of God, is in reality the prolongation of onto-theo-logy.

6. This end of metaphysics leaves a chance for the thinking of being, which would no longer be ontology.[7] Heidegger no longer uses the word "ontology," which is still tied to logic (whereas, in the first period of his thought, the task was that of a *fundamental ontology*). This abandonment is due to this memory of logic, that is, to the manner by which being was translated as the Being of beings. Logic would still bear the mark of onto-theo-logy. On the other hand, that which is coming, that which can come, Heidegger calls *the thinking of being.* There is a new epoch, marked by the death of God and the end of onto-theo-logy.

⁓

Here too it is a matter of finishing with onto-theo-logy. But a question arises: did onto-theo-logy's mistake consist in taking being for God, or rather in taking God for being?

To pose this question is to ask whether being, in the verbal and the nominal senses, is the ultimate source of meaning. Being, that is, being *and* nothingness; and as we have known since Hegel, nothingness is not the result of a purely negative operation that would repel being—the negation keeps, on the soles of its shoes, the dust of the ground it left behind it. All nothingness is the nothing of something, and this something, whose nothing remains nothingness, remains thought. Being and nothingness are linked.

Does not God signify the *other of being*? Does not signifying thought signify, in the image of God, the bursting and subversion of being: a dis-inter-estedness (a departure from "essement")?[8] Does not the other, as irreducible to the Same, allow us to think, within a certain (ethical) relationship, that other or that beyond?

Ethics, that is, not a simple layer or covering but something more ancient than onto-theo-logy, for which the former must account.[9]

What is meaningful does not necessarily have to be. Being can confirm thought, but thought thinks meaning—the meaning that is exhibited by being. This thought enlarges disinterestedness.

To contrast [*opposer*] God with onto-theo-logy is to conceive a new mode, a new notion of meaning. And it is from a certain ethical relationship that one may start out on this search.

Being and Meaning

Friday, November 14, 1975

The theme of onto-theo-logy attaches the coming of God into philosophy to the thought of a certain signification of being, understood in the sense of the foundation of beings. (It is Heidegger who poses the question "How has God come into philosophy?")[1] For Heidegger, that notion of a foundation of beings by beings characterizes metaphysics. That is, it characterizes the epoch of philosophy in which the foundation of the being is itself a being, in which being is understood in the form of a being, and in which the ontological difference is forgotten. This is the metaphysics that is completed and at the same time fulfilled in our European science extended by technology. An opportunity is then offered to thought to rediscover a possible thinking of being. It is not a question of going backwards, or of again seizing this possibility of thought after the end of this epoch (without purely and simply effacing this metaphysical epoch), by separating thought from onto-theo-logy.

Heidegger's thesis consists in positing that being is at the origin of all meaning. This immediately implies that one cannot think beyond being. All that is meaningful comes back to the understanding of being. It is against such a thesis that a question arises here: Is thinking of God by way of onto-theo-logy the wrong way of thinking about being (the Heideggerian thesis), or is it the wrong way of thinking about God? Does not God signify *the beyond being*? (Now that is what, for Heidegger, would be scarcely defensible, although there is a philosophical tradition—Platonic and Plotinian—of thinking of a God beyond being.) To the degree that God signifies, does not all meaning go back to God? Is meaningful thought not a subversion of being, a disinterestedness (that is, a stepping out of the Order)?[2] In that sense, beyond being signifies a transcendence and not a superlativity, unless one derives the superlativity from a *height* that, as such, is not inspired by being.

To separate God from onto-theo-logy is to conceive the notion of meaning in new ways. Here in particular, it is found in the relationship of the Same to the Other. The Other as Other has nothing in common with the Same; it is not thinkable in a synthesis; there is an impossibility here of making comparisons and synchronizations. The relationship between the Same and the Other is a *deference* of the Same to the Other, in which we can recognize the ethical relationship (from the Same to the Other: without a common measure, but not without relation—and the relation that there is is one of deference). And the ethical relationship no longer has to be subordinated to ontology or to the thinking of being.

In what sense is a rationality other than ontological rationality thinkable; in what sense is it possible? What structures does a thinking beyond being take, a thinking that thinks more than it can think? Here, the correlation, the equality of the *noesis* and the *noema*, is put back into question. Here, there would be a relationship, but one that would not be a relation of equality.

The relationship of equality is Greek. Nevertheless, if I speak, if I speak of the other relationship,[3] then the same Greek rationality, that of equality, will be demanded by the very discourse that wanted to relativize the relationship of equality. The discourse on the beyond of being that is sought here intends to be coherent.

For the Greeks, discourse is the site where meaning is communicated and clarified, but already offered to him who thinks. And it is in this coherence of discourse that thinking itself is thought. There is not thought first and discourse afterward, but discourse in thought itself. We recall that, in Plato, the sole condition Socrates sets such that he can teach the slave is *the knowledge of Greek*; of Greek and not a barbarian language; of Greek, which is an articulated language, which possesses a syntax, and not a language made up of syllables bound together.[4] Here, there is a difficulty: for one could make a logical relation relative only in a logical discourse.

In the Western tradition, linguistic expression has importance for meaning as meaning: there is no meaning if there is no language. And this meaning *qua* meaning is a manifestation of being. (But "a manifestation of being" is a tautology for the Greeks![5] Being is manifestation, "to be" = "manifestation"—and Heidegger preserves this position.) The grammatical categories are thought by Greek thought as the categories of being and as being's very intelligibility. And Kant finds in the modalities of expressed judgment the table of his categories.[6] Logic is already in some fashion ontological; it is, at least, in logic that the fundamental forms of being are found.

To speak is to speak Greek.[7] But if it is correct that meaning is only shown in language, must we likewise argue that logical exposition does not contain a *manner of speaking* [*pour-ainsi-dire*]? Must we not ask ourselves whether the logical exposition of meaning does not call for an unsaying [*dédire*]—where the *saying* [*dire*] calls for an *unsaying* [*dédire*]—must we not ask whether speaking shows a gap between meaning and that which is manifested of it, between meaning and what, in manifesting itself, *takes on the ways of being*? Does the meaning that shows itself not distinguish itself from this appearing, from the epic of being, from the train of being that, in the form of positing or the thesis, mingles with it? Indeed, in proposing, I posit, and it is in this way that I show, and there is already there an intervention of being. All meaning thus seems to be doxic. But can we not speak also of a para-doxical meaning (that is, a meaning that would not be a doxic thesis)?[8]

In other words, it would be necessary to think of language as a question. But is the question itself only the diminution of affirmation? In questioning, do I limit myself to doing less than affirming? Is the question *only* that? For Greek thought, the answer is "yes": the question is a minus. The question is *posed*; it is posed in view of a response. But is language as a question only a diminution of affirmation? Does the gap between the meaningful and what is expressed—which appears as the "manner-of-speaking," in

the unsaying—signify *only* negation? Does it signify only a negation that would be immediately taken, in its turn, for a position,
and still expressing an ontology, albeit negative in the sense in
which we speak of negative theology? In the latter case, negation is
not really the contrary of position; it is *a negative position*. And the
priority and primacy of the affirmative or positive judgment remains (in negative theology, we *posit* what God is *not*).

This putting in question of the ontological priority is a question
that is posed, philosophically, against philosophy. The question obliges us, at the same time that we seek another source of meaning,
not to repudiate philosophy. Here, there is at the same time a divorce and no divorce. This is what characterizes the situation of all
contemporary thought that at once seeks something other than
doxic position and yet, insofar as it speaks, still philosophizes. (This
would be like the realization of Aristotle's remark: not to philosophize is still to philosophize.)[9]

Philosophy traces all signification and all rationality to being, to
the epic or adventure of being carried out by beings inasmuch as
they assert themselves as such. (The term "epic of being" [*la geste
d'être*], which expresses the ess*a*nce of being, emphasizes the verbal
aspect of the word "to be.")[10] This epic of being coincides with the
assertion that resounds in the proposition as language. This being,
this act, or this event of being asserts itself—so firmly that it resounds as a proposition and shows itself in the proposition. Being
asserts itself, bears itself out, to the point of appearing and of making itself into presence in a consciousness. The fact that we speak
is the very emphasis of being. The fact that we think and assert is
the fact that being itself asserts itself.

This assertion is the position on firm ground, on the firmest of
grounds: *the earth*.[11] In this idea of being that posits itself, there is
a condition: the very firmness of the earth. The very assertion of
ess*a*nce supposes this repose, this sub-*stance*, beneath all movement
and all halting of movement. In the verb "to be," which grammar-
ians too lightly call "auxiliary," the reign of a fundamental repose
resonates, and this repose supposes the earth. It is the indication
of an activity that indicates no change—neither of quality nor of

site—but only being: nonrestlessness, repose, identity as the act of its repose. There lies an apparent contradiction in the formula "act of repose," which the Greeks did not hesitate to call pure act. Beneath the agitation of the pursuit of beings [*chasse aux êtres*], there reigns an imperturbable repose. Behind everything that we do, is this repose. That reign is at once a necessity enacted, that is, it is at once presupposed everywhere—and it is not a violence.

What is proposed here may therefore appear as a scandal, if it consists in tracing a dis-quietude.

Being and World

Friday, November 21, 1975

In our project of detaching thinking from onto-theo-logy, we have asked ourselves whether intelligibility is possible without reference to being, to the ess*a*nce of being. While recognizing the impossibility of any presentation of meaning outside of a Said, in which the Saying is absorbed and before which it often abdicates, one may ask oneself whether, in the comprehension or the presentation of meaning, there subsists a gap between the form of the Said and this meaning itself—that is, whether the call of the Unsaid is not inside the Said. In this way, a situation appears in which—even if the answer to the question we raised is positive—we are not freed of a critical confrontation [*explication*]¹ with Greek philosophy. It is for us, more precisely, to look for a notion of being—always understood as presence—and of positivity in the repose of the world that would thus determine ontological intelligibility.

In the Western tradition, meaningful thought is thetic. It thinks what is posited (to think is to posit), and it thinks the repose of what posits itself. This rest or repose, which is fundamental—fundamental because it is the support of all movement and all arresting of movement—is expressed by the verb "to be." Through this repose, the manifold thought or reflected, the manifold of thought [*le divers pensé, le divers de la pensée*], has its place, discovers itself again, recognizes itself there, is presence, is identified with this immobility—and thus forms a world (the world is place; it is the site). In the world, positivity has all its meaning. The identity of beings thus comes from a profound and fundamental experience, which is also an experience of the fundamental, the profound, and the foundation. That repose is an experience of being *qua* being— it is the ontological experience of the firmness of the earth. This identity is a truth unsurpassable for our traditional thinking (our Western, or Greek, thinking).

According to the *Timæus*,[2] the circle of the Same encompasses and comprehends that of the Other. We must not believe that this amounts to an outdated astronomy: even the Copernican geometry, and that which charts our interplanetary voyages, will preserve the identity of the *Timæus*'s cosmos. (The interplanetary voyage does not shake the identity of repose, but it suppresses the transcendence of Height, which for the Ancients was an essential thing, for Height marked a distance impossible *to walk*; we should think, in this regard, of Icarus's dream. The gaze directed upon the stars is immediately adoration, idolatry—and, as such, forbidden by monotheistic religions. Interplanetary voyages, with their thoroughly disappointing results, show these idols as common stones, on which one can *walk*—a sign that the divine assumes another meaning.)[3]

The idealism of modern thought, which, against this repose of being, seems to privilege the activity of a synthesizing thought, does not dismiss this stability, that is, this priority of the world— and, indirectly, this astronomic reference. Philosophic thought is thought in which all meaning is drawn from the world. The activity of the subject in modern philosophy is hyperbole or an emphasis of this stability of the world. That presence is to such a degree presence that it becomes presence to ... , or representation. The firmness of the repose grows firmer to the point of appearing; it is so firm that one affirms it. *Esse* itself is an *esse* that we understand, which shows itself to someone; the *esse* is itself ontological: being that posits itself to the point of appearing, to the point of bursting. The psyche is a superlative form of this ess*a*nce of being.[4] That firmness, that repose, come to disclose, in subjectivity, in the synthetic activity of transcendental apperception, the energy of presence that gives rise to them.

In Heidegger himself, the being of the world becomes the subject's activity. It is there that repose is act and that it is active. The essance of repose is repeated in the positivity of thematization and of synthesis. It is in the nature of repose to show itself, and in the nature of its activity to be synthetic.[5] Science itself, which must be considered as a reflection of being, comes from being; it comes from a light that is being's light. In Heidegger likewise, it is being that gives rise to man, the energy of being, its *energeia*. Positivity (the act of positing an unshakable foundation, or holding a content firmly: the mundanity of the world) preserves its value as a virtue even in those philosophies that mistrust positivism. The idea and the sign are restricted to a content; positive thought and language alone deserve consideration. (Recall, in this regard, the critiques addressed to Buber: your concepts are not positive.)

Negation, which claims to refuse being, is still—in its opposition to being—a position that reposes upon the earth, one that is based on it. This reference of negativity to the positive within the contradiction is Hegel's great discovery: negativity is still a positivity. Hegel will tell us that all negativity preserves, in its negativity, that by which it is a negation. In the *Phenomenology of Spirit*, the immediate is nameless singularity, which returns to the absolute repose of identity in Knowledge, across the diverse figures of mediation. It is because it rests upon nothing that singularity is not thought. To Hegel we owe the fact that every overflowing of the Same by the Other that does not return to the Same passes for an incomplete or a romantic thought. The two adjectives (romantic and incomplete) have a pejorative value. Such an overflowing is a moment of thought, where we could not remain, for it is a thought without foundation that does not rejoin the essance of being.[6]

We might wonder whether formal logic (which asserts no reality but remains in the forms of something in general, void of all content, as the *Etwas überhaupt*—Husserl noted that our logic is one that has formalized but not generalized), in its pretense to the purity of what is void, is possible in the true void if this formal logic (otherwise named, by Husserl, formal ontology: the study of being emptied of all content) does not already sketch out the contours of a material ontology. We might wonder as well whether the very idea of form does not require the stability of the Same, the repose of the world, and the astronomic order that it guarantees. For Husserl (who, in his first works, nonetheless wanted to establish a strict division between formal and material logic), to found formal logic we must show its birth from material ontology; we must return to the experience of things, and to sensation in particular. We have not understood formal logic philosophically until we have understood how it is born.[7]

In Husserl, within the encompassing and synthetic activity of transcendental consciousness, rationality amounts to the confirmation, by the given, of what is simply aimed at [visé], of what Husserl calls signitive intentionality. (I read a book. I may find therein letters inserted accidentally; I can read words without syntactic connections between them; in reading I can find a meaning, or a certain meaning, in the sequence of words; then, it can happen that a correctly constructed proposition is false; finally, a correctly constructed proposition, having a meaning that we understand, can be true: it is true when it is confirmed by reality. So the meaning we thought is confirmed; there is vision to confirm the intended.) The intention is itself an identification; the intentional order is, for Husserl, a series of confirmations that tell me: "This is the same object, it is the same, it is the same, it is the same. . . . " Rational thought is a thinking that rediscovers a stable and coherent reality. And Husserl's thought searches [fouille] every horizon in which the Other who would escape the Same might be hiding.

That which goes by, that which goes by temporally, or that which passes (i.e., the present, which is already past, which we must retain), is retained at first immediately; thereafter it is recalled thanks to memory; and finally it is rediscovered through history and reconstructed by history, or by prehistory.[8] The rational work of consciousness is, from Plato to Husserl, *reminiscence*, which is the ultimate force of the identity of being or, at least, the normative program of ontology. (It is in reminiscence that identity is produced, or reconstructed.) That is, reminiscence or, for the future, anticipation. The Husserlian theory of time is a theory of what is stable and firm, where all the operations of retention and protention in which the present is constituted are rational acts.

The same holds true for Heidegger, in whom we again find the same ideal of the Same. The same ideal in Heidegger—who nevertheless sought to destroy the identification of presence and being. Yet in Heidegger the Same is still the rational, the meaningful.

To Think God on the Basis of Ethics

Friday, December 5, 1975

Heidegger opened the path to a rationality of disquietude or of nonquiet. Being is in question in man; it is at stake. The question is not an interrogation held by man with curiosity but the manner by which being is in question, by which it is a bottomless abyss, the nonfoundation. For being is always to-be [*à-être*]; it is a task of being, that is, the possibility of (being) grasped or (being) missed [*(se) saisir ou de (se) manquer*]. With such thoughts, a rupture is produced with the rationality of repose, a rupture with the Greek tradition. If being is itself a task, if it is to-be or to-abandon (and this, in such a way that even when one abandons being, one is still inside being), then it is no longer the being of the Greeks, the Platonic "being." And the "being" of the pre-Socratics would be close to a biblical, and singularly Christian, conception. It is the *question* of being that is the comprehension of being.

All that is found in Heidegger; and yet, as far as the ultimate question is concerned (death), the question of being turned toward its end, the relationship is no longer a question but a *confronting* [*affrontement*]. "Death is the possibility of impossibility," as *Being and Time* will say. In this question, there is therefore a positivity. Death is no longer a question but rather something to be seized. There is, consequently, a taking charge of death, about which *Being and Time* moreover asserts that it is the most certain thing (*gewissen*).[1] In this respect again there is a rupture with a tradition, for in the Middle Ages, with the ideal of the *scientia divina*, it was the knowledge of God that gave the greatest certitude, at the same time that it was the most excellent of knowledge. (In Aristotle, there is but one theologian, God.[2] And theology is the manner by which God possesses himself. In the Middle Ages, grace opens to all men the theology that God alone possessed in Aristotle.)

～

Let us now come back to the questions of this course. How was God "retrieved" by the ontology whose characteristics we sketched out in the preceding lectures? How did he get introduced; "how did he enter" into an intelligibility of this type? And again: is it possible to think of God outside of onto-theo-logy? Is it possible to formulate a model of intelligibility that would permit such a thinking? Or more precisely, since this is what our question shall become: on the basis of an *ethics* that would no longer be the corollary of a simple vision of the world, could we not formulate a model of intelligibility such that we could think God outside of onto-theo-logy?

In the philosophical tradition, ethics was always conceived as a layer covering that of ontology, itself asserted to be primordial. It was thus from the outset referred to the Same, to that which is identical to itself. But does not ethics provide us a meaning without reference to the world, to being, to knowledge, to the Same and to the knowledge thereof? Does it not signify a *transcendence* that would not come down to the fulfillment of an aiming by a vision?[3] Indeed, the very fact of knowing [*connaître*] is to transcend oneself toward the other, to go from the Same to the Other. But, in Husserl—and this is the foundation of his phenomenology—transcendence is the aiming of thought, which a vision "in flesh and blood" must come to fulfill. In this sense, transcendence is *appropriation*, and, as such, it is or remains *immanence.*

But transcendence as such would be an aiming that would remain an aiming. In this sense, it would be not a doxic transcendence but para-doxical. There would be a paradoxical manner of passing from Husserlian transcendence, which remains immanence, to the transcendence toward the Other. The Other, who is invisible, and of whom one awaits no fulfillment, would be the uncontainable, the nonthematizable. An infinite transcendence, for the idea of fulfilling an aiming or intending by a vision is out of the question and out of proportion here. A dis-proportionate transcendence. That is to say that here something other than intentionality is at stake. And this transcendence could not be brought back to the models of negative theology.

Ethics is a relationship with another [*autrui*], with the neighbor (whose nearness could not be confounded with a neighborhood in the spatial sense of the term). "Neighbor" emphasizes firstly the *contingent* character of this relationship; for the other [*autrui*], the neighbor is the first come.[4] This relationship is a nearness that is a *responsibility* for the other [*autrui*]. A relationship that obsesses, one that is an obsession, for the other besieges me, to the point where he puts in question my for-me, my in-itself [*en-soi*]—to the point where he makes me a *hostage*.[5] And this uncondition of a hostage is the condition without which one could never say a simple "After you, Sir." (This means that in the present-day crisis of morality only *responsibility for the other* remains,[6] a responsibility without measure, which does not resemble a debt that one could always discharge, for, with the other, one is never paid up.) This responsibility goes to the point of fission, all the way to the e-nucleation of the "me" [*la dé-nucléation du moi*]. And therein lies the subjectivity of the "me."

To signify is to signify the one *for* the other [*l'autre*]. There is a priority in this *one*; it is the priority of immediate exposure to the Other [*Autrui*], an exposure in the first person, who is not even protected by the concept of the I [*Moi*]. For there does indeed exist a constituted I [*Moi*], protected by its concept in some fashion in legal society. But the unprotected *I* [*je*] is *outside the I* [*hors du Moi*], outside the concept.[7] The "I" [*"je"*] is already thought as I [*Moi*], and yet it remains unique in the impossibility of eluding the other man. It is impossible to elude the other man in his exigency, in his *face*, which is extreme immediate exposure, total nudity—as though the other were from the first, without protection, the wretched, and as such, from the first, entrusted to me.

The I [*le Je*], my I [*mon Moi*], eludes this exposure, to the point of seeking its condition beyond the uncondition, in the time composed of instants where every I [*je*] seems to make itself an individual, or become an individual within a genus. We could say this: *The I [Je] eludes, but it remains I [je].* This is I [*Moi*], as deposed within myself, as a putting in question to the point of overflowing the condition of being, but in which the time composed of instants is struck by the disquiet of the *all of a sudden*. Through suddenness, this trauma agitates rest, arresting time. In this sense we have an opening of the time of suddenness, which is the *beating of the Other in the Same*, and which, precisely, agitates rest. (Recall that in Hebrew, the *blow* [*coup*] and the [striking or beating][8] of the *clock* have the same etymology: the verb "to agitate."[9]

In this time of suddenness, there is a *patience*. This is a patience that is the *length of time*, and an awaiting of this patience whose intentionality as awaiting is repressed or expelled [*refoulée*]. This is because awaiting aims at something, whereas patience waits without waiting for; that is, it is an awaiting without anything being awaited, without the intention of awaiting. All that is intentionality is always proportionate to thought (there is an agreement between the noesis and the noema), and every intention is the intention of ... , or in other words, *willing* [*vouloir*]. It is not the same with patience, which has, as it were, swallowed its own intention.

Patience swallows its own intention; time is attested in being deferred [*se réfère en se déférant*]. Time is deferred, is transcended to the Infinite. And the awaiting without something awaited (time itself) is turned into responsibility for another. There we find a notion of transcendence *without aiming* and *without vision*, a "seeing" that does not know that it sees. A pure patience, a pure undergoing, an awakening that is awakening in regard to the neighbor, a suddenness that becomes the nearness of the neighbor.

The Same and the Other

Friday, December 12, 1975

From the other to the one, there is a relation, even if it is a relation without a link. Cannot the other, irreducible to a content, or in the form of infinity, concern my identity as "me" [*moi*], which would thus contain, paradoxically, more than it could equal? Concretely, this eventuality signifies not knowledge but the relation with another, whatever might be the nodes of this intrigue[1] or this relation. "To concern" is a general term that does not necessarily mean "contact." In fact, it is perhaps much stronger than contact, for it perhaps indicates a fission, a deposing.

Indeed, in ethics, in responsibility for another, it is a question of the nearness of the other who obsesses me without measure, to the point of placing in question my in-itself and my for-itself. All the way to me, who am not only the singularized concept of I [*Moi*]. When I say "I" [*je*], I am not the particular case of a concept of the I [*Moi*]: to say "me" ["*moi*"] is to escape this concept.[2] In that first person, I am a hostage, a subjectivity supporting all the others, yet unique, without the possibility of having someone replace me, or in an impossibility of hiding before responsibility, which is more *grave* than the impossibility of escaping from death. It is on this basis that we can think the significance of notions that the philosophy of the Same reduces to incomplete or romantic thoughts—but which are, in effect, non-con-ceiving concepts.[3]

A time made of fits and starts [*un temps fait d'à-coups*], in which the Same is woken up by the Other, as if the Other knocked on his walls from within. Indeed, there is a special passivity to this intrigue of the other-in-the-same:[4] a patience. Patience that is a length; it is the very duration of time. "Patience and length of time"[5]—this is patience or length of time, patience as length of time. This is a patience that is not an awaiting, for awaiting is intentional, an intentionality that is equal to what it awaits in its awaiting. As in all intentionality, there is in the awaiting an equality between what is thought and what comes to fill thought.

~

The awaiting is expelled in patience, too modest to understand [*entendre*], and too timorous, for therein lies a patience that fears. And what is feared is in this patience, like the fear of the religious where one does not fear punishment before all else.[6] In its perfect correlation between the noesis and the noema, intentionality opens onto a discouraging parallelism; in its patience, however, time is attested or deferred to infinity. And in this awaiting without anything being awaited, intentionality turns back, or inverts into responsibility for another. We must therefore think time and the other together.[7]

Time would signify the difference of the Same and the Other. This difference is a nonindifference of the Same to the Other and, in some way, of the Other *in* the Same. But this *in* can destroy the difference: if the Same can contain the Other, then the Same has triumphed over the Other. Here, with time, the Other is in the Same without being there; it is "there" in disquieting the Same. There lies an insurmountable difference, lacking a common ground, which nevertheless is non-in-difference. A difference insurmountable for intentionality, which only knows how to invest being with its thought.

In pure passivity, patience, responsibility under the shock [*coup*] of the neighbor, in the diachrony of time, there lies coiled up a thinking that is more than a thought one can think, more than a thought can think. It is there that this "phenomenon" lies, which would be the "phenomenon of transcendence."[8] This is the transcendence to the infinite, based on responsibility for the neighbor, in the nearness of another; there lies, literally, a meaning without vision or even aiming. An awaiting with nothing awaited, which translates or signifies not a void to be filled but a thinking more thoughtful than knowing [*connaître*]: the way by which the infinite can signify without losing its transcendent meaning.

In contemporary thought in Europe, this significance of a meaning *before knowledge* [*savoir*] is beginning to be formulated in philosophy. There are no doubt conceptual potentialities to be found in Heidegger. But this possibility began to be articulated before him: since Kierkegaard, since Feuerbach in a certain sense, in Buber, Rosenzweig, Gabriel Marcel, or Jean Wahl.[9] In the so-called "dialogical" thinking of these last four figures, it is not certain that the fundamental investigations proceed only from a moralizing concern.

The Cartesian ontology, in itself adopting the idea of the infinite, thinks the Same as a totality that integrates every Other—in such a way that the "in" signifies the triumph of the Same over the Other, the equality of the unequal, and the identity of identity and difference. It integrates every Other and thereby suppresses all that could exceed the totality; it suppresses all transcendence. But the idea of the infinite taught by Descartes (an idea *placed in us*) makes possible the thinking of this transcendence in a passive subject. It is Descartes who will say to Mersenne: "I have never treated of the infinite, except to submit to it."[10]

In question here is a singular "placing in us": the "placing" of the beyond-measure into the measured and the finite, by which the Same undergoes without ever being able to encircle [*investir*] the Other. There is something like heteronomy here, which one can also call *inspiration*—and we will go as far as speaking of *prophecy*, which is not some kind of genius [*génialité*] but the very spirituality of the spirit. That is the meaning of the verse from Amos, "The Lord God has spoken, who can but prophesy?"[11]—as if prophecy were simply the fact of having an ear.

In this way, and since Descartes, a relationship has become thinkable with the more-than [*avec le plus*], with the uncontainable, which is not, for all that, less than the investment by thought. A patience of the *question* is thus and finally rehabilitated. A patience of the question that is a relationship with that which is too great for a response. Philosophy is brought to see in this question a privation of answers, possession, or enjoyment—while it signifies the infinite.

It is not a matter of using this signification to seek to find therein a new "proof of the existence of God"—for that would be to come back to positivity itself. (Simone Weil said, in this regard, that God does not exist, that existence is not enough for him.) It is a matter of thinking the heteronomy of the Other in the Same, where the Other does not subjugate the Same but awakens it and sobers it up. The Other sobers the Same by way of a sobering that is a thought more thoughtful than the thought of the Same, in a waking up that disturbs the astronomic repose of the world. It is that thought of disquietude as a relation that, no doubt outside any theological concern, Maurice Blanchot expressed when he wrote, "We have the presentiment that the disaster is thought." In these words, we must understand the disaster as a dis-aster, that is, a not being in the world under the stars.[12]

The Subject-Object Correlation

Friday, December 19, 1975

It is a question here of thinking the significance of transcendence as a movement of the Same to the Other. Now the significance of signification rests not only in the resting of the Same in itself where it finds itself fulfilled but in the disquieting of the Same by the Other, which wakes up the Same. The idea of the infinite is found *in* thought, but the "*in*" here makes the identity burst open. The *in* indicates at once interiority and the impossibility of interiority.[1] This surpassing is duration, at once as the *in*-cidence of the Other in the Same and as the noncoincidence or the *diachrony* of time. This model of time signifies not a mediation between being and nothingness but a relationship with what thinking could not contain, that is, with the uncontainable (or the *infinite*). It must be thought outside of being and nothingness, in the form of the "overfull" [*"trop-plein"*], as a modality in which the more disquiets the less, which gives to desire, or to searching (which would designate an emptiness), a signification *better* than the being that is found, asserted, and confirmed. This more in the less is waking up, or waking is the meaning of this more in the less. This nonrepose can be concretized as responsibility for another, a responsibility without escape, and an irreplaceable uniqueness. This waking up is the intrigue of ethics or the nearness of the other man. It is not the outcome of the ontology founded upon the fixity of the stars, but, to use the term of Blanchot we cited in the previous lecture, *disaster.*

Is there not in this bursting of the Same under the shock [*coup*] of the Other all the violence of alienation? We would respond in the affirmative if the self-sufficiency of the identical had to be the ultimate meaning of what is thinkable and rational. But the Other intervenes as a trauma; that is the manner peculiar to it. Consequently, before signifying the ess*a*nce of being, does not subjectivity state its unthinkable wakefulness [*veille*], does it not "show" its unthinkable watching in the trauma of the waking? This is the waking that would then settle into being, grow sluggish there, fatten up, go *bourgeois*, and content itself with the unrelenting boredom of the Same; such is the waking that rests in its *state* of waking. Subjectivity would then have to be thought of as an awakening in the waking, as a waking up of this waking. It would be prophecy, not in the sense of brilliance or genius, but as the waking up of the one by the Other.[2]

But a question arises. How would the subject, as correlative to the object, come to be absorbed in the object, when subjectivity is not reducible to the intentional subject but, in the form of waking up, expresses the meaning that would be *better* than being, that would be the Good itself? How could there be such an absorption, when subjectivity bespeaks [*se dit*] an exceptional unconditionality: the nonstatus, the noncondition (or uncondition of the hostage), and the unconditioned as unconditional, as irrecusable, and as inevitable? We shall therefore confront today the problem of the subject-object correlation.[3]

～

We must recall the way in which being carries on on the side of the object, absorbing the subject in correlation with the object, and, in the truth of its epic [*sa geste*], in triumphing over both the primacy of the subjective and the subject-object correlation. That man is able to think being means that the appearing [*apparoir*] of being[4] belongs to its very train of being, or that phenomenality is essential, and that being cannot dispense with a consciousness to which its manifestation is made. But although ess*a*nce and manifestation go together, and although ess*a*nce (as the epic of being that appears) is the very truth of the true, ess*a*nce is in no way inscribed as some sort of property in the quiddity of what appears. The truth of the true, its being uncovered and the nudity of this being uncovered, is not a property, nor something that being would receive. If something came from consciousness, it would only be a delusion. This nudity must belong to the train or the game that being conducts as being. Objectivity protects in some sense the unfolding of being from what would come to trouble the procession of ess*a*nce. As a mode of being, objectivity signifies the indifference of what appears in regard to its own appearing.

The ess*a*nce of being in truth is a permanent presupposition of our philosophical tradition. Being's *esse*, by which beings are beings, is the *affair of thought* and abides from the first in the Same. This explains the indifference in regard to a thought that takes place outside of being—and, at the same time, a certain poverty of the being obligated to an other than itself, that is, to a subject called to gather up the manifestation, this receptivity being necessary to its train of being. It is in this sense that there is in being a *finitude*.[5]

However, outside of this function of reception or receptivity, any game that consciousness would play for itself, any instant in which it would play its own game outside of being, could only be a concealment, an obscuring of the ess*a*nce of being, a lie or an ideology. The status of this ideology is difficult to establish unequivocally: in the *Phædo*, it is death that puts an end to all ideology and allows being to appear gloriously.[6]

Ideology and the lie may be interpreted both as the pure effect of being's finitude and as the effect of a ruse. But we must push this analysis farther. The disclosure [*dévoilement*] of truth is not stated only in terms of optics. If the visibility of beings that show themselves is not inscribed in the form of an attribute of their visibility, then it is their *copresence*, their position in regard to one another, the relativity in which they become signs of each other, and the regrouping of significations—or the structure, the system—that are intelligibility and disclosure itself. The intelligibility or the systematic structure of the totality allow the totality to appear and would protect it against every alteration that would come from the gaze. But a *shadow* veils the terms taken outside of the relation in which they are implicated. The shadow covers the structures, taken by surprise outside the system that encloses them.

Structure is an intelligibility, a signification whose terms by themselves have no signification outside of the identity that language gives them. Yet, in relation, they receive a grace, a transparency and a lightness, while they grow heavy and hidden the moment they are separated from it. We may therefore differentiate between intelligibles separated in their thematization and the intelligibility itself of the system. We can also distinguish, in the movement that goes from this thematization to intelligibility, a hesitation, that is, good or bad odds for the structures to find an arrangement [*s'arrimer*]. We can reduce subjectivity to these good odds. Subjectivity is then entirely subordinated to the arrangement of structures; it is rational theoretical consciousness, which we will call spirit. Intelligibility signifies, as much as does manifestation, the arrangement into a system in which beings signify.

The present is contemporaneousness itself, and the manifestation of being is a permanent representation. The subject would thus be essentially a power of representation, in the active sense of the term. The subject unites time into a present by way of retention and protention: what seems to disappear is retained; time is retained by the subject. This subject acts in a time that is dispersed. And an isolated structure cannot be exhibited without growing obscure in its insignificance. Subjectivity thus intervenes to unite disparate elements; this spontaneity of the subject that calls for exhibition to assemble what is dispersed is the moment in which the intention ceases to be blind. It is therefore because the gathering of elements into a structure involves risks, delays, and hesitations; because it incurs good or bad fortune; it is because being is in this sense finite that there intervenes the spontaneity of the subject who gathers (who *sammelt*, to use Heidegger's term) the nonsimultaneous and that in this way vision occurs. The spontaneity of the subject gathers the manifold into an intelligible structure, and in this way light is produced.

Led to seek out this intelligible arrangement, the thinking subject interprets itself, despite all its spontaneity, as a detour that being must take to truly appear. It is thus that intelligibility is immanent in being. This possibility of absorbing the subject to which ess*a*nce entrusts itself is what is proper to ess*a*nce. Understood this way, subjectivity is subjection to being before which it effaces itself.

The Question of Subjectivity

Friday, January 9, 1976

Let us take up the question again: can we think of God outside of onto-theo-logy, outside of God's reference to being? To articulate this question, we are going to look for forms of thought different from intentionality, that is, forms of thought solicited by what overflows them. Thus the Kantian ideas are forms of thinking that overflow knowledge and point toward a subjectivity awakened by what it could not contain.[1]

We must come back, however, to the description of subjectivity's being absorbed in being or the object that it thinks, and finishing by understanding itself on the basis of being. We pass *from* the fact that being is thinkable *to* its manifestation, to the phenomenality essential to its train of being,[2] although the fact of being thinkable, of being a phenomenon, of showing itself, is inscribed in no attribute of the being that appears and comes in no way from the subject.

This indifference of being, surpassing its manifestation, allows us to speak of a finitude of being, which is different from the finitude of the subject. But we can speak of finitude in yet another sense, in thinking of the reference of being to a knowledge that is always less than being, a conceptual knowledge that negates the individual. There cannot be a concept of being except by way of death. There again, the subject exhausts itself in receptivity to being, in knowledge, and every game that consciousness might play for itself would be an ideological cover-up.

Yet manifestation also signifies the intelligibility of the terms of the structure that shows itself—where it is understood that these terms refer to other terms, that is, they constitute a system in which meaning is attached to the position of every term in the system (and it is thus that meaning is structure)—and this intelligibility appears paradoxical in that each term in itself is without meaning, and they receive their meaning from the way they are arranged with respect to one another. Within these groups a hesitation may occur, and it is then up to the subject to bring together the terms in search of each other. The subject would thus be this hesitation or this invention. But he will think that he has invented something, whereas he has only allowed the system to realize its own arrangement [arrimage]. Here again the subject is considered entirely in relation to the object, or to being.

The thinking subject, called to seek out this intelligible arrangement, interprets himself, despite its spontaneity, as a detour that the act of being [l'acte d'être] takes, one that the essance of being takes in order to appear in truth. Intelligibility or signification is [font] part of the reign of being. Everything is on the same side— on the side of being—and this possibility of absorbing the subject to which the reign of being or essance is entrusted is what is proper to essance. Subjectivity effaces itself before being; it is subordination to being. It lets being be—it is Seinlassen, as Heidegger would say[3]—inasmuch as it is the gathering of structures into significations uttered in a Said, which is the great presence of synopsia,[4] where being shines in all its brilliance. However subordinate it might be, the subject thus plays a role in the train of being; insofar as it participates in the event of being, the subject also manifests itself: there is a self-consciousness of consciousness. Subjectivity discloses itself in disclosing. Subjectivity shows itself to itself, and thus shows itself as an object to the human sciences (in Hegelian terms, we could say that the I, as mortal, conceptualizes itself). Yet, as other in relation to the being that shows itself, as different from monstration, subjectivity is nothing. Despite, or because of, its finitude, being will show itself, like the visible gods of the Greeks.[5] Despite its finitude, it has an encompassing and absorbing essence. The truth of the subject is in its veracity; subjectivity has no other meaning than its effacement before presence, or than its work of re-presentation.

But would not the subject have another meaning, which could arise if we insisted upon the *communication* to another person of the manifested ess*a*nce?[6] If we take the Saying as pure information, as the simple transmission of a content or of a Said (as in the Anglo-Saxon analytic philosophy, where language dispenses with exegesis and interpretation), then the question does not even come up. The manifestation *to another* and the interhuman understanding about being can be interpreted as playing their part in this manifestation and in the train of being: speaking would then be a condition of manifestation. The message would be the price that finitude costs being. Communication would be entirely reference to a monstration of being, or communicating would go back to no proper meaning that the subject would produce independently of the truth that he serves. A science would be capable of totalizing being at every level of its essence. Communication would be an event *of being*, where the putatively subjective representation of being would operate. Here, the Saying has grown silent in the Said, as if no one had spoken.

We can again envision a third possibility, where the Said would be prior to communication. As in Heidegger, where being has a meaning, that is, where it would manifest itself in a silent and nonhuman language: this is what the famous expression *Die Sprache spricht* ("Language, or speech, speaks") means.[7] In its reign of being, being is language[8]—and it is a silent language or the voice of silence, *Läute der Stille*. (In this way, without realizing it, Heidegger would have "Judaïzed" the Greeks!)[9] This voice of silence is that which is heard by the poet, who transposes it into human language. To make the evocation of being resonate in the poem is to make a Said resonate. The λέγειν, or the very meaning of the λόγος, would be gathering.[10] Signification, intelligibility, and spirit reside in manifestation and in the synopsia of presence; consequently, all dia-chrony is excluded. Meaning is thought as revelation, as the manifestation of being. The psychic life of the subject consists then in its gift for synchronization, or for re-presentation, thanks to which nothing is outside. Psychic life would thus be a consciousness excluding all trauma: being as precisely that which shows itself before striking, or which strikes only to show itself thereafter, and resolve into knowledge the violence of its shock.[11]

The circumstances in which one is responsible for the other, the ethical relationship that philosophy knows but that it treats as derivative, this relationship that we are accustomed to found in ontology, shall here be approached as irreducible, as structured as the one-*for*-the-other, and as signifying outside the finality and reasons of the system. This responsibility appears at first sight to be *paradoxical*: no present in me can encompass the other; no engagement made in a present is the place or the surface that would have this responsibility as its underside. Yet no slavery is included in the obligation of the Same for the Other. There is so little slavery that the uniqueness of the "me" [*moi*] is required by and in this responsibility: no one could replace me.

Kant and the Transcendental Ideal

Friday, January 16, 1976

We are attempting, here, to think about God without the help of ontology. That is, we are looking for a thinking that contrasts with the philosophical tradition in which God is understood as being [*l'être*] *par excellence*, as being that is in a superior sense being, and in which the idea of God draws its philosophical signification from its conformity with the rational rules of knowledge. Nevertheless, it is with Kant's *Critique of Pure Reason* that the "beginning of the end" of the onto-theo-logical conception of God is marked. In that work, there is a critique of all thinking that overflows the given; and the given remains the prototype of being for Kant. To think is to subsume an intuition under a concept, and the concept without intuition can only lead to an aberration [*égarement*]. "Without sensibility, no object would be given and without understanding none would be thought. Thoughts without content are empty, intuitions without concepts are blind,"[1] as the Introduction to the "Transcendental Logic" notes.

Much more important, however, is the fact that Kant acknowledges the existence of rational ideas that foist themselves upon thinking with necessity; he admits the existence of thoughts that speak of being and that are obligatory for reason, *but that do not rejoin being*. What Kant therefore discovers in the *Critique of Pure Reason*, and particularly in the "Transcendental Dialectic," is the fact that *thinking*, without falling into arbitrariness, and indeed in order to satisfy the needs of reason, *can fail to reach being*. This discovery of Kant's is the transcendental ideas, which "are concerned with the unconditional unity of all conditions in general," and aim at "the synthetic unity of the variety of empirical knowledge in general." These include the psychological ideas ("absolute unity of the thinking subject"), the cosmological ideas ("the absolute unity of the series of conditions of appearance"), and the theological idea ("the absolute unity of the condition of all objects of thought in general").[2]

Surpassing the given, these ideas to which no intuition corresponds can lead us to an illegitimate or dialectical use of reason, but it is just as possible to make good use of them:

> The ideas of pure reason can never be dialectical in themselves, only *their abuse* is necessarily a cause of their being a source of deceptive appearances to us, for they are given to us through the nature of our reason, and it is impossible that this supreme tribunal of all the rights and suppositions of our speculation itself contain original illusions and marvels. It is therefore probable that they will have a purpose both good and fitting to some end in the natural constitution of our reason.[3]

The proper use to which we can put these ideas is their *regulative* use, where they do not have the function of determining being—where they *must not* end up at being—but where they direct and orient the work of the understanding:

> If, then, it can be shown that the three transcendental ideas (the *psychological*, the *cosmological*, and the *theological*) although they do not directly relate to, or *determine*, any corresponding object corresponding to them, none the less, as rules of the empirical employment of reason, lead us to systematic unity, under the presupposition of such an *object in the idea*; and that they thus contribute to the extension of empirical knowledge, without ever being in a position to run counter to it, *we may conclude that it is a necessary maxim of reason to proceed according to ideas of this sort.*[4]

Despite everything, there is a return to onto-theo-logy in Kantian thought, in the way in which it determines the idea of God. On the basis of experience, God is posited as the totality of reality (*omnitudo realitatis*). Kant calls this set of all possible predicates of reality a *transcendental ideal*. It is required not because a cause is necessary but because of the individuality of the thing and its determination, which gives it the right to be. To determine a thing completely, to determine it in its individuality, "it is not only the predicates that we compare logically amongst themselves, but we also compare transcendentally the thing itself and the set of all possible predicates."[5] Each thing must be determined in relation to this *ideal*, which is the ideal relation of the causal series. The determinate thing is determinate insofar as it rejects all the rest and, at the same time, aspires to the whole. There is something of a tension in the individual, at once torn from the whole and aspiring to that whole. This whole or ideal is not given in an intuition but constitutes an idea necessary for reason. It is *in concreto* and *in individuo*. It is, as the totality of what is, the supreme form of concreteness and individuality. It is not a thing (on the contrary, all things suppose it), and yet it is "something" that is. Kant identifies it with God.[6] This is fully in line with Western thought, where the totality of being is thought of as a being, even if Kant here distinguishes his claim, asserting that one cannot prove the existence of this concrete supreme entity, of this individual: "We remain in complete ignorance about the existence of a so eminent superiority."[7] One cannot therefore demonstrate speculatively (by theoretical thought) the being of the transcendental ideal, but Kant keeps the idea that the ultimate meaning of a notion is in its being; he does not grant to the thinkable any other norm than that of being.

~

It will be a matter here not of enlarging the notion of being beyond things themselves but of proposing a radical questioning. Is not the human being *otherwise than being*? Is being what most interests man? Is being the meaning of what is meaningful? These questions are addressed not only to Kant but to all of the philosophy handed down to us. They are posed on the basis of the idea that that we must look for signification in the one-for-the-other; we must look for signification in nearness, where it is brought about as the Saying and not as the communication of a Said. The intelligibility of rationality would originally be not in the language of what is Said, in the communication of contents but in the Saying itself—in the word given to the neighbor—which is the intrigue of responsibility.

For Western philosophy, it is not the approach of the other person that poses a question, it is the communication of what is communicated. Signification is a mode of representation of being in the absence of being; being is absent, and yet there is a relation to being thanks to which signification is meaning: there is an allusion to being. Signification would thus be accomplished with the appearance of the given. What we are seeking here is a signification that is prior to, and independent of, every content and every communication of contents, and that can be fixed by the term *"Saying"* as a Saying to another, as the one-*for*-the-other. The *"for"* is what we must consider; it has a meaning different from what it would have at the thematizable level of ontology. In the thematizable it surmises a nonstatus and signifies a rupture with the rationality of the foundation.

Signification as Saying

Friday, January 23, 1976

In the expression "the one-for-the-other," the "*for-*" cannot be reduced to the reference of one thing said [*un dit*] to another thing said [*un autre dit*], or of one theme to another. To make that claim would be to remain with the idea of signification as a Said. But we are going to look for what signification might mean as Saying.[1]

The "for-" is the way in which man approaches his neighbor, the way in which a relationship with the other is set up that is no longer proportionate to the one. It is a relation of nearness where the responsibility of the one for the other is played out. In this relation there is a nonthematizable intelligibility; this relationship is meaningful [*sensée*] by itself and not by the effect of a theme or a thematization. That means—here, at least—that intelligibility and rationality do not belong by first right to being. In the relationship of the one for the other, a rapport is traced that cannot be thought on the grounds of the rationality of a foundation.[2]

~

In the one-for-the-other that is signification and responsibility, there is a certain subjectivity. It is that of a subject unique in its identity, indiscernible from without, and who is not defined by properties or by reference to predicates, but who has instead the identity of the *assigned*, of him who is responsible and cannot be replaced. It is to this subject that the neighbor is entrusted, and its identity is formed by way of the impossibility of fleeing in the wake of this responsibility. This is as impossible as fleeing before death in Heidegger, for whom death is always my death to die and no one can die in my place, any more than I can die in the place of another.[3]

Here, however, the impossible escape is not before *my* death, before my being and the end of my being. It is something other than this attitude before death; it is an exacerbation, a supervaluing [*surenchère*] of the uniqueness of the subject—this comes to pass not in an excess of presence but in the passive exceeding that is more passive than any passivity, the transcendence of the one who is *for* the other. This signifies neither intentionality nor a property of the "me" [*moi*] that would be responsibility for the other. It is, on the contrary, as responsibility and in responsibility that the "me" gains its uniqueness.

Even in the first person, the I [*Moi*] is a concept. Within the intrigue of responsibility, everything happens as though I escaped from the concept of the I [*Moi*] to become "me" [*moi*] in my uniqueness. This uniqueness is that of the hostage, for whom no one could substitute himself without transforming that responsibility into a role played on a stage. If that were so, then this unconditional responsibility could be *chosen* by the subject, who could keep his own personal reserve [*quant-à-soi*], and all the sanctuaries of its inner life would be preserved. Here, on the contrary, subjectivity, the psyche, is passively structured as for the other, as the one-*for*-the-other. My basic posture is the for-the-other. That is, it is my expiation for the other (for there is no compensation possible in responsibility). The subject is thus he who has lost his place. Without that loss, the I [*je*] always remains a point, and a firm point. Here, the last remaining point is dis-appointed.[4]

The one for the other is not the situation of an engaged subjectivity. Engagement always supposes a theoretical consciousness, despite the facticity and the already-there of *Dasein*.[5] In engagement, consciousness has the possibility of taking charge of all that is passive within the limits of what can be assumed. This is the nerve of Sartre's thinking on freedom, where one must assume or take charge even of what one has not chosen. For Sartre, one ends up by having chosen everything right up to one's birth. There, extreme vulnerability, being-seized or "susception" [*susception*]⁶ is taken up again by a project, within an intentional thinking that knows how to survey its horizon.⁷

In this vulnerability [*susception*] of the one for the other, there was no engagement, and there is no debt to acquit. From the outset, I am not exonerated. I am originally in default. The I [*je*]— or me [*moi*]—approached as responsibility, is stripped bare, exposed to being affected, more open than any opening, that is, not open upon the world that is always proportionate to consciousness but open to the other that it does not contain. In this responsibility, the "me" does not posit itself but loses its place; it is deported or finds itself deported. Substitution for the other is like the trace of exile or deportation. The "me" finds himself only in his skin, but skin is no longer a protection; it is a mode of being exposed without protection.⁸ It is this passivity that is expressed or suggested by the verbs "to be exiled" [*s'exiler*], "to be deported" [*se déporter*], or again "to surrender oneself" [*se livrer*].⁹ There, a tearing away [*arrachement*] and the excess of a tearing away is expressed, whose violence Simone Weil accurately measured when she wrote, "Father . . . tear this body and this soul from me . . . to make of these your things, and let nothing remain of me, eternally, but this tearing away itself."¹⁰

Ethical Subjectivity

Friday, January 30, 1976

Onto-theo-logy consists in thinking of God as a being [*étant*] and in thinking being [*être*] on the basis of this superior or supreme being. The Heideggerian critique concerns this way of misunderstanding being and consists in saying that we must ultimately think being without beings; we must not think of being, as all of metaphysics has done, *on the basis of beings* and only as the being *of beings*.[1] The inquiry carried out here also begins from a critique of onto-theo-logy, but it seeks to think God without making being or beings intervene in the relation with God. It seeks to think God as a beyond-being.[2]

Being as being binds together an intrigue from which all meaning is suspended. Being reigns; not only *is* it, but it *west*—just as the world not only is but also reigns in the Heideggerian proposition *Die Welt weltet* ["the world worlds"].[3]

The knowledge of being, in which being is manifested, itself belongs to the train of being, to its epic, to this drama or this intrigue. In Hegel, the manifestation of being to consciousness is a moment of the unfolding of that being, which Hegel calls Logic: "Logic, which becomes speculative, takes the place of the metaphysics that one treated as a science separate from it."[4]

Nevertheless, the history of thought shows a scission between knowledge [*connaissance*] and being. This is why there is in Hegel an advance of consciousness toward Spirit, which only at the end attains Knowledge [*Savoir*]. In Heidegger, the manifestation of being takes place by way of forgetting, concealment, and dissimulation, and this errancy (which *is* the manifestation of being) concerns not only the history of philosophy but history *tout court*. It is in this sense that we find a certain kinship between Heidegger's thinking of history and Marx's philosophy of history.[5]

The theoretical character of philosophy makes the *question* of being inevitable. Being is the correlate of knowledge. Knowledge is occasioned by being as its manifestation. Yet we might wonder whether the manifestation, in which all signification has the form of an ontological event, exhausts the significance of signification, whether everything is exhausted by this form, whether, in this event, *nothing* else comes to pass. If one could counter this line of interrogation positively, then one could perhaps deduce the theory itself from what surpasses this form. It is here that the interrogation about the signification that comes to pass in the one-for-the-other finds its place—a signification capable of providing other models of intelligibility.

The relationship with another is a relationship that is never finished with the other; it is a difference that is a nonindifference and that goes beyond all duty, one that is not resorbed into a debt that we might discharge. The intelligibility in play in this relationship is not a theoretical knowledge; it does not imply the thematization of something thematized. It alludes to a meaning that does not result from a disclosure that one might gather into synchrony. In the situation of the face to face, there is no third party that thematizes what occurs between the one and the other.

I am for the other in a relationship of deaconship: I am in service to the other. In other words, the relationship of responsibility with another signifies as Saying. The Saying, prior to any language that conveys information or content, prior to language as a Said, is exposure to that obligation for which no one can replace me, and which strips the subject right down to his passivity as a hostage. In the Saying, the way in which I appear is an appearing-before or a co-appearing: I am placed in the accusative case, in the place of the one accused—I lose all place. In this sense the I [*je*] does not posit itself but is impoverished to the point of substituting himself, of suffering and expiating for another, and even for the other's wrongs, to the point of expiation itself. This is in no sense an act of reflection upon oneself; it is a passivity that is not even opposed to activity, for it is beyond the passivity that would merely be the reverse side of the act.

Assigned, placed in the accusative, the "me" [*moi*] is not a particular case of the universal. It is not a particular case of the concept of the I [*Moi*]; it is the first person, that is, the first to give up its place. As soon as we speak of the subject, that subject is indeed, in a certain sense, universal. Yet in signification, I am unique, and my uniqueness consists in the impossibility of my slipping away. The Saying is the only way by which the "me" [*moi*] is stripped naked in its return into itself [*récurrence*], in substituting itself on the in-side of its own identity; in this way alone does it show its uniqueness. The subject thus cannot be assimilated to transcendental subjectivity in its openness to the world that it equals. The Saying is not held in consciousness or in the engagement, and it does not trace a connection with him to whom it is addressed. The Saying is, rather, a manner of being completely exposed, of exposing oneself without limit.

The subject as a hostage has no beginning; it lies on this side [*en deçà*],[6] or the in-side, of every present time. This is why memory does not manage to synchronize its subjectivity. The subject as hostage is a referral to a past that was never present, to an immemorial past, that of its preoriginal affection by another.[7] This subjectivity is implicated in the intrigue of nearness as the approach of the neighbor. A paradoxical approach since, with it, distance increases in relation to the approach, and the closer one gets, the farther away one finds oneself. Yet this paradox inscribes the glory of the Infinite [*l'Infini*] in the relationship habitually called "intersubjective." From this relationship, the Infinite rises up gloriously.

Transcendence, Idolatry,
and Secularization

Friday, February 6, 1976

We are attempting here to describe thoughts that cannot be reduced to containing what is thought by them, but which should allow us to think properly what the word "transcendence" means. It
is *ethics* that must make this investigation possible—concretely possible. Now ethics, when proposed as a modality of transcendence,
can be thought on the basis of the secularization of the sacred.[1]

Transcendence signifies a movement of traversing (*trans*) and a
movement of ascending (*scando*). In this sense, it signifies a double
effort of stepping across an interval by elevation or a change of level.
Before any metaphor, the word is therefore to be thought in its
sense of a change of site. In an age in which movement toward the
heights is limited by the line of the summits, the heavenly bodies—
stars fixed in their positions or traveling along closed trajectories—
are intangible. The sky calls for a gaze other than that of a vision
that is already an aiming and proceeds from need and to the pursuit of things. It calls for eyes purified of covetousness, a gaze other
than that of the hunter with all his ruse, awaiting the capture. Thus
the eyes turned toward the sky separate themselves in some fashion
from the body in which they are implanted. And in this separation
the complicity of the eye and the hand, which is older than the distinction between knowing and doing, is undone. Raising itself toward the sky, the gaze thus encounters the untouchable: the sacred.
(The untouchable is the name of an impossibility before being that

of a taboo.) The distance thus traversed by the gaze is transcendence. The gaze is not a climbing but a deference. In this way, it is wonder and worship. There is an astonishment before the extraordinary rupture that is height or elevation within a space closed to movement. Height thus takes on the dignity of the superior and becomes divine. From this spatial transcendence, crossed by vision, idolatry is born.

Unlike the agitation in which covetousness struggles (*epithemitikon*), and unlike those shifts toward the intended object wherein the eye anticipates the movement of the hand, the heavenly vault confirms the imperturbable repose of the *terra firma*. That repose reigns, and toward the authority of the sovereign rises the allegiance that is prior to any oath: religion.[2] The normative ennobles the commanding power of norms, the excellence of the hierarchy, and the order established forever—which excludes commerce and novelty, and which no stranger disturbs.

Aristotle interpreted "the wonder that things might be what they are"[3] as the recognition of ignorance by itself, and thus as the origin of philosophy, thereby making knowledge [*savoir*] proceed from the love of knowledge [*savoir*]. In so doing, he denies to knowledge any origin in the practical difficulties of life, in the difficulties of commerce between men who do not manage to communicate with one another. The origin of knowledge is not in need but in knowledge itself. Yet, in the wonder or astonishment it provokes, in the idolatry of its wonderment, is the reign of astronomical repose not an ignorance that would know itself as an anticipation of knowledge and as some beginning of rationalism? Is not this religion prior to any sermon older than every history and like the secret of the intelligibility of the Same? Would this not be a secret whose identity is still unknown, a synthesis of judgment to which this reign of the identical would already be necessary?

Is not the knowledge of the West, consequently, the secularization of idolatry? In the extraordinary rupture of transcendence that is idolatry, the repose of the earth under the vault of the sky prefigures the reign of the Same. Wonder is the admission of a knowledge that ignorance suspects, and that consists in identifying the identical. It is the birth of the reason that embraces the rational, a birth of the comprehension that gathers the manifold. We have here the birth of thought at the price of a narrowing, which gathers into a point the volume of the human body, which no longer projects a shadow. Everything here comes to pass as though the eyes no longer had their place in the cavity of their orbits, but became the unity of the concept, set down in the very space that this concept comprehends.

We will not ask whether another transcendence is announced in this end of idolatry, whether, that is, in this secularization, no social site is found. Contemplation passes from its hieratic sense to its obvious sense, which is that of knowledge and intuition; we pass from admiration to philosophy, from idolatry to astronomy, to rationality, and to atheism. In this astronomic fixity, the immanent epic and the reign or the kingdom of being is unfolded. A repose or positivity, a displaying within knowledge upon the flat surface of a theme, indifferent to any height and present to the foreground of the display. Being as presence recommencing, being as being as the act of rest, in the form of identification. Being as being coming to pass in its very identification, being its being [*étant son être*] by way of its intelligibility, and thus being in the form of ontology. The emphasis of its being as being *is* ontology. The transcendence of idolatry shows through in the knowledge to which it brings the serenity of theory. This idolatrous transcendence in a world at rest is a state of affairs that is not itself based upon the empirical. In the epic of being, this past is the positivity in which all rationality takes on meaning and foundations.

~

This secularization of the transcendence that is becoming the reign of being finds in wonder only its possibility. In order that knowledge effectively come out of wonder, in order that ignorance be recognized as such, in order that being occur as being, it was necessary that the light of the heavens also illumine the ruse and industry of men. The light whose brilliance the eyes admired is the same light that directs those eyes toward the given. And those eyes —which are bound to their innate covetousness, which aim at things and perceive, and which have the ruse of hunters—learn patience and become an industrious gaze. There is consequently an affinity [*convenance*] between the secularization of the idolatry that becomes ontology (i.e., the intelligibility of the cosmos, representation and presence measuring and equaling each other) and the good practical sense of men gnawed by hunger, inhabiting their houses, residing and building. Every practical relationship with the world is representation, and the world represented is economic. There is a universality of economic life that opens it to the life of being.[4] Greece is the site of this intersection, and despite the diversity of cultures, Messer Gaster, companion to Prometheus, is the world's first master of arts.[5] Nothing is therefore more comprehensible than European civilization with its technologies, its science, and its atheism. In this sense, European values are absolutely exportable.

No one is mad enough to fail to recognize technology's contradictions, but the balance of gains and losses that we habitually draw up rests upon no rigorous principle of accounting. The condemnation of technology has become a comfortable rhetoric. Yet technology as secularization is destructive of pagan gods. Through it, certain gods are now dead: those gods of astrology's conjunction of the planets, the gods of destiny [*fatum*], local gods, gods of place and countryside, all the gods inhabiting consciousness and reproducing, in anguish and terror, the gods of the skies. Technology teaches us that these gods are of the world, and therefore are things, and being things they are nothing much [*pas grand-chose*]. In this sense, secularizing technology figures in the progress of the human spirit. But it is not its end.[6]

Don Quixote:
Bewitchment and Hunger

Friday, February 13, 1976

To think God outside of onto-theo-logy, in other words, to think no longer on the basis of positivity—that is, from the point of view of the world—is the question this course is seeking to articulate. The world is always proportionate to our knowledge or to the thought to which it is always given. In this way, it can always be apprehended and comprehended [*pris et compris*] by thinking. Thought contains the world or is correlative with it—and let us emphasize that here "correlative" amounts to being prior-to[1]— and this thought, thinking in the form of apprehension and comprehension, disqualifies all thought that would be otherwise than proportionate to the world, all thought said to be "romantic" or "theological" in its inception.

Now, that disqualified thought, passing as a privation relative to what is awaited and hoped for, can signify—in the manner of a *question* or in that of a *hope*—a *disproportion* between what contains and what is contained. (In truth, only God is a metaphor sufficient to state the *dis-proportion*.) This would be the thought of an outside that is not the outside of the world; a thought of a *nonspatial outside*, or of an outside whose extraneousness is more external than externality, which is itself not external enough.[2] And since everything is accounted for in the world, and nothing resists, our question is how and to what degree one can be affected [*affection*] by what is not equal to the world, how one can be affected by what can be neither apprehended nor comprehended.

As destructive to the *gods of the world,* the *god-things* [*dieux-choses*], technology has a disenchanting effect. Yet technology does not shelter us from all mystification. There remains the obsession with ideology, by which men delude each other and are deluded. Even sober knowledge, or that which means to be, that knowledge contributed by the human sciences, is not exempt from ideology. But above all, technology does not shelter us from the amphibology that lies within all appearing, that is, from the possible appearance coiled at the bottom of all the appearing of being. From there comes modern man's persistent fear of allowing himself to be bewitched.

This is what Cervantes expresses so admirably. The first part of his *Don Quixote* has, as its principal theme, bewitchment; the bewitchment of the appearance that sleeps in all appearing. Here, we should think especially of chapters 46 and following in this first part. There the "Knight with the Sad Face" lets himself be bewitched, loses his understanding, and assures everyone that the world and he himself are the victims of bewitchment: "Sancho my son," he said, "now you will realize the truth of what I have many a time told you, that everything in this castle is done by means of enchantment."[3] In this affair, Sancho alone maintains a certain lucidity and appears stronger than his master ("Yet his gullibility never reached so high a pitch that he could persuade himself that it was not the plain and simple truth, without any deception whatever about it, that he had been blanketed by beings of flesh and blood and not by visionary and imaginary phantoms, as his master believed and proclaimed."[4] Or again, "Of all those present, only Sancho was simultaneously in his senses and in his own veritable shape, and he, though not far from sharing his master's infirmity, did not fail to perceive who all these disguised shapes were."[5] These "disguised shapes" that Sancho doubts are a priest, a barber, and a whole group that had decided to take Don Quixote back to his country, where he could be cured, and that, in order to do this, had fancied entering into his madness and passing themselves off as spirits, which the Knight, in his diminished understanding, had little difficulty believing.[6] Thus the adventure of Don Quixote is the passion of the bewitchment of the world as the passion of the enchantment of the Knight himself. We must understand that the whole of Descartes's Evil Genius is present in these pages![7] But we must again emphasize the modernity of this passage, in which enchantment functions in the form of an imprisonment within a labyrinth of uncertainties, lacking any connection between faces, which are only masks or appearances.[8]

In the midst of his confinement within a labyrinthine enchantment, Don Quixote experiences, in his way, the *cogito* on which a certitude is founded: "I know and feel that I am enchanted, and that is enough to ease my conscience, for it would weigh heavily on it if I thought I was not enchanted and that in a faint-hearted and cowardly way I allowed myself to lie in this cage, defrauding multitudes of the aid I might offer those in need and distress, who at this very moment may be in sore want of my aid and protection."[9]

Perhaps there is no deafness that allows one to hide from the voice of the afflicted and the needy, a voice that in this sense would be disenchantment itself. Such a voice would lead to an other secularization, whose agent would be the humility of hunger. A secularization of the world effected by the deprivation of hunger, which would signify a transcendence beginning not as a first cause but in man's corporeality. A transcendence, consequently, that is not ontological, or that at least has neither its origin nor its measure in ontology. Ontology reduces the visible gods, but it would place us in Don Quixote's position and in his labyrinthine confinement if it were not for this other transcendence.

How to get outside the circle that encloses Don Quixote in the certainty of his enchantment? How shall we find a nonspatial exteriority? Only in a movement that goes toward the other man, and that is from the outset responsibility. At a very humble level, in the humility of hunger, we can see taking shape a non-ontological transcendence that begins in human corporeality. In this sense, the empirical world of man's animal nature must be conceived as a *bursting* of the epic of being, a bursting in which a break, a fissure, or a way out is opened, in the direction of the beyond where a God that is other than the visible gods would abide.

Have we plumbed the depths of the hunger where, in a first moment, the Same of the "me" [*moi*] seeks only to confirm its identity?[10] We are never sufficiently amazed by the voiceless language of hunger ("the famished stomach has no ears," says the proverb); hunger is deaf to every reassuring ideology, deaf to every equilibrium that would be that of the totality alone. Hunger is, in itself, need or *privation par excellence*, which constitutes the materiality or the great frankness of matter.[11] (Logic conceives privation on the basis of hunger, and not the reverse.) A privation that keeps one from taking consolation from this privation in the image of a spiritually ordered world; a hunger that no music appeases, and that secularizes all that romantic eternity. This is a privation whose acuteness consists in despairing of this privation itself. Here is a despair struggling against the same rocky surface, or a head striking against a wall, as though it appealed to some hidden side of nothing [*à quelque envers du rien*]; an appeal without reason or oration; neither aiming nor thematization, this despair is like a preintentional turning, like a departure out of the world. A preorational prayer, a demand as mendicancy, a question without a given, a question that is not even the posing of this very question, a question *beyond*—and this, not in the direction of some world behind the world. A question lying within the oscillation between the terms of an alternative, an oscillation between death and God. This is a question irreducible to the mode of a problem, in which some assertoric *doxa* would be lodged; it is a para-doxical question that struggles in the depths of its own interestedness, for of all the appetites in which our *conatus essendi* asserts itself, hunger is the most interested. A question in which it is a matter not of taking but of begging infinitely, and in this sense, a question in the direction of a nonspatial outside, of a beyond of ontology.

Secularization through hunger is a question about God and to God [*à Dieu*], and thus at once more and less than an experience. It is a pre-orational question, a question without response, like an enigmatic or ambiguous echo of a question. We should say explicitly, however, that it is a question not of making transcendence subjective in this analysis but of being astonished by subjectivity.

Note that here the world's first master of arts, Messer Gaster, does not reign single-handedly. Here, in the *conatus essendi*, hunger is astonishingly sensitive to the hunger of the other man. The hunger of another awakens men from their well-fed slumber and their self-sufficiency. We cannot wonder enough over the transference, which goes from the memory of my own hunger to suffering and compassion for the hunger of the other man. This is a transference in which an untransferable responsibility is expressed, and with it the impossible evasion that individuates even him who, sated, does not understand the hungry one and does not cease escaping his own responsibility without also escaping himself. Individuation is this impossibility of hiding even as we slip away; it is the condemnation to be oneself. The uniqueness of the "me" [*moi*] is the trace of this impossible evasion and of this untransferable responsibility, which —in the midst of his own enchantment—Don Quixote still remembers. In the possibility of being *I* [*je*], life holds its breath and its vitality as a force on the move. The one listening to the other, the one stepping out of itself toward the other, is the response to the question and the pre-orational prayer of hunger.

It is thus that, in hunger, at a very humble level, transcendence progressively appears.

Subjectivity as An-Archy

Friday, February 20, 1976

The non-onto-theo-logical approach to the idea of God goes by way of the analysis of the interhuman relationships that do not enter into the framework of intentionality, which, always having a content, would always think in proportion to itself. Thoughts overflowing their limit, like desire, searching, questioning, hope—these are thoughts that think more than they can think, more than thought can contain. The same goes for ethical responsibility for other human beings. Ethics contrasts with intentionality, as it also does with freedom: to be responsible is to be responsible before any decision. Therein lies a breaking-away, a defeat, a defection from the unity of transcendental apperception, just as there is here a defeat of the originary intentionality in every act. It is as though there were here something before the beginning: an *an-archy*.[1] And that means placing the subject as spontaneity into question: I am not my origin unto myself; I do not have my origin in myself. (We should think of the popular Russian tale in which a knight has his heart outside his body.)[2]

This responsibility for another is structured as the one-for-the-other, to the point of the one being a *hostage* of the other, a hostage in his very identity of being called irreplaceable, before any return to self. For the other in the form of one-self, to the point of *substitution* for another.[3] And we must understand that here is a relationship unintelligible within being, which also means that this substitution is an exception to essence. Compassion is, to be sure, a natural sentiment on the part of him who was hungry once, toward the other and for the hunger of the other. But with substitution, there is a break in the mechanical solidarity that has currency in the world or in being. "Who is Hecuba to me?" we must ask with Shakespeare.[4]

~

We are seeking to describe subjectivity as irreducible to the transcendental consciousness that thematizes being. Nearness appears as a relationship with another who cannot be resolved into images or presented as a theme. The other person [*Autrui*] is not beyond-measure but incommensurable; that is, he does not hold within a theme and cannot appear to a consciousness. He is a face, and there is a sort of invisibility to the face that becomes obsession, an invisibility that stems not from the insignificance of what is approached but from a way of signifying that is wholly other than manifestation, monstration, and consequently, vision.

Indeed, contrary to what the philosophy handed down to us teaches, signification does not necessarily imply thematization. The one-for-the-other is not an absence of intuition but the *surplus* of responsibility that is expressed in the *for* of the relationship. In this *for* there beckons [*fait signe*] the significance of a signification that goes beyond the given, and that is to be distinguished from the famous *Sinngebung* or "meaning bestowal."

Signification is this one-for-the-other or this responsibility for another. It is not the inoffensive knowledge relation in which everything is equalized, but an assignation of me [*moi*] by another, a responsibility in regard to men we do not even know. An assignation of extreme urgency, prior to every engagement and every beginning: *anachronism.* This is what we are calling *obsession,* a relationship prior to the act, a relationship that is neither act nor position, and that, as such, contrasts with the Fichtean thesis, which holds that all that is in consciousness is posited there by consciousness.[5]

Here, it is entirely different: not all that is in consciousness is posited by consciousness. Obsession crosses consciousness against the current and is inscribed in it as *foreign* [*étrangère*], to signify a heteronomy, a disequilibrium, a delirium overtaking the origin,[6] rising earlier than the origin, prior to the ἀρχή, at the beginning, being produced before any glimmer of consciousness. An anarchy stops the ontological game in which being loses itself and finds itself anew. In nearness, the "me" [*moi*] is anarchically late for its present and incapable of covering up that lateness. This anarchy is *persecution*; it is the hold of the other upon the me, who leaves me without speech.

This persecution designates not the content of a mad consciousness but rather the form according to which the me [*moi*] is affected. It expresses the inversion of consciousness, a passivity that will not be defined in terms of intentionality—where undergoing is always a *taking charge*. However, in the consciousness that is all freedom, or is so at least in the last instance (because, in it, everything is taken charge of intentionally), how is a *suffering* [*pâtir*] possible as a *passion* [*passion*]?[7] How can madness and obsession enter into consciousness? This is the paradox of the intrigue of consciousness.

The heteronomy of which we are speaking—a nonobjective, nonspatial (if it were spatial it could still be recovered by consciousness), obsessional, nonthematizable, anarchic exteriority—points to the intrigue or the meta-ontological drama of anarchy undoing the *logos*, the speaking, the reason that becomes an apologetic recovery of self-possession in which the me [*moi*] comes to the defense of the self [*soi*]. A matter of extreme passion, in at least three aspects. First, through this passion, consciousness is struck or wounded *despite itself*; in it, consciousness is seized without any *a priori* (the other is always encountered in an unexpected fashion— he is the "first come"). With this passion, consciousness is touched by the *nondesirable* (the other is *undesirable*, and this includes here the meaning that some give to this term when speaking of foreigners! Second, there is no libido in the relationship with the other; it is the anti-erotic relationship *par excellence*).[8] Third, there is here a putting into question prior to all questioning.

In contrast with the vision of Heidegger, Fink, or Jeanne Delhomme, each of whom calls for a freedom without responsibility,[9] a freedom of *pure play*, we are here distinguishing a responsibility that rests upon no engagement and whose inscription in being is made *without our choice*. (The other is the oppressed—as for "me," I can only be obligated!) Before the pair freedom/nonfreedom, a vocation is set up that goes beyond the limited and egoistic designs of the one who is only for-himself and who washes his hands of the misfortune and offenses that did not begin in his present time.[10] There is a relationship with a past that was never present. This is the investment, or *investiture*, of a being who is not for-itself but *for all being*. Therein lies his dis-inter-estedness (*Sein* is not only *esse*, it is likewise "-estedness" ["*essement*"]—or *conatus essendi!*).

It is the exceptional uniqueness in the passion of the self that is this incessant event of subjection to all and that expresses subjectivity. Subjectivity of a being who detaches himself, who empties himself of his being, who turns himself inside out—who "is" *otherwise than being*. Otherwise than being is dis-inter-ested; it is to carry the misery of the other all the way to the responsibility that the other can have for me. Here there is no "human commerce," nor a simple swapping of responsibilities! To be oneself—as the condition or uncondition of a hostage—is always to have one more responsibility. The responsibility of the hostage should be understood in the strongest sense. *For it remains incomprehensible to me that another concerns me*: "Who is Hecuba to me?" Stated otherwise, "Am I my brother's keeper?"[11] Such questions are incomprehensible within being.

In the prehistory of the I [*Moi*],[12] the "me" [*moi*] is, from top to bottom, a hostage—in a way more ancient than is the *ego*. For the self, in its being, it is not a question of being. There lies the religiosity of the me, preoriginally tied to another. And it is only this hostage's uncondition that makes pardon, pity, or compassion possible. Let us recall Paul Celan by way of closing: *Ich bin du, wenn ich ich bin.*[13]

Freedom and Responsibility

Friday, February 27, 1976

Suffering the weight of the other man, the "me" [*moi*] is called to *uniqueness* by responsibility. The superindividuation of the me consists in being in one's skin without sharing the *conatus essendi* of all the other beings that are in themselves. I am *in respect* [*à l'égard*] to all that is, because I am *through respect* [*par égard*] for all that is. The me who *expiates for* all of being is not a being capable of expiating, or paying for all the others. Its in-itself is an originary expiation, prior to the initiative of the will.[1] As though the uniqueness of the me [*moi*] were the gravity of the hold of the other upon me.

We can call *goodness* what gets tied together in this intrigue: under the demand that I abandon all having, all for-myself, I substitute myself for the other. Goodness is the sole attribute that does not introduce multiplicity into the one. If goodness were distinguished from the one, it would no longer be goodness. To be responsible in goodness is to be responsible on the inside or the outside of freedom. Ethics slips into me before freedom. Before the bipolarity of Good and Evil, the I as "me" has thrown its lot in with the Good in the passivity of bearing. The "me" has thrown its lot in with the Good before having chosen it. This means that the distinction between free and nonfree would not be the ultimate distinction between the human and the nonhuman, nor that between sense and nonsense.

It is as though there were in the "me" a past, always irreducible

176

to presence, on this side of every past;[2] an absolute and unrepresentable past. The present is the site of initiative and of choice. But has not the Good *elected* the subject before any choice? Has it not elected the subject with an election that is the responsibility of the "me," who cannot hide from it and takes from this election its uniqueness?[3] This priority of responsibility relative to freedom signifies the goodness of the Good [*la bonté du Bien*]: the Good must elect me before I may choose it. The Good must elect me first.

There is, therefore, at the bottom of me a preoriginary vulnerability or being-seized [*susception*],[4] a passivity prior to all receptivity, a past that was never present. This passivity transcends the limits of my time and is a priority prior to any representable priority. As if the "me" as responsible for another had an immemorial past; as if the Good were before being, and before presence.

This is the strong sense of what we are calling *diachrony*.[5] It is an irreducible difference that does not enter into the unity of a theme; an untraversable difference between the Good and me; a *difference without simultaneity of unmatched terms*. Yet this is an irreducible difference that is still a non-in-difference: a relationship with the Good that has invested me in *assigning me* to responsibility for another. This assignation to desire for the undesirable, assignation to a desire that is nonerotic or without sensuous appetite [*concupiscence*]—the same appetite that, diabolically, never stops seducing us with the appearance of the Good presenting itself as the equal of the Good, but in this very appearance, admits its subordination to the Good. In this way, concupiscence suggests that Good and Evil *are not on the same level.*

In this relation of the Good to me, which is an assignation of me to another person, something comes to pass that survives the death of God.[6] For we can understand the "death of God" as a "moment" in which *one can reduce every value giving rise to an impulse to an impulse giving rise to a value.*[7] On the other hand, if we do not accept this equivalence or this reciprocity, if the Good declines the "me"[8] by inclining it toward the neighbor, then the difference of diachrony is maintained in the form of nonindifference to the Good, which elects me before I welcome it.

In responsibility for another, the fact that the "me" [*moi*] is already a self [*soi*], obsessed by the neighbor, signifies this anachronistic election. The "me" does not begin in the self-affection of a sovereign I, susceptible in a second moment to feeling compassion for the other; instead, it begins through the trauma without beginning, prior to every self-affection, of the upsurge of another. Here, *the one is affected by the other*. There is an inspiration of the one by the other that cannot be thought in terms of causality.[9]

We have described the notion of a *finite freedom* starting from the situation of a responsibility that is not utopian.[10] There exists a co-possibility of freedom and the other, which allows us to give meaning to this notion of finite freedom without striking a blow against freedom in its finitude. Yet how can freedom be, while also being limited? How can a free or Fichtean I [*Moi*] undergo the suffering that comes to it from the non-I? Would this be to the degree that freedom wills, in a given situation that limits its power? That is not enough. In "finite freedom" a region of freedom breaks loose, which finitude or limitation does not affect in willing, even if finitude affects it in its power. Finite freedom is not an infinite freedom, acting in a finite field and for that reason, limited. Yet it is the freedom of a "me" [*moi*], whose unlimited responsibility (not measured by freedom and irreducible to nonfreedom) demands subjectivity as that which nothing and no one could replace, and strips this subjectivity bare like a passivity, like a self in an accusative form without a nominative. "Finite freedom" is neither first nor initial, for the willing that it animates wills on the ground of a passivity more passive than any passivity, on the ground of a passivity that cannot be taken charge of. This freedom is finite because it is a relationship with another; it remains freedom, because this other is another person [*cet autre est autrui*].

Finite freedom consists in doing what is our vocation, that is, in doing what no one other than myself can do. Limited in this way by the other, it remains freedom. It comes from a heteronomy that is inspiration—an inspiration that would be the very *pneuma* of psychic life. The subject's *for-the-other*, which is this finite freedom, could not be interpreted as a guilt complex, or as natural goodwill (like a "divine instinct"), nor again as a tendency to sacrifice. This finite freedom, which, ontologically, has no sense to it, is the *rupture of being's unrendable essance.*[11] As such, responsibility frees the subject from boredom; it frees him from the gloomy tautology and the monotony of essence, or delivers him from the attachment in which the "me" smothers under itself.[12]

In effect, responsibility signifies an inequality to self in sensibility's suffering [*subir*] beyond its capacity to suffer. This sensibility is a vulnerability that comes about in the form of the other in me—that is, as inspiration itself. The "me" is an ipseity without any match; it is without a return to self. Here, the hard and closed core of consciousness—in which the equality and equilibrium between trauma and act is always reestablished—is fissured. The other awakening the same is the other *in* the same without alienating him, without slavery. Therein lies the excellence of goodness.

This way is possible because, since time immemorial (that is to say, an-archically), the *by-the-other* [*par-l'autre*] has also been the *for-the-other* [*pour-l'autre*]. In suffering *through* or *by* the fault of the other there glimmers the suffering *for* the fault of the other. It is to suffer *for* the others in suffering *by* the others. The recurrence of the subject is therefore not the freedom of a game but an exigency coming from the other over and above the active dimension of my powers, so as to become a departure without limits in which the self spends itself without counting (and in this sense, freely so). If *essance* fills every interval of nothingness that would interrupt it in a rigorous accounting where nothing is lost or created, then finite freedom contests this accounting by way of a gratuity. For gratuity must be understood not only as the absolute distraction of a game without trace or memory, but also and firstly, as *responsibility* for another, or expiation.

The Ethical Relationship as a Departure from Ontology

Friday, March 5, 1976

The witness or account whose notion we are seeking to give here does not accompany a perception. It does not consist in presenting what one has seen or heard; more specifically, it contrasts with the denatured and unctuous concept of the witness of a "religious experience," comparable in its structure to the experience that one may have of the world. The witness, not subordinated to perception, constitutes a proper and irreducible mode of access.

We are looking to formulate here notions that have meaning only in the relationship with another. And we are seeking a mode of access to a non-ontological notion of God, on the basis of a certain dis-inter-estedness. We are looking for a way to get outside of ontology starting from the relationship with the other in his difference, which makes objectivity impossible (since objectivity always implies containing a content), and which is a responsibility for the other in which the Saying itself is like a supplement of exposure without the slightest protection. This Saying itself is a way of surrendering oneself [*se livrer*].[1] And this way of surrendering oneself is not the result of a foregoing engagement, or a measured responsibility, but is expressed in the word "hostage." Hostage means *substitution*. But substitution does not come to pass as though "I put myself in the place of someone," such that I sympathize with him; substitution signifies a suffering for another in the form of *expiation*, which alone can permit any compassion.

The notion of *subjectivity as hostage*, studied in its formal schema, is a reversal of the notion of a subject that is characterized by position, and that one may call I [*Moi*].[2] The I [*Moi*] posits itself in, or facing, the world, and this position is presence of the I to itself. The subject as I is what abides with itself and possesses itself; it is the master of itself as of the universe. This subject is, consequently, a *beginning*, as if it were before all things. It guarantees the universe, as if it were the beginning of the universe. Even if it comes late, it is as though it were before everything else: by way of history, it can know what was before it. But, as beginning, it is also fulfillment: the end of history is the full possession of self by self, a full presence to self.

In the relationship with the Other [*Autrui*],[3] which the self has not yet interpreted, this presence to self is, from the start, defeated by the other. The subject—the famous subject resting upon itself —is unseated by the other [*autrui*], by a wordless exigency or accusation, and one to which I cannot respond with words, but for which I cannot deny my responsibility. The position of the subject is already his deposition. To be me (and not I [*Moi*]) is not perseverance in one's being, but the substitution of the hostage expiating to the limit for the persecution it suffered. It is necessary to go all the way to that point. For it is only then that we witness [*assistons*] a dereification of the subject, and the desubstantialization of the condition, or uncondition, which qualifies the subjection of the subject.

We must therefore emphasize here the fact that *freedom is not first*. The self is responsible before freedom, whatever the paths that lead to the social superstructure. The for-oneself, in the accusative, is responsible prior to freedom through an untransferable responsibility that makes it unique. Freedom can here be thought as the possibility of doing what no one can do in my place; freedom is thus the uniqueness of that responsibility.

The dissymmetry of the relationship keeps me solitary and unmatched [*dépareillé*] in regard to the other. In the social superstructure, in justice, the "me," as deposed, shall again find the law and, by way of the law, autonomy and equality. But the me is firstly substitution. To articulate this proposition is not to state the universality of a principle or to fix a concept; it is to think the me inasmuch as it has rejected every generalization. The subject is not an opaque being equipped with the structure of egoity, as though it had an essential eidetic structure, for this would permit us to think of it as a concept whose realization would be the singular being. *Through substitution, it is not the singularity of the me that is asserted, it is its uniqueness.*[4] What is proper to this situation of the me-as-hostage is to flee the concept that immediately gives it a framework and places it.

The grandeur of modern antihumanism—which is true beyond its own rationale—consists in making a clear space for the hostage-subjectivity by sweeping away the notion of the person. Antihumanism is right insofar as humanism is not human enough. In fact, only the humanism of the *other man* is human.[5]

It is difficult, to be sure, to abandon the notion of the free ego [*moi libre*]. Even if one grants us that the world weighs with all its suffering and all its weight upon the self [*moi*], it will be countered that only a free self [*moi*] could be sensitive to the weight that presses down upon it, and capable of opting for solidarity with others. Let us accept this for a moment: if Cain *is* not his brother's keeper, then it would be necessary to *commit oneself* as one's brother's keeper. We should then recognize, at least, that freedom has no lapse of time in which to *assume* that urgent weight. In the impossibility of hiding from the call of the neighbor, in the impossibility of taking distance, the assumption of the offense and the suffering of the other does not encompass passivity. This passion is not an assumption. The uncondition of the hostage will thus be, at least, a fundamental mode of freedom, and not some accident of an I [*Moi*], of itself haughty and proud.

~

In any given society,[6] my responsibility for all may, and even must, manifest itself in limiting itself. This excess of the responsibility of the hostage carries the limit in its excess. The me can be brought, in the name of its unlimited responsibility, to be concerned with itself. Through the fact that the other [*l'autre*] is also a third party [*tiers*], in relation to an other who is also his neighbor (in society, one is never two but at least three), through the fact that I find myself before the neighbor *and* the third party, I must compare; I must weigh and evaluate [*pèse et soupèse*]. I must think. It is therefore necessary that I become aware [*prenne conscience*]. Knowledge appears here. I must be just. This birth of consciousness,[7] of knowledge, and of justice is likewise the birth of philosophy as the wisdom of love. The initial unlimited responsibility that justifies that concern for justice[8] can be forgotten. In this forgetting, consciousness is born as a pure possession of self by self, yet this egoism, or egotism, is neither primordial nor ultimate. A memory lies at the bottom of this forgetting. A passivity, which is not only the possibility of the death of the being-there (the possibility of its impossibility), but an impossibility prior to that ultimate possibility of the "me" [*moi*]: the impossibility of hiding, an absolute susceptibility, a gravity without frivolity that is, in reality, meaning within the dullness of being, which is constituted within that forgetting.

The institutions and the State itself can be found on the basis of the third party's intervening in the relationship of nearness. Can we deduce institutions from the definition of man as "a wolf for man," rather than the hostage of the other man? What difference is there between institutions arising from a limitation of violence and those arising from a limitation of responsibility?[9] There is, at least, this one: in the second case, one can revolt against institutions in the very name of that which gave birth to them.

In this initial passivity, in this accusative preceding every nominative, the self [*soi*] abrogates the imperialism of the Same and introduces *meaning* into being. In being as such, there cannot be meaning. Mortality renders meaningless the care that the me [*moi*] takes of its destiny. To posit oneself as "me" [*moi*] persevering in its being, when death awaits, resembles an evasion within a world without exit. Nothing is more comical than the care that a being takes of its being when destruction is certain; it is as absurd as questioning the stars in view of taking action, when the verdict admits of no appeal. Yet the comical is also tragic, and it belongs to man to be a character at once tragic and comical.

On the other hand, the approach in the nearness without limits confers a meaning upon death. In this approach, the absolute singularity of the responsible one encompasses the generality of death. Life is not measured by being; death cannot introduce the absurd into it. To pleasure, death brings a denial. Yet we can have attachments through which death takes on meaning, though we say this without thereby being so hypocritical as to pretend to take away death's sting. Simply, the other affects us despite ourselves, and this passivity is the subjectivity of the subject.

Just as Kantianism finds a meaning to the human without measuring it against ontology, and outside of the question "How is it with?" which is the ontological question itself,[10] here, we seek a meaning outside the problem of immortality and death. The fact that immortality and theology do not belong to what determines the categorical imperative signifies the novelty of the Copernican revolution. Meaning is not determined through the to-be or the not-to-be. It is being, on the contrary, that is determined on the basis of meaning.

The Extra-Ordinary Subjectivity
of Responsibility

Friday, March 12, 1976

Subjectivity is the everyday extra-ordinary dimension of my responsibility for other men, for what is not in my power (for the
other is not like the objects in the world under my power). Consequently, there is in this responsibility a failure or undoing [*défaite*]:
something that comes undone in transcendental subjectivity's actuality as acting, in its being in act. Something comes to pass whereby
the spontaneity of the subject finds itself broken.[1]

What guides our research, which is seeking out ways to elaborate nonpositive concepts, are human relationships, ethical relationships—improperly called ethical if ethics, as *ethos*, means habit
and second nature.[2] Outside of their dense material aspect, which
only sociology retains, human relationships are structured according to another model than that of being. They signify the otherwise than being.

What we call "God" can take on meaning[3] only on the basis of
these other relationships. It is only with them as a basis that God
can be "manifest." Yet let us emphasize that to think God on the
basis of ethics is in no sense a self-righteous thinking. On the contrary, it is a matter of accentuating human relationships as the extra-
ordinary in which a nonspatial outside signifies, and in no wise
thinking about God as cause of the world, a God who, as such,
would still be of the world. Yet we can recognize that this attempt
to think otherwise than according to being is thinkable; all of struc-

turalist thought, on the contrary, is a struggle against the idea that for thinking there could be models other than being.

~

Passivity has no sense other than in the one-for-the-other, pushed to its end (to the point of the one hostage of the other), in which man finds himself in his identity as unique and irreplaceable: for the other, without a return toward oneself. In his *basic posture* [*son port de soi*], the subject is expiation, and what one might be tempted to take for my being is expiation. Therein lies, within ess*a*nce, an exception to ess*a*nce.

To fix this relationship or this deference, we have had recourse to the word "substitution." This substitution is not transubstantiation. It is not a question of entering into another substance and establishing oneself in it. Substitution remains a relationship with another, and as such it stays in discontinuity, in diachrony, without coincidence. Substitution is not a result and does not signify a lived state. It is like a process on the reverse side of the ess*a*nce that posits itself. Substitution, in which responsibility does not cease, thus remains otherwise than being.

It is not out of the question that the extra-ordinary that is responsibility could float above the waters of ontology. It is not necessary to seek status for it at all costs. Responsibility does not signify a synthesis; rather it signifies in the one-*for*-the-other, that is, in the one separated from the other by the interval or the meanwhile of difference, which the non-in-difference does not efface. Responsibility is not an *Erlebnis* (Experience), which always has an ontological status.[4] But neither can it be reduced to a revelation, and it has no cognitive character. Responsibility is not a knowledge.

Phenomenology has begun to find a meaning in what is not cognitive. A sentiment, an act, or a decision also have a meaning. Husserlian phenomenology expressed this in stating that these psychological states are not only states but intentions: every sentiment is already a sentiment of something sensed. Intentionality thus signified an outside-oneself, but one that always preserved a cognitive character and opened onto an experience-of-something, an information-about-*x*. One was always committed with the intended, and in this commission, one learned something. The lesson of the *Ideas* [*Ideen*] is that everything can always be transformable into knowledge; every axiological thesis is always transformable into a doxic thesis. At the bottom of all psychological life, there is always this theoretical vision. And the *Logical Investigations* [*Logische Untersuchungen*] took up Brentano's thesis afresh, according to which "every intentional experience either is itself a (simple) representation, or it has a representation for its basis."[5]

~

The search we are here carrying out is for a relationship that might be *meaningful* without being founded in a theoretical aiming such as Husserl described. The ethical relationship is not a disclosure of something given but the exposure of the "me" [*moi*] to another, prior to any decision (every decision is a decision about something to be decided, about a conclusion). Here, a sort of violence is undergone: a trauma at the heart of my-self [*moi-même*], a claiming of this Same by the Other, a backwards movement of intentionality. The extreme tension of the command pressed upon me by another; a command prior to any opening on my part; a traumatic hold of the Other upon the Same. This is a hold that I discover in the extreme urgency that calls for my help, to the point where I always come too late, for there is no time to wait for me.

We can call this way of laying claim to me, of stirring within me, *animation* (which is not a metaphor; I am animated by the other), or again, *inspiration*. And it is in the ethical situation that the latter word receives its proper sense; it is when one uses it in speaking of a poet that it is metaphorical. In our sense, it is an *alteration without alienation*. The psyche is that animation and inspiration of the Same by the Other; it is translated into a fission of the core of the subject's interiority by way of its assignation to respond, which leaves no refuge and authorizes no escape. It is like a *despite myself* that is more me [*moi*] than myself: it is an election. Every me is elected or chosen: no one else can do what it must do. This is the meaning of "and I more than all the others" in Dostoyevski.[6]

If this alteration is the psyche, then the psyche is a seed of madness—or every psyche is a psychosis, and it is as such that it qualifies not the I [*Moi*] but "me" under assignation.[7] Under assignation, the pronoun "I" [*je*] is in the accusative: it signifies *here I
am*.[8] It is as if, declined prior to any declension, prior to any position within a nominative, the "me" were awakened as one possessed by the other. And this is why the Bible can say, "I am sick
with love."[9] "Here I am" [*me voici*] is the saying of that inspiration
that could not be confused with the gift of fine words or with that
of the song (the inspiration of the poet is not the first of inspira-
tions). The *here I am* signifies a being bound to giving with hands
full, a being bound to corporeity; the body is the very condition of
giving, with all that giving costs. Therein lies the sense of money,
so that Léon Bloy could even say that he called his friend him who
gave him money.[10]

For Descartes, the union of the soul and the body presupposed
a miraculous intervention, for it was sought according to the rationality of representation; it was a question of thinking the gathering
and the simultaneity of two distinct substances. But, approached
on the basis of responsibility for the other man, the psyche of the
subject is the one-for-the-other, the one having to give to the other,
and thus the one having hands for giving. Human subjectivity is of
flesh and blood. More passive in its extra-dition to the other than
the passivity of the effect in a causal chain. It is here a question of
being torn out of oneself in a giving that implies a body, because to
give to the ultimate degree is to give bread taken from one's own
mouth. Subjectivity is here all the gravity of the body extirpated
from its own *conatus*.

How can the Saying, which is a modality of responsibility, come
to modulate responsibility? Why does my responsibility for the
other become a Saying instead of limiting itself to the giving? What
more is there in the Saying that is not found in the giving? Why
do we speak of the other? What does language signify in the relationship with another? Is it because *dialogue* is the privileged
mode of the relationship with another? No![11] Here, the Saying is
understood not as dialogue but as a bearing witness of the infinite

to the one to whom I open myself infinitely. In the relationship with another, this dimension of witnessing signifies, and it does not rest upon a foregoing cognition or familiarity. (To limit the witnessing by a foregoing cognition would make us fall back into ontology.)

The Sincerity of the Saying

Friday, March 19, 1976

Let us take up the question again. To give is to give the bread taken from one's mouth; giving has from the outset a corporeal meaning. But why do we not limit ourselves to this giving, and why does a Saying come to modulate responsibility? Why is this Saying necessary? This Saying is formulated as *here I am* (*me voici*), which formulates the accusative case of the subject that presumes no nominative case. There is therefore a passivity in this Saying, whereas the Saying seems to be an act, and a denial of the passivity of the subject. Yet this Saying must also be the Saying of a Said. Is there not, then, surreptitiously reintroduced into responsibility, a reference to a truth that would be prior to responsibility? Do we not hereby reestablish a priority of representation? In other words, *what does language as Saying signify?*[1] What is being presented here could pass for a "philosophy of dialogue." In fact, we contest that dialogue is the first form of language. Before that, language is witnessing, in the sense specified in the preceding lectures.

Despite its prohibiting us from closing up in ourselves, exposure can be turned back into position in pain itself, or in complacency when it swells with substance and pride (with pride consisting in the fact of finding repose in the self). In the turning of persecution back into substance, there is something like an unabsorbable residue of activity in subjective passivity, something like a residue of the activity of the I [*moi*] who has the possibility of being a presented personage, and of representing himself in the form of the saint. Thereby, obligation in regard to another seems to have a limit, a stopping point, and can be discharged.

By contrast, the impossibility of being discharged in regard to the other, the approach of the other, becomes a stricter and stricter obligation the greater the distance one covers. It is like something that would become increasingly distanced or that would distance itself more and more as one approached, like a distance that is more and more untraversable. The Infinite [*l'Infini*] is what makes for the increase of obligation. It is a *glory*, or the fact that the more the distance is covered, the more there remains to cover.

If the approach is of this sort, then in order that passivity not revert into activity, and in order that subjectivity might signify without reserve (that is, by way of a deficit), a passivity of passivity is necessary; under the glory of the Infinite, an ash is necessary in which activity could not be reborn. This passivity of passivity, this dedication to the other, is a *sincerity*, and this sincerity is *Saying*.

The Saying is therefore not a communication of something Said. When Talleyrand claimed that language exists to dissimulate thought, he was pointing to language as a Said. When the Saying has meaning only through the Said, the Saying is covered over and absorbed by the Said.

To the Saying without a Said an opening is necessary that does not cease to open, and that declares itself as such. The Saying is that declaration. (We must give the lie to everything that is constructed as an internal world, as interiority.) It is necessary that the Saying be a Saying of the Saying itself, a Saying that goes without thematization, but that exposes itself ever more. This is a Saying turning back on itself as though it were a matter of exposing the exposure, rather than standing there as in an act of exposing.[2] To Say is thus to exhaust oneself in exposing oneself, to make a sign of that of which one makes a sign,[3] without resting in its form of a sign. The Saying would thus be a passivity of the obsessional extradition, where this extradition surrenders to the other, rather than being established in a position or in a substance.

There is, then, an *iteration of the Saying*, which is pre-reflective iteration and which designates the Saying as a Saying the Saying [*Dire le Dire*].[4] That is the utterance of the *here I am*, which identifies with nothing if not the voice that utters and surrenders. Here is where we ought to search for the origin of language.

To make signs to the extreme point of making oneself a sign is not a language of stammering; it is the extreme tension of language, the for-the-other of nearness that surrounds me from everywhere, down to my very identity. This is the tension of language, whose potential the *logos*—whether of monologue or of dialogue—has already slackened by dispersing it into the possibility of being. The sign that is made to another is already a sign of our giving [*donation*] of signs, without affecting any attitude or behavior. It is, in other words, the impossibility of keeping silent—which is the whole scandal of sincerity. In this sincerity there is witnessing, and a witnessing that does not presuppose an experience.

Sincerity is not an attribute of Saying; the Saying accomplishes the sincerity that must be joined with giving. It is inseparable from giving, for it is sincerity that opens our reserves. (Sincerity is not a hyperbolic sort of giving; no extrapolation could be the source of infinity; on the contrary, extrapolation and projection suppose the dimension of infinity to which they supposedly gave rise.) The hand that gives exhausts its reserves without being able to dissimulate anything.

Sincerity annuls the absorption of the Saying in the Said wherein, beneath the cover of words, information is exchanged, wishes are uttered, and responsibility recedes. In the Said there is presence, and being. No Said equals the sincerity of the Saying; no Said is adequate to the truthfulness that is before the true;[5] no Said is a beyond presence and representation. Sincerity would thus be a Saying without a Said, a "speaking to say nothing in particular,"[6] a giving of the donation of signs. It is like the transparency of the avowal, the recognition of a debt, an indictment of oneself.

To what does the donation of a sign refer (a donation that is perhaps present in salutations)? To what does the sincerity in which one exposes oneself to the other without holding back refer, and to what again does the approach of the other refer, that responsibility that cannot be reduced to anything ontic or ontological? To what does this sincerity bear witness? What is accomplished in this accusative? Does the meaning of this sincerity not refer to the glory of the infinite, which is fulfilled in nearness itself?

This glory could not appear. The regime of appearing [*l'apparoir*] and presence would make of this a theme, and it would be necessary that glory then have its beginning in a present of representation, whereas this infinity comes from a past more distant than that which, within reach of memory, is aligned with the present. The "debt" was never contracted. It comes from a past that was never represented, and that is refractory to representation and has never left behind it the mark of a beginning. This glory could not become a phenomenon without immediately entering into conjunction with the subject, without closing itself up in the immanence of being and in its finitude. We will dare to say that this glory is without principle: there is in this infinity an *anarchical* element.[7] To represent glory to oneself would make the theme, in which it was supposedly closed up, burst open. But glory signifies on this side, or the in side [*en deçà*][8] of every *logos* that is thematization, and it signifies the extradition of the subject.

The subject is sensitive to the pro-vocation that was never presented but that struck it with a trauma; sensible to the immemorial, to the unrepresentable, to a "deep yore."[9] Glory is only the other side to the passivity ordained to the first come. Therein lies a heteronomy, in this relationship with another where I am, myself, torn from my beginning in me, from my equality with myself. This heteronomy is an alteration that is not alienation, not slavery, nor a loss of uniqueness, since precisely no one may replace me, since I am chosen.

To seek a relationship with the Infinite in the midst of nearness is the manner by which witnessing bears witness, by leaving to the Infinite its infinitude. To bear witness to the Infinite without bringing it back to being is a relationship in which the Infinite is not acquired by way of presuppositions or in some simple extension. One can speak of a non-ontological God only by bringing nearness and God together. To think God without this thought taking its model from a relationship of immanence is a thinking that is contradictory from the outset. There is no model of transcendence outside of ethics. The sole manner by which an otherwise than being could signify is in the relationship with the neighbor—which the human sciences reduce to being. The search for a non-onto-theo-logical God does not come out of a thinking that is adequate to its object [*d'une pensée adéquate*]. This search must understand that it starts from a model without a world, and that the relationship with the other is a *contra-diction* [*contre-sens*].

Glory of the Infinite
and Witnessing

Friday, April 9, 1976

Inspiration—which is the psyche—is not *presence* of the Other within the Same. Presence applies to consciousness [*connaissance*] and to intentionality, which are always consciousness in proportion to its own powers, a correlation and equality between what is thought and thinking itself. Here, we are speaking of a bursting of the Same, whom the Other disturbs or tears out of his repose. Responsibility cannot be stated in terms of presence. Responsibility for the other in me is an exigency that increases as one responds to it; it is an impossibility of acquitting the debt and thus an impossibility of adequation: an *excess* [*excédence*] over the present. This excess is glory. It is with glory that the Infinite is produced as an event. The excess over the present is the life of the Infinite. This inherence of the Other in the Same, without the presence of the Other to the Same, is temporality by way of the irreducible non-coincidence of the terms of the relation.[1]

The way in which the Infinite is glorified (its glorification) is not representation. It is produced, in inspiration, in the form of my responsibility for the neighbor or ethics. This is an ethics that does not presuppose some sort of ontological layer as its substance. The "me" [*moi*] implied in this intrigue is a fissured subject, one without a core who does not have to-be, but rather has to-substitute-itself. There is no refuge for this subject in the secrecy that would protect him from obsession by the neighbor, or in the short-circuiting of his interiority. This glory is glorified by the subject's stepping out of the dark corners of his reserve [*quant-à-soi*], which resembles the thickets of Paradise where Adam hid upon hearing the voice of the Eternal.[2] The glory of the Infinite is anarchy in the subject driven out of hiding, with no possible escape. It is expressed in the sincerity making a sign for the other before whom I am responsible. This manner of being driven from hiding—this *here I am*—is a Saying whose Said consists in saying "Here I am!"—this is a witnessing of that glory.

A witnessing that is true by a truth irreducible to the truth of disclosure[3] and that recounts nothing that shows itself. This witnessing occurs not in the form of dialogue but in dissymmetry, in the fundamental inequality of that originary relationship. It is a difference that is increasingly great and that is at the same time a non-in-difference: the double negation that defines difference. In this bearing witness, there is no recovery of self by self; there is neither shelter nor screen.

The sign dedicated to the other is a sign of the signification of signs. In this way the sign loses its material and its plasticity—the moment the other becomes material, he loses his face. The impossibility of hiding is an extra-ordinary situation that escapes the concept in which I take refuge unceasingly. Contrary to what Kierkegaard thought, the "ethical stage" is not universal;[4] rather, it is the stage in which the "me" [*moi*] forgets its concept and no longer knows the limits of its obligation. One would prefer, on the contrary, to take refuge in one's concept in which the limits of obligation are found.

Here, however, it is a question of an exposure without shelter, as under a leaden sun without protective shade, where there vanishes every residue of mystery or of a notion at the back of our minds by which escape might still be possible. An exposure without reserve, or the "cheek turned toward the blow that smites it,"[5] where it is the *first* cheek that is turned, in a gesture that designates the one who is just. Contrary to Gyges, who sees without being seen, here I am seen without seeing.

Bearing witness does not thematize that of which it is the witness, and as such it can be a witnessing only of the Infinite. All other acts of witnessing are secondary or derived, and draw their truth from an experience. Here, bearing witness is the exception to the rule of being: in it the Infinite is revealed without appearing, without *showing* itself as Infinite. The Infinite does not appear to the one who bears witness to it; it is the witnessing that belongs to the glory of the Infinite. It is by the voice of the witness that the glory of the Infinite is witnessed (and it is in this sense alone that "God needs men"). No present is *capable* of the Infinite. In Descartes, the idea of the Infinite that lodges itself—a difficult tenant —in a thought that cannot contain it expresses that disproportion between glory and the present.

The passivity expressed here is more passive than any passivity that still *assumes* the act that bursts out [*éclate*] in Saying or that witnesses. Exteriority becomes interiority in resounding [*éclatant*] in the sincerity of witnessing: prophetism is the ground of the psyche. Interiority is not a secret place somewhere in me; it is this reversal of the external event, incapable of entering into a theme. The Infinite takes exception to ess*a*nce, and yet it concerns me and encircles me and commands me by my own voice. The infinitely exterior becomes infinitely interior, in the guise of my voice bearing witness to the fission of the interior secret, to the fission of the very giving of the sign.

As his epigraph to the *Satin Slipper*, Claudel wrote this Portuguese proverb: "God writes straight with crooked lines."[6]

Witnessing and Ethics

Friday, April 23, 1976

Bearing witness is not expressed in or by dialogue but in the formula *here I am*.[1] As a dedication of oneself, this witnessing is an
opening of self that expresses the surplus of exigency that expands
as the exigency of responsibility is filled.

It is by way of this witnessing that glory is glorified [*la gloire se
glorifie*]. It is the way in which the Infinite surpasses the finite,
and the way in which the Infinite *comes to pass* [*se* passe].[2] The Saying without a Said of witnessing thus signifies the *intrigue* of the
Infinite, which is an intrigue and not experience, an intrigue that
is not experience. The word "intrigue" denotes that to which one
belongs without having the privileged position of the contemplating subject.[3] The intrigue attaches us to that which detaches itself [*rattache à ce qui se détache*]; it attaches us to the ab-solute,
but without relativizing it. This way of detaching itself within the
relationship itself is what characterizes Illeity.[4] That the Infinite
comes to pass in the Saying is what allows us to understand [*entendre*] the Saying as irreducible to an act or to an attitude of mind,
to a mood or to one thought among others, or again to a moment
of ess*a*nce.[5]

Language does not double or repeat thought. The Saying is, in
itself, bearing witness, whatever its later destiny by which it will
enter into the Said in the form of a verbal system. From the Saying,
such as it is grasped in the *here I am*, we can remove every Said.

The Saying is not the stammering infancy of what will become the Said, in which information will circulate. The Saying without a Said is a sign given to another, by which the subject comes out of his subjective clandestinity.

Bearing witness does not come to be added on, like an expression, or some information, or a symptom; and it does not refer to an experience—who knows which—of the Infinite. At no moment has the Infinite been thematized. There is no experience of the Infinite that is not thematizable. But there can be a relationship with God, in which the neighbor is an indispensable moment. We understand this much from the Bible: to know God is to do justice to the neighbor:

> "Did not your father eat and drink and do justice
>   and righteousness?
> Then it was well with him.
> He judged the cause of the poor and needy;
> then it was well.
> Is not this to know me?
> says the Lord."[6]

And the New Testament expresses the same thing:

> When the Son of man comes in his glory, and all the angels with him, then he will sit on his throne of glory. Before him will be gathered all the nations, and he will separate them one from another as a shepherd separates the sheep from the goats, and he will place the sheep at his right hand, but the goats at the left. Then the King will say to those at his right hand, "Come, O blessed of my Father, inherit the kingdom prepared for you from the foundation of the world; for I was hungry and you gave me food, I was thirsty and you gave me drink, I was a stranger and you welcomed me, I was naked and you clothed me, I was sick and you visited me, I was in prison and you came to me." Then the righteous will answer him, "Lord, when did we see thee hungry and feed thee, or thirsty and give thee drink? And when did we see thee a stranger and welcome thee, or naked and clothe thee? And when did we see thee sick or in prison and visit thee?" And the King will answer them, "Truly I say to you, as you did it to one of the least of these my brethren, you did it to me."[7]

The sign given to another is sincerity, veracity according to which glory is glorified. The Infinite has glory only through the approach of the other, through my substitution for the other, or through my expiation for another. The subject is, in its very psyche, *inspired* by the Infinite; the subject contains more than it can contain. Therefore, there is no *correlation*, as in Hermann Cohen, between man and God.[8]

That the way in which the Infinite comes to pass might have an ethical meaning does not imply a project of constructing the transcendental foundation of ethical experience. There is no ethical experience; there is an intrigue. Ethics is the field sketched out by the paradox of an Infinite in relation, without correlation, to the finite. A relation such that there is no encompassing but rather an *overflowing* of the finite by the Infinite, which defines the ethical intrigue.

Ethics signifies the bursting of the unity, originally synthetic, of experience, and therefore a beyond of that very experience. Ethics requires a subject bearing everything, subjected to everything, obedient with an obedience that precedes all understanding and all listening to the command. Therein lies a reversal of heteronomy into autonomy,[9] and this is the way in which the Infinite comes to pass. It is inspiration: to have received from who knows where, that of which I am the author.

Prophetism could be the name of this reversal in which the perception of the order coincides with the fact that he who obeys it also signifies it. Prophetism would thus be the very psyche of the soul, the Other *within* the Same, where the *within* signifies the *waking up* of the Same by the Other. And this, without the Infinite being present! It is a thought [*arrière-pensée*] too far back—or too high up—to push itself into the front ranks, or into the rank of a theme. In the *here I am*, that is, in the first phrase in which God is attested, "God" is not uttered. Here, one could not even say "I believe in God." To bear witness to God is not to utter that word, as though glory could be posited as a theme or a thesis, or as the ess*a*nce of being.[10]

The order that commands me [*l'ordre qui m'ordonne*] leaves me no possibility of putting the wrong side right, or of going back to exteriority as though I were confronting a theme, or, as in dialogue, of again finding a being in the Thou [*Tu*]. The nonphenomenality of the other who affects me beyond representation, unbeknownst to me and like a thief, is the Illeity of the third person. I hear an order in my own voice and not from someplace where the gaze could come to look for its authority as it would before an idol. One here recalls the errant cause in Plato.[11]

The obedience that precedes listening to the other is the anachronism of inspiration, more paradoxical than any prediction. It is the singular obedience to the order to surrender *prior to* hearing an order. This allegiance before any oath is the Other in the Same; that is, it is *time*, the *coming to pass* [*se passer*] of the Infinite.[12]

From Consciousness to Prophetism

Friday, April 30, 1976

Bearing witness can and must be understood as a manifestation that does not refer to disclosure, a manifestation that is not presence or the representation of presence. It is a manifestation that is, in this sense, anarchical and, as such, a "manifestation" of the In-finite. Ethics is the field wherein the para-dox (i.e., what is not a *doxa*, not a position) of the infinite in relation to the finite progressively appears. For every experience is comprehension, and if bearing witness is understood as a relationship of the infinite with the finite, then we may speak here of a *bursting of experience in witnessing.*

At stake in this investigation is the attempt to descend from *con-sciousness* and *knowledge* (which, in the form of con-*sciousness* [con-*science*], is the structure of consciousness), and from the Same that is confirmed in knowledge (since knowledge rediscovers the Same in the various and the multiple). It is a matter of descending from this level where, for us and at first sight, the psyche of the subject unfolds (as the depths of consciousness) toward *prophetism*, toward inspiration, toward a spirituality in which the Same does not confirm itself, does not set itself up, but wherein the Other *agitates* the Same.[1]

In prophetism or in inspiration, the Other is not *within* the Same according to the structure of comprehension, but the Other agitates the Same to the point of the fission of its core. There is here a non-coincidence (one that is, in this respect, contrary to the instant as a coincidence with oneself and as the stability of the identical), and this noncoincidence is fission and overflowing.

This agitation of the Same by the Other is what *scans* [*scande*] the diachrony of time itself in its impossibility of closing on any final syllable.[2] This scanning is an *ascent* [*montée*] of time toward the infinite, the distance of infinity, a turning toward its height, which is time in its *dia-chrony*. As such, far from signifying the corruptibility of being, time would signify the ascension toward God, *dis-inter-estedness* [*dés-inter-essement*], the passage to being's beyond, the stepping out of "ested-ness."

The infinity that signifies in bearing witness is not before its witness, and we cannot speak of it as we would of a name. It is attested in its beyond-measure [*démesure*] by the accusative of the "Here I am!"[3] that responds to its call. The command that commands me leaves me no possibility to ascend to the infinite as toward a name posited in a theme.[4] In this way God escapes objectification and is not even found in the I-Thou relationship; God is not the Thou [*Tu*] of an I, is neither dialogue nor in dialogue. But neither is God separable from responsibility for the neighbor, who, himself, is a Thou [*Tu*] for me. God is thus a third person or *Illeity*. And the command [*l'ordre*] to which, as a subject, I am subjected, comes from the understanding [*entente*] that I hear [*j'entends*] in my own Saying alone.[5]

The commandment [*commandement*] that commands in my own Saying is neither domination nor coercion, because it leaves me outside of any correlation with its source. Indeed, God is not in the correlation where a gaze would come to look for him. As Illeity, God is in-finite, outside of the structure wherein the gaze might take charge of his shock and include him in a *logos*. What God signifies is the unrepresentable, the without-beginning, anarchy: an immemorial past irreducible to objectification.

Yet the movement beyond being in the relationship with the neighbor can become ontology and theology, thereby marking a halt in the halt-less quality [*non-arrêt*] of the relationship in which the infinite is traced. From this halting flows an idolatry of the beautiful in its indiscreet exposure, in its motionlessness of the statue, in its plasticity. Here, the gaze substitutes itself for God. With theology, which is linked to ontology, God is fixed in a concept. With art, which is iconography in its essence, the movement beyond being is fixed in beauty. Theology and art hold fast to the immemorial past.[6]

The investigation being carried on here is the strange search for God without onto-theo-logy. The *word* "God" is unique in that it is the only word that neither extinguishes nor smothers nor absorbs its Saying. It is only a word, but it overwhelms semantics. Glory can be enclosed in a word, and therein it becomes being, but already glory undoes its dwelling. Immediately unsaid, the word "God" does not fit grammatical categories (it is neither a proper name nor a common noun).[7] This Said that is the word "God" derives its meaning from witnessing, which pure thematization—forgetting the ethical intrigue whence it arises or else inserting that intrigue into linguistic systems—seeks to recapture; yet immediately this excessive utterance prohibits itself. Here, not-to-be is not simple nothingness but the excluded third [*tiers-exclu*]. There is a refusal of presence, which immediately is converted into my presence thought through to its end: in a commandeering of my presence.

But since the unnamable God is named "God," since philosophy thematizes him through theology or onto-theo-logy, that is, since it makes him come back to the *esse* of being as the source of all meaning, we must ask ourselves what is the relationship between this non-ontological God and philosophy, whose discourse *is* ontology. Philosophical discourse claims an ultimate encompassing and comprehension. When "theology" snatches some domain from philosophy for the benefit of religion, that domain is immediately recognized as philosophically invalid, or as something to be recaptured and invested. Philosophy claims a coincidence between its thinking and being, to which it holds fast. This coincidence signifies for thinking that it does not have to think beyond that which depends on the act of being, nor venture toward what might modify its prior belonging to the process of being. In this way an expression like "the thinking of being" (i.e., thinking that has meaning) is a *tautology*, which can be justified only by the adventures to which this identification of thinking and being (i.e., meaning) is exposed, and through which it is obliged to pass.

This thinking or philosophical discourse must therefore be able to embrace God, whatever the form of its notion of God.[8] And for this thinking, to think about God signifies first that God is situated in the midst of the process of being, from which thinking does not depart. It signifies that God is situated as a being—through his belonging to the process of being—and conceived as the being *par excellence*, as the "supreme being," and as what is *par excellence*. It is in this way that God "comes into philosophy,"[9] by being thematized and brought into the course of being. By contrast, the God we are seeking here signifies, in an *unlikely* way, a beyond being. How then could a relationship exist between man and that which transcends him? How is the beyond being thinkable in its transcendence? The history of philosophy is the destruction of transcendence, the affirmation of immanence, and rational theology—profoundly ontological in nature—expresses this transcendence through adverbs of height: God would exist eminently, signifying a height or elevation that is above all heights.

But is this height still dependent on ontology? Is it not in a rupture with immanence? Is not the modality of height not borrowed from the sky, extended above our heads? "The starry heavens above me and the moral law within me": does not this Kantian formula express the nonthematizable?[10]

The problem posed here consists in asking ourselves whether the meaning that holds to the *esse* of being—philosophical meaning—is not already a restriction of meaning, something derived or adrift [*un dérivé ou une dérive*], or again a shadow of meaning. Is not the meaning that is equivalent to ess*a*nce, to the *esse* of being, already approached on the basis of presence, which qualifies the time of the Same? This is a question that implies the possibility of going back, on the basis of this meaning, to a meaning that would no longer state itself in terms of being or of beings. It is a question that asks whether, beyond the intelligibility of immanence and of identity, beyond the consciousness of the present and of being, we might make out a significance that would be an *other rationality*, one that would be a rationality of transcendence. It asks whether, beyond being, a meaning is not shown whose priority shall be said to be prior to being—and this, even when it is translated into ontological language.

And we must note that with this, in speaking beyond being and beings, we do not necessarily fall back into the discourse of opinion, nor even say that faith characterizes our language. On the contrary, faith and opinion (or the opinion of faith) speak the language of being. And perhaps nothing is less opposed to ontology than opinion and faith (and the *opinion* of faith).[11]

In Praise of Insomnia

Friday, May 7, 1976

Our seminar now comes back to the question posed at the outset: Can we not think, or speak, of a rationality or a meaning that would not be a reference to being and to ontology?

We rejoin this question at the end of a journey on which we passed through the notion of a witnessing that was not referred to an experience, a bearing witness in which the infinite, in relation with the finite, disquiets or awakens the finite, which is equivalent to the psyche *qua* inspiration and which was understood concretely in the sense of an ethical intrigue. We then interpreted this breaking open of experience in witnessing, this agitation of the Same by the Other, as the *diachrony* of time. This is a time that would lend itself [*se donnerait*] to our understanding as a reference to God—as the *to-God* itself [l'*à-Dieu* même]—before being interpreted as a pure deficiency or as a synonym of the perishable or the noneternal. That is, what gives itself to be understood as that which is diametrically opposed to the traditional idea of God. It is as if, within temporality, there were produced a relationship with a "term" or end (but is it properly speaking a *term*?) that is third to being and to nothingness—an *excluded* middle or third and, in this way alone, a God who would not be thought in an onto-theo-logical manner. And we again noted that, within the intrigue of the relationship with God, in which God distances himself in the guise of the third person (as He, that is, neither being nor nothingness) from both objectification and dialogue, this term nonetheless undergoes—if only in the discourse ventured here—the thematization and objectification wherein rational theology found its departure point. A thematization that even naive faith undergoes.[1] In this way we are brought back to the initial question of the possibility of a non-ontological meaning.

~

We must now take up in a more radical fashion the distinction between awakening—as the nonquietude that is the shaking up of the Same by the Other—and the notion of the spiritual, or the reasonable, that constitutes this thinking on the measure of the world, which we call consciousness. Consequently, we must also approach the correlation consciousness/being in a direct way so as ultimately to justify ontology.

For philosophy, meaning coincides with manifestation, as though the business of being—its work [œuvre], its deeds, or its epic—were carried out in the form of intelligibility. This is why philosophy remains an attachment to being (whether it is a matter of the being or entity, or of the being of the entity). Philosophy is the intrigue of cognition, the adventure of experience between clarity and obscurity. In that sense, this adventure is not the mere accidental enterprise of a handful of men; rather it carries the spirituality of the West, in which knowledge is the production of being.

Here knowledge, thought, or experience are not reduced to some sort of reflection of exteriority before the tribunal of conscience [for intérieur]. The notion of the reflection does not belong to knowledge. To understand the intelligible, as defined on the basis of what is reflected, we must go back to something higher or earlier than consciousness itself. Consciousness refers to a more ancient modality, from which it derives, and in which it justifies itself and is justified by its source. This modality is precisely *wakefulness* or *keeping watch* [*la veille*], which does not consist in keeping watch *over* [veiller-*à*] (something).[2]

The entire opening of consciousness would already be a turning toward the something over which wakefulness watches. It is necessary, however, to think an opening that is prior to intentionality, a primordial opening that is an impossibility of hiding; one that is an assignation, an impossibility of hiding in oneself: this opening is an *insomnia*. ("Insomnia" is a good word, for we can never envision speaking of an insomnia-*over* [insomnie-*à*]!) It is already as a modality or modification of the wakefulness of insomnia that consciousness is a consciousness-of and, as such, an assembling into being and into presence; it is a necessary modification, and one that justifies itself at a certain depth of awakening [*veiller*].[3]

Insomnia is not defined as a simple negation of the natural phenomenon of sleep. Sleep is always on the verge of waking up [*réveil*];[4] it communicates with wakefulness [*la veille*], all the while attempting to escape it ("I sleep but my heart awaketh," says the Song of Songs);[5] sleep remains attentive to the wakefulness that threatens it and calls to it by its exigency.

The categorial of insomnia is not reduced to the tautological affirmation of the Same. If the awakening that, within consciousness, is already paralyzed should be inflected toward a content that is assembled into a presence, then awakening does not come down to the watching-over that is already a search for the identical, which absorbs us and in which we sleep. Insomnia as a category or a meta-category (and it is here that the "meta" takes on its meaning) is not inscribed in a table of categories on the basis of a determinant activity, which would be exercised upon the Other as on a given (itself based on the unity of the world) and in order to consolidate or guarantee the gravity of the Other [*l'Autre*]. Insomnia is disquieted at the heart of its formal equality by the Other who cores out [*dénoyaute*] all that which, within insomnia, makes up a core [*noyaute*] in resting, in presence, in sleep[6]—all that which is identified. Insomnia is the tearing of that resting within the identical.

Such is the irreducible character of insomnia: the Other *within* the Same who does not alienate the Same but who awakens him (and, as we have seen, this *within* must be understood as the diachrony of time). It is an awakening that is an exigency or demand, a more within the less, such that the "within" must be set between quotation marks, since it is at the same time on the outside [*en dehors*]. To put it in terms out of date today, here lies the "spirituality of the soul," but of a soul that is ceaselessly woken up in its state, its *state of soul.* Here we find the passivity of inspiration, a passivity lacking a taking charge, or the subjectivity of a subject sobered out of its perseverance in being. The formalism of this insomnia is more formal than that of the form that encloses in a presence; this is a formalism of the void, a formalism of a piercing or a fission.[7] This is because the insomnia, or the awakening without intentionality, the disinterested awakening (in the etymological sense of the term: dis-inter-estedness),[8] is not an appeal to a form (it is not a materiality calling for form). And here form does not arrest its own design as a form, any more than it encompasses its content; instead, this form signifies the absolutely noncontained (or the *infinite*).

～

Consciousness has already broken with this intrigue: it is identity—presence of being and presence of presence. Yet presence is only able to be, thanks to the waking up of consciousness itself, outside of all sleep. Thus, consciousness descends from insomnia even if that descent toward itself, in the form of self-consciousness, is fundamentally the forgetting of the Other, and even if the freedom of the Same is still only a waking dream. Presence is able to be only as the incessant taking up anew of presence: as re-presentation. Re-presentation is the very possibility of the return, of the presence of the present. The unity of apperception, the *I think,* is in no way a manner of rendering presence purely subjective. The synthesis accomplished by the unity of the *I think* behind experience constitutes the act; presence as act and in act. This synopsia is necessary to the actualization of the present.[9] The actuality of the phenomenon is precisely the activity of consciousness.

There is therefore, within the subject's experience, an extreme tension of presence that goes to the point of its bursting into the experience of a subject. There is an emphasis of presence in which presence comes back to itself and is actualized [*revient sur elle-même et se comble*]. There is an emphasis of being, a supervaluing [*surenchère*] of presence, which is without escape routes or subterfuge. One therefore finds, here, a reference to awakening taking the form of lucidity. But, then, it is always a matter of a watching-over-being, of an attention-*to*, rather than an *ex-posure* to the other [*l'autre*]. So it is already a matter of a modification of the empty formalism of insomnia.

All that goes on into the past is retained, recalled, or rediscovered in history. All that is apt to fill the field of consciousness was in its time received or perceived. For consciousness, the past is always a modification of a present: nothing could have come about without *presenting* itself. Transcendental subjectivity is the figure of this presence. Consequently, within consciousness, the process of the present unfolds in what is a *de jure* simultaneity.

The process of subjectivity does not come from outside. It is the presence of the present that contains or implies consciousness, or the subjective. And not only is philosophy a cognition or understanding of immanence; it is also itself immanence. The notion of experience refers to the unity of apperception; it is inseparable from presence; it is tied to the notion of gathering together (in the Heideggerian sense of *Sammeln*).[10]

However, not all signification is resolved into manifestation. The one-for-the-other does not come down, straightway, to a *showing itself.* "To suffer for another" has a meaning, in which knowledge is purely adventitious. It is therefore necessary to understand that the adventure of cognition is not the only mode, nor the first mode, of meaning. *It is necessary to put experience in question as the source of all meaning.* We do not mean in so saying to contest that philosophy itself is cognition. But the possibility for knowledge to be meaning is not equivalent to the necessary reduction of all meaning to exhibition. It is on the basis of this that we propose the idea of a *diachrony of truth* in which the Said must be unsaid, and in which the resulting Unsaid must be unsaid anew.

⁓

Let us again note that immanence and consciousness, as the recollection or contemplation [*recueillement*] of manifestation, are not subverted by the phenomenological interpretation of those affective states that place emotion or anguish at the heart of consciousness. In the phenomenology originating with Husserl, there was no true shaking of the representation: representation is at the basis of all life affective and voluntary; the psyche is representative; and it is so to the degree to which it is intentional. In Heidegger, the question is much more complex, but we nevertheless still find in him that idea of monstration and manifestation, which remains the corollary of meaning.

But we must at least recall the situation of the Cartesian idea of the infinite, in which the *cogito* bursts under the impact of something it cannot contain.

Outside of Experience:
The Cartesian Idea of the Infinite

Friday, May 14, 1976

The correlation of being and consciousness does not result from a contingent addition of a thought that might receive the reflection of an event. The correlation is tied to the fundamental rationalism of the energy of being. The affirmation (that is, the affirmation of being) unfolds as manifestation and becomes the consciousness that affirms it. Consciousness is persistence within the abiding or dwelling of being [*le demeurer de l'être*], its very immanence. The presence of being is affirmed and confirmed within representation, as though representation were an emphasis of presence, a retaking and a repetition of presence. In this sense consciousness is representation, and its structures are not shaken by the discovery of the intentionality of the affective and the voluntary [*l'intentionnalité de l'affectif et du volontaire*].

Phenomenology's discovery has consisted in insisting upon the irreducible *aiming* of these states, upon the anxiety capable of overturning the impassiveness of representations. Capable of overturning the impassiveness: that means not simply to provide a nuance but to constitute an access—and that, in the way in which fear and trembling constitute an access to the sentiment of the sacred.[1] In this way phenomenology has provided new elements for the comprehension of the psyche, but the privilege of representation has not been put into question for all that, for we have continued to speak of these affective states as affective *experiences*.

It is no accident if, in Husserl, the representative ground remains.[2] This representative ground, which Husserl brings to light
in nonrepresentative states, consists less in a serenity of some sort
than in the always and ever active activity of *identification* of a
unity across the multiplicity. What remains is at once the *gathering*—by which the contents of consciousness are something identified, something brought to their identity—and the *lucidity* of the
consciousness that lets nothing escape. The priority of ontology is
not put into question by intentionality.

The interpretation of affectivity that holds that the latter rests
upon representation is successful to the degree to which affectivity
is taken as a tendency whose aspirations can be satisfied in pleasure
or remain unsatisfied in suffering. Every aspiration that is concupiscence (in the Pascalian sense of the term)[3] is reducible to representation; however, it is not certain that every aspiration might be
concupiscence. Ontology is always discovered beneath the affectivity that is consciousness, and fulfilled desires are the desires that
connote the identical. But, elsewhere than in the site of consciousness where tendencies proceed to an end, an affectivity can break
out that does not conform to this sketch of consciousness and that
tears us out of experience; this is an affectivity that, otherwise put,
does not reduce to experience: an affectivity *that is transcendence.*

One might wonder what a thinking, born of religious preoccu-
pations but not wanting to limit itself to the mere authority of the
Churches, can gain from referring to religious *experience.* A thinking of this nature is already, *qua* experience, referred to the *I think*,
and is entirely turned toward the philosophy of experience. The
narrative of religious experience, inasmuch as it is a narrative, does
not shake what philosophy will say in purifying the narrative;
therefore it could not disrupt the present whose fulfillment is philosophy. It is possible that the word "God" could have come to
philosophy from the religious [*à partir du religieux*]. But philosophy understands the religious discourse in which the word "God"
is inscribed as composed of propositions concerning a theme, as
invested by a meaning resting upon unveiling or disclosure. The
messages of the religious experience conceive no other significance

for meaning. The religious revelation is already assimilated to the disclosure effectuated by philosophy. That a discourse might speak otherwise than to state what has been seen and understood, seen and understood outside or internally, that there might be a meaning other than the appearing of being—all this remains unimaginable and unsuspected. It follows that the religious human being interprets what he has lived as experience, and as a consequence, he interprets God, whom he claims to experience, in terms of being. In this way there is an inevitable return to immanence, and it is not an accident that the philosophy of God in our tradition is an ontology.

Hence the importance of the question posed by this lecture: Can discourse signify otherwise than by signifying a theme? Does God signify as a theme of the religious discourse that names him?

The thematization of God within religious experience has already missed the beyond-measure [*la démesure*] of the intrigue of infinity that disrupts the unity of the *I think*. This possibility of missing or conjuring away the beyond-measure signifies a division of truth into two times: that of the immediate and that of the reflected. But this division, which should incite us to prudence, does not lead to the subordination of the one to the other. Within this division or this duality, there is a structure specific to meaning: meaning as diachrony, as necessarily in two times, and thus a meaning that repels synthesis. This diachrony—to coincide and, at the same time, not to coincide—is perhaps what is proper to transcendence.

~

In meditating upon the idea of God, Descartes sketched, with an unequaled rigor, this process (in two times) of a thinking going to the point of the breaking up of the *I think*. Thinking, first, God as being, Descartes thinks of him as *eminent* being [comme être *éminent*], as the being who is *eminently*. Before the approximation of the idea of God and that of being, we must ask ourselves whether the "eminently" qualifying the being of God does not refer to height, which would signify the height of the sky above our heads, the dis-inter-estedness of this height, and thus an overflowing of ontology. Be that as it may, Descartes here maintains a substantialist language by interpreting God's beyond-measure as existence in the superlative mode.

Yet it is not there that Descartes's unsurpassable contribution resides. This is found in the breakup of consciousness; this is a breakup that is not repression into the unconscious but a sobering or a waking up. It is a waking, as it were, out of the "dogmatic slumber," but we must be aware that in using this expression we are stating a tautology. In the Cartesian analysis of the idea of the infinite, we always find these two times:

1. God is the *cogitatum* of a *cogitatio*; there is an *idea* of God;

2. God is what signifies the uncontainable *par excellence*, what surpasses all *capacity*.

Thus the objective reality of God causes his formal reality of cogitation to break apart; and perhaps there lies that which, before its time, reverses the universal validity and the original character of intentionality. God escapes the structure of the *cogito cogitatum* and signifies what cannot be contained. It is in this sense that the idea of God explodes the thinking that remains ever synopsia or synthesis, the thinking that always encloses in a presence or that re-presents, and brings back to presence or lets be.[4]

Here the idea of God is *placed in us*. In this *placing*, there is an incomparable passivity, for it is a placing in us of the unassumable. It is perhaps in this passivity beyond every assumable passivity that we must recognize the *waking* [le *réveil*], and there we must recognize the *insomnia* of which consciousness is already a modality stupefied by being, an insomnia that is the impossibility of dogmatic slumber.[5]

Everything unfolds in Descartes as though the negation, included in the *in*-finite, signified not some vague negation but precisely the idea of infinity, that is, the infinite *in* me. It is as though the psyche of the awakened subjectivity were equivalent to the infinite in the finite; as though—without any play on words—the *in* of infinity had to be understood at once as a *non-* and as an *in*. The birth of negation resides not here in the subjectivity that denies or negates but in the very idea of infinity, or in subjectivity as the idea of infinity. It is in this sense that the idea of infinity is a

veritable idea, and not simply what I conceive through the negation of the finite.

The actuality of the *cogito* is thus interrupted by what takes the
form of an idea of infinity [*en guise d'idée*], by way of the unencompassable, which is not thought in the sense of intentionality
but *undergone*—where the unencompassable carries, in a second
time of consciousness, that which, in a first time, claimed to carry
it. In effect, after the acquisition of the *cogito*'s certitude, and then
the sudden halt that Descartes deals himself in the last lines of the
second *Meditation*,[6] the third *Meditation* asserts:

> And I must not think that, just as my conceptions of rest and dark-
> ness are arrived at by negating movement and light, so my perception
> of the infinite is arrived at not by means of a true idea but merely by
> negating the finite. On the contrary, I clearly understand that there is
> more reality in an infinite substance than in a finite one, *and hence
> that my perception of the infinite, that is God, is in some way prior to my
> perception of the finite that is myself.*[7]

The idea of the infinite in me can only be passivity, and a passivity that one could not assimilate to receptivity, for it is a breaking apart, whereas receptivity is regaining possession of self (one
"can take a blow" in receptivity). The rupture is a passivity more
passive than any passivity; it is like a trauma by which the idea of
God would have been placed in me. And this "placed in me" is a
scandal in the Socratic world! This idea of "placed in me" abjures
all its Socratic honoraria.[8]

In the idea of infinity there is described a passivity that is surprise, an unassumable vulnerability or being-seized [*susception*], one
more open than any opening. The placing in me of an idea reverses
the presence to self that is consciousness, forcing through the bar-
rier and the checkpoint to which everything that enters consciousness is held, and overflowing the obligation to adopt all that penetrates from outside.

It is thus an idea that signifies with a significance prior to presence: an an-archy. An idea signifying within the trace, not ex-
hausting itself in exhibiting itself, and not deriving its meaning

from manifestation. Breaking with the coincidence of being and appearing wherein philosophy resides, breaking up this synopsia, this idea thus expresses diachrony itself. A signification more ancient than the recollectable thought, which representation retains in its presence.

What can this significance more ancient than exhibition mean? What can the antiquity of this signification mean? How can we specify concretely this antiquity, which is the trauma of awaking? We may do so in grasping it as though the idea of the infinite in us were an *exigency*; as though significance were an *order given*.

A God "Transcendent to the Point of Absence"

Friday, May 21, 1976

It is not in the negation of the finite by the infinite (negation as an event of judgment, understood in its abstraction and logical formalism) that we should interpret the idea of infinity or the infinite *within* thought. It is, on the contrary, the idea of infinity that is the proper and irreducible figure of the negation of the finite. The *in* of infinity is not some sort of "non-," but its negation is the subjectivity of the subject, its subjectivity behind, or prior to, intentionality.

The difference between the infinite and the finite is in this sense —in the manner of a very fine thread—a non-in-difference of the infinite with regard to the finite and the secret of subjectivity, or if you will, what is "proper" to it [*son "propre"*]. The figure of infinity placed in us—and this "placing" is, according to Descartes, contemporaneous with my birth[1]—would signify that the not-able-to-comprehend-the-infinite-through-thought is not a negative relationship but a relationship with that thought (of which we do not know whether we can still call it thought), with that thought as *passive* cogitation, which is half dumbfounded, and which does not understand its *cogitatum*. This is a thinking that does not hasten to establish an adequation between the term in the teleology of consciousness and that term given in being, going to its intentional term and rejoining presence in representation.

Here we do not find that spontaneous movement. The not-able-to-comprehend-the-infinite-through-thought would signify the condition (or the uncondition) of thought; as though stating the in-comprehension of the infinite by the finite came back to uttering the commonplace that the infinite is not the finite; and as though their difference should have to remain at the stage of this verbal ab-straction. In fact, the infinite need add nothing to itself anew in or-der to affect subjectivity. It is its very infinity, its difference in regard to the finite, that is already its non-in-difference in regard to the fi-nite. This comes down not to a cogitation that does not understand its *cogitatum* but to a cogitation that the infinite merely *affects*. The infinite affects thought and devastates it at the same time; it affects it in devastating it, and in this way it calls to it. It puts thought back in its place, and in this fashion puts thought in place: the infinite wakes thought up.

This waking is not a *welcoming* of the infinite; it is neither con-templation nor taking charge, both of which are necessary and suf-ficient to experience—which the idea of infinity places in ques-tion. The idea of infinity is not assumed, like the love that awakens at the end of the arrow that strikes, but it is like the state of soul in which the bewildered subject immediately finds himself again within his own immanence. The infinite signifies precisely the in-side [*l'en-deçà*] of its manifestation, its meaning not being reduced to manifestation even if the signification of the in-side must show itself in some sense.[2]

What, then, is this intrigue of meaning that is other than the in-trigue of representation and that is tied up in the monstrosity[3] of the infinite placed in me, this idea that is no longer an idea? What is the meaning of the trauma of awakening, in which the infinite can neither be posited as a correlate of the subject nor become his contemporary? How is transcendence as a relation thinkable if it must exclude the ultimate and most formal copresence that every relation guarantees to its terms? How can a relation refuse con-temporaneousness to its terms? A problem, to be sure, that is for-mally insoluble!

Yet the *in-* of infinity designates the depth of the affection by which subjectivity is affected through this *placing* of the idea, which is a placing without grasp [*une mise sans prise*]. The *in-* bespeaks the depth of the undergoing that no capacity contains, that no foundation supports any more, in which every process of investing runs aground, and in which the locks securing interiority's rear guard [*arrières*] are burst open. A placing without contemplation devastating its site like a devouring fire, laying waste to the site. The Bible expresses this in its manner:

> For behold, Yahweh is coming forth from his place,
> and will come down and tread upon the high places
> of the earth.
> And the mountains will melt under him and the valleys
> will be cleft,
> like wax before the fire,
> like waters poured down a steep place.[4]

What supports gives way to what is supported. It is like a dazzling in which the eye holds more than it can hold; like an ignition of the skin that touches and yet does not touch—beyond the graspable—what burns it.

A passivity or passion in which we recognize the *Desire* that is a more within a less and that awakens with its most ardent and most ancient flame a thought given to thinking more than it thinks. Here is a Desire of a different order than that of affectivity or the hedonic activity by which the desirable is invested, attained, and identified as an object of need—and in which the immanence of representation and the immanence of the world again find each other.[5] The negativity of the *in-* of infinity hollows out a desire that could not be filled, that nourishes itself from its own growth, that exalts itself as desire, and that grows distant from satisfaction insofar as it approaches the desirable. A desire that does not identify as need does. A desire without hunger, and also without end [*sans faim et aussi sans fin*]: a desire for the infinite *qua* desire for what is beyond being, which is stated in the word "dis-inter-estedness." This is transcendence and desire for the Good.

But if the infinite in me signifies desire for the infinite, are we then certain of the transcendence that comes to pass there? Does desire not restore, here, the contemporaneousness of the desirable and the desiring—and, even though there is neither vision nor aiming here, there is, doubtless, a very fine thread but a thread all the same? Does not the desiring one derive from the desirable a satisfaction in desiring, as if he had already seized the desirable? Is the dis-inter-estedness of desire for the infinite not interested? Does the transcendence of the Good beyond being not imply an indifference, while the Good signifies simultaneously a non-in-difference?

Love is possible only through the infinite placed in me, through the more that devastates and awakens the less, diverting theology, destroying the fortune and happiness [*l'heur et le bonheur*] of the end. Plato obliges Aristophanes to admit, "It is such reunions as these that impel men to spend their lives together, although they may be hard put to it to say what they really want with one another."[6] But Aristophanes knows what this is all about: to become a single being out of the two that they once were ("Likewise it is to desire and to this searching for that nature of a single piece that one gives the name love").[7] He thus wants to restore to love its end, and in this way satisfy a nostalgia. But why are the lovers themselves incapable of saying what they ask of each other ("and indeed, the purely sexual pleasures of their friendship could hardly account for the huge delight they take . . . both their souls are longing for a something else—a something to which they can neither of them put a name").[8] Diotima, for her part, will place love's intention over and above this unity, but she will find it needy and unhappy.[9] Love draws satisfaction in awaiting the beloved; one delights in the representation that lights up in anticipation. That is perhaps what pornography is. In any case it is in this way that love is concupiscence, an investment by the *I* [*je*]. In love, the *I think* reconstitutes presence.[10]

~

Is the transcendence of the desirable—beyond interestedness and the eroticism in which the beloved stands—possible? Affected by infinity, the *I* cannot go to an end that it could equal in his desire. The approach increases the distance, and enjoyment is only the increase of hunger. The desired one thus remains transcendent to desire. It is in this reversal of terms that transcendence, or the dis-inter-estedness of desire, comes to pass. But how?

Through the transcendence of infinity, which the word "Good" expresses. In order that disinterestedness be possible in desire, in order that the desire beyond being not be an absorption, the desirable (or God) must remain separated within desire: near, yet different—which is, moreover, the very meaning of the word "holy."[11] This is possible only if the desirable commands me to what is undesirable, only if he commands me to the undesirable *par excellence*: to the *other person* [*à autrui*].[12] The referral to the other is an awakening to nearness, which is responsibility for the neighbor to the point of substitution, which is the enucleation of the transcendental subject.

Here we find the notion of a love without eros. Transcendence is ethical, and subjectivity—which, ultimately, is not the *I think* and which is not the unity of transcendental apperception—is subjection to the other person [*autrui*] in the guise of responsibility for the other [*autrui*]. The "me" [*moi*] is a passivity more passive than any passivity; it is self, straightway in the accusative, without having ever been in the nominative. Self in the accusative, under accusation by another, albeit without fault, faithful to an engagement that it never contracted, to a past that has never been present. As such the "me" is a wakefulness or an opening of a self absolutely exposed and sobered from the ecstasy of intentionality.[13]

This way that the infinite has of referring, in the midst of its own desirability, to the nondesirable nearness is denoted by the term "Illeity." Therein lies the extraordinary reversal of the supreme desirability of the desirable who appeals to the rectitude of desire; the reversal by which the desirable escapes desire. The goodness of the Good inclines the movement to which it appeals to set it aside from the Good as desirable and to orient it toward the Other [*Autrui*]—and only thus toward the Good. There is, in this, an irrectitude going higher than the intangible rectitude; in this irrectitude the desirable separates itself from the relation to desire it called forth, and, through this separation or this holiness, the desirable remains a third person, a He at the base of the Thou [*Tu*]. He does not fill me with good but compels me to goodness, better than the good to be received. To be good is a deficit, it is withering and stupidity within being; but it is excellence and elevation beyond being. What this signifies is not that ethics is a moment of being but that it is, rather, otherwise and *better* than being.

~

In this reversal and this referral of the desirable to the nondesirable, in this strange mission commanding the approach of the other person, God is torn out of the objectivity of presence and out of being. He is no longer an object or an interlocutor in a dialogue. His distancing or his transcendence turns into my responsibility: the nonerotic *par excellence*!

And it is on the basis of the analysis just carried out that God is not simply the first other but other than the other [*autre qu'autrui*], other otherwise, other with an alterity prior to the alterity of the other person, prior to the ethical compulsion to the neighbor. In this way God is different from every neighbor. And transcendent to the point of absence, to the point of his possible confusion with the agitation of the *there is*.[14] A confusion in which the substitution for the neighbor grows in disinterestedness, in nobility,[15] and in which the transcendence of the infinite is raised to its glory. A transcendence that can be called true with a diachronous truth, without synthesis, higher than the truths one confirms.

In order that this expression, "transcendent to the point of absence," not remain an expression, it was necessary to return it to the signification of every ethical intrigue, to the divine comedy in which responsibility is implicated and without which the word "God" could not have arisen.

Postscript: On the Other Man: *Time, Death, and God*

Jacques Rolland

The two lecture courses whose text we have just read are, as I noted in the foreword to this book, strictly interconnected by way of their shared belonging to the philosophical space dominated by *Otherwise than Being* in all its severity. The one like the other requires commentary, but commentary of a different nature in each case, just as they each require a set of notes that are different. The few clarifications proposed here take up the essential points—and complete—the postscript written for the pocket edition of *Death and Time*.[1] We may hope that, in conjunction with the notes, and particularly those around "God and Onto-Theo-Logy," these clarifications will allow the reader a proper understanding of texts whose difficulty we would above all not wish to mask.

To Make History

Death, time: these are not themes but questions; questions that thinking cannot fail to encounter. They are words that philosophy has not ceased to pronounce over the course of its history, all the while forgetting to name being. And this—since Plato, who in a certain fashion was born to writing with the death of Socrates, with the end of his living word, and who later had to commit his famous parricide. Yet this is the Plato whose first question is, more than that of the death of soul, that of its immortality—and the Plato who knows, as if from the very beginning, what time is: a moving image of eternity—immobile eternity.[2] It is as though these questions were from the outset present to philosophy but, at the same time, held apart by it or too quickly resolved. And they are questions that are reborn with an unequaled vigor in the two works— that of Hegel and that of Heidegger—that claim to assemble, and in a sense surmount, the entirety of Western thought, whose history they traverse with ardor.

It is therefore not astonishing that it is to these two thinkers that Levinas turns when he turns toward those questions, in order to take them on in struggle. That, however, gives to the first of the two courses, "Death and Time," an entirely peculiar status within the work of Levinas (for I maintain that they are a part of his philosophical work), when we compare it with the philosopher's published works. In the latter, the history of philosophy is present on each page, but it is present without ever leaving the background and presents itself more in the mode of allusions than in that of analysis. To take but one example, let us recall the strange sentence from *Otherwise than Being* that follows:

> The multiplicity of unique subjects, "beings" immediately, empirically encountered, would proceed from this universal self-consciousness of Spirit [*Esprit*]: bits of dust collected by its movement or drops of sweat glistening on its forehead because of the labor of the negative it will have accomplished, forgettable moments for which alone counts their identity accruing to their position within the system and which are reabsorbed into the Whole of that System.[3]

As we have no doubt understood, it is here a matter of a debate or conflict with Hegel. But let us admit that there are more conventional manners of speaking of the thinker of Jena and, more generally, of carrying on a debate in philosophy!

A surprising situation. For us, for the post-Heideggerians that we inevitably are,[4] and more surprising still when we recall that we are here dealing with a philosopher who published the first book in French on Husserl and the first substantial study of Heidegger, and who introduced Rosenzweig into France.[5] But recall precisely that Rosenzweig—regarding whom Levinas never hid the fact that he had been decisive for the origin of his own thought, incommensurably more so than was Buber—is said in the preface to *Totality and Infinity* to be "too often present in this book to be cited."[6] As though there were, for Levinas, a strict distinction set down between his studies of the history of philosophy, relegated to a sort of preliminary status, and the proper development of his thought, which could assuredly find assistance in recalling past philosophies but which did not feel the need to enter into an explicit debate or a real dialogue with them. (In this situation, Husserl alone would be the exception.) This manner of thinking seems to me clearly stated in the following proposition: "But to fix one's positions relative to Hegel, corresponds, for a philosopher, to what would be for the weaver the setting up of his craft *prior to the work that would therein be created and re-created.*"[7] That comes first; and it is only afterward that the work itself begins. Fundamentally, had he been Aristotle, perhaps the *Metaphysics* might still not have included Book A in its corpus.

This is perhaps the first thing we should observe in regard to that course: indeed, if the thought that unfolds there is precisely that pursued in Levinas's books as well—more precisely, the thought that had just been inscribed in *Otherwise than Being*—then for once this thinking is woven into dialogue and debate with the great predecessors and the great contemporaries. First among them is Heidegger, whose crushing presence will have been noticed; but likewise present are Kant, Hegel, Bloch, Bergson, and selected others. This was, no doubt, because what was at stake was a series of lectures. Yet this itself seems to me to constitute another reason for the interest of these texts for publication (as perhaps a unique trace of the philosopher's professorial activity, to which he came so late in life), texts through which passes, I hope, by virtue of their character as lectures, something of the word of this man of letters.[8]

From a Distance of Thirty Years

We must shortly underscore the crucial points or principal intersections of the thinking that unfolds here in dialogue; likewise, we must situate this course within the evolution of Levinas's thought.

But before that we must note the way in which the meditation here conducted underlines—over and above the inevitable shifts in emphasis, whether these are translated by the deepening or the abandonment of a notion—the remarkable continuity, and thereby the remarkable unity, of Levinas's thought over more than a half century. We will bring this to light here in regard to the two terms that compose the title of the course in question: death and time.

Although the question of time is absent from the brief work of 1935, *On Evasion*, which represented the veritable launching of this adventure of thought, and although that work merely alluded—negatively—to death,[9] the works immediately following World War II, *Existence and Existents*[10] and *Time and the Other*,[11] placed these two questions at the heart of their reflection. The themes of time and death are respectively found there, each in itself as a question and together in the relations that unite them. It seems to me that, in order to comprehend fully what was then being thought, and to know how what was occurring in the early works corresponds with, while diverging from, the problematic unfolded in the present course, we must turn to the lectures Levinas gave at the Collège Philosophique, created by Jean Wahl, from 1946 to 1947. These lectures were subsequently published under the title *Time and the Other*.

While death is not announced in the title, nor pronounced in the initial sentences of *Time and the Other* ("The aim of these lectures consists in showing that time is not the achievement of an isolated and lone subject, but that it is the very relationship with the other"),[12] death occupies a determinant place in that work, where it is already understood essentially in the sense it will receive in the 1975–76 lectures. That is, if death is always and undeniably annihilation, it is still, and more profoundly, characterized by its unknowable quality [*son inconnu*]. Now, "the unknown of death signifies that the human relationship with death cannot take place in the light,"[13] and, consequently, "the subject is in relation with that which does not come from him."[14] This is a relation that cuts across all those that come to pass in light, where "the illumined object is something one encounters, but from the very fact that it is illumined one encounters it as if it came from us."[15] On the contrary, the encounter with death is a relation with what in no way comes from us. Thus death betrays the "passivity of the subject" at the same time as it "announces an event over which the subject is no longer master, an event in relation to which the subject is no longer a subject."[16] In that sense, death can be called a *mystery* (later on, Levinas will prefer to use the term *enigma*), if by this term we mean "something"—in truth, it is the non-object *par excellence*—which cannot be possessed, cannot be comprehended, cannot be grasped even by anticipation alone. Thereby the relation with the mystery or the unknown quality of death is a relation with the *other*: "This approach to death indicates that we are in relation with something that is absolutely other, something bearing alterity, not as a provisional determination . . . but as something whose very existence is made of alterity."[17] This is why death, as an ungraspable event, "is never now" but shows itself as an "eternal futurity [*éternel à venir*]."[18] For "that which is in no sense grasped"—in the sense of death, and in the sense of the other—"is the future." In other words, or inversely, "the future is what is not grasped, what befalls us and lays hold of us. The future is the other. The relationship with the future is the very relationship with the other."[19]

Thus the relation with the other as he is concretized in the event, or in the mystery of death, allows us to think the future concretely, that is, quite simply to think it. Yet this future, "the future that death gives, the future of the event, *is not yet time*."[20] In order that it become time, it would at least be necessary that this future allow a certain relationship between itself and the present (as presence of the future in the present or the "encroachment" of the present into the future). This is a relationship excluded precisely by death understood in its mystery or its alterity. Death, which permits us to think the future, is insufficient to thinking time. For this, there must be another relation, another situation—another *circumstance*, as Levinas will say later on. A situation is necessary "where, at the same time, the event happens and yet the subject, without welcoming it, as one welcomes a thing or an object, faces up to the event."[21] A situation, then, wherein, without any grasp of the unknown or any anticipation of the future, there would nevertheless be a rapport between the present of the subject and the future of the event that comes to him without his assuming it. This situation, Levinas writes, is "the relationship with another, the face-to-face with another, the encounter with a face that at once gives and conceals the other."[22] And this situation in which another is substituted for the other *überhaupt* [above all], for the other pure and simple, for the other in general, allows us to pass from the future alone to time itself, where present and future can and must maintain a relation. (We will have observed that, in this description, the past is not yet taken into account.) "The relation with the future, the presence of the future in the present, seems as yet to be accomplished in the face-to-face with another. The situation of the face-to-face would be the very *accomplishment of time*; the encroachment of the present on the future is not the feat of a subject alone, but the intersubjective relation. The *condition of time* is in the rapport between humans or in history."[23]

This extremely succinct summary of the central pages of the lectures of 1946–47 (and of these pages alone; that is, we shall have passed over in silence both the preceding pages, in which the birth or hypostasis of the subject is described, and those pages that follow, in which the attempt is made to think the alterity of the other on the basis of the feminine, taken there as a sort of model of alterity) will not have been useless insofar as it may constitute a good introduction to the reading of the lectures of 1975–76. Indeed, although certain analyses were modified over the course of the thirty years separating the two texts, the fundamental themes have remained unchanged, and, above all, the basic thematic—in which time and death are related to each other, by implicating the alterity of the other person in their relationship—has been strengthened and deepened. We may thus make a few remarks on the lectures of 1975–76.

Death on the Basis of Time

We thus come to the lecture course "Death and Time," not to propose an explication or a commentary but only to extend the reading of it with some brief notes. The first of these concerns the structure of this text, which could be called circular since it begins (the first part comprising the lectures from the 7th to the 21th of November 1975) by posing the terms of the question. From there the text passes to the reading of a certain number of philosophic works (the second part comprising the lectures from November 28, 1975, to May 7, 1976), and concludes with a meditation (the third part comprising the lectures of the 14th and the 21st of May, 1976), which recapitulates, while deepening, the questions of the first part. These three parts call, in their turn, for certain remarks. In the first place, we note that the position of the question in the first part is in no sense neutral, but that it situates the problem within the proper horizon of Levinas's thought. Thus, "This search for death within the perspective of time," as the first lecture puts it, "does not signify a philosophy of *Sein zum Tode* [Being-toward-death]. It is thus differentiated from the thought of Heidegger." The question situates the problem, more precisely, within the horizon opened by *Otherwise than Being*. For this reason, the second part will consist not in merely exposing a certain number of philosophical positions whether past or contemporary, but rather in interrogating them on the basis of the initial questioning and in view of taking up this questioning anew in the third part. (This, after all, is why one could not reduce these pages to a course in the history of philosophy, and it is indeed why they must be understood as an integral part of Levinas's philosophical work.) Another word on the structure of the second part of the lecture course is in order. This structure (which I here restore in a schematic fashion) is such that the second part rests as if upon two pillars, upon two critiques: those of Heidegger and of Hegel. First, Heidegger—to whom Kant is essentially opposed; then Hegel, whose critique is followed by a highly favorable evocation of Bloch. Aristotle, Husserl, Bergson, and Fink —as well as a few others!—intervene in a minor mode and a punctual fashion.

If, however, in the midst of this circular structure, it is a matter of thinking death and time in their relationships to each other, then it is evidently toward Heidegger—the "great antagonist," as

one commentator put it, thinking no doubt of how Levinas himself once qualified Rosenzweig as the "great contemporary"[24]—
that Levinas must first turn; the same Heidegger in whose work
"the close relationship of death and time is asserted." Yet Levinas
will turn to Heidegger only to take his distance immediately by in-
verting the Heideggerian sequence and attempting "to think death
on the basis of time, and no longer time on the basis of death." To
comprehend this other relation between death and time, it seems
to me important to underscore certain aspects of these two concepts such as they are thought in Levinas.

First, death: Levinas in no way denies its significance as ending
and annihilation. But in this regard he will ask whether the nothingness [*le néant*] that death opens has been sufficiently thought,
that is, thought radically enough within the philosophical tradition. That means nothingness as such, a nothingness that "like
that of death . . . *is pregnant with nothing at all*"; in other words, if
we may put it this way, a nothingness devoid of any being, and
separated from all being—or, be that as it may, a *pure* nothingness. Now, in these lectures, Levinas wants to demonstrate that
nothingness has defied Western thought—from Aristotle, who situated nothingness in the couple generation/corruption, to Hegel,
for whom "pure being and pure nothingness are the same" (not to
mention Bergson, who asserted that the idea of nothingness as the
abolition of the whole "is as absurd as that of a square circle"). The
West has not managed to think the nothing [*le rien*].[25]

Things would be otherwise with Heidegger—at least in *Being
and Time*, the work primarily considered in these lectures—where
death is properly nothingness in virtue of being the end of the
being-there whose property is to comprehend being. But this pure
nothingness [*néant*] itself—which nonetheless can be anticipated
—would not yet reach the measure or beyond-measure of death.
This is precisely because Heidegger's nothingness would determine or delimit the unlimitedness and indeterminateness of death
understood as an end, as nothingness or annihilation—and that
alone. Yet, whence comes our certainty that death is nothing other
than nothing [*rien d'autre que rien*]? Or, why do we refuse to take

into account what is *unknown* in this nothing [*rien*], in the nothingness [*néant*] of death? ("I even wonder how the principal trait
of our relation with death could have escaped the philosophers'
attention. It is not with the nothingness of death, of which we
precisely know nothing, that the analysis must begin, but with the
situation where something absolutely unknowable appears."[26]
This remark, found in *Time and the Other*, could find its place in
the present lectures if modified only slightly, but modified, nonetheless, from its formulation at least, since the 1975–76 lectures
take the nothingness of death more firmly into account.) In this
way, and to be properly thought, death would require—and this
is Levinas's major proposition—a nothingness [*néant*] that would
be more nil [*néant*] than the "pure nothingness" [*le pur néant*]:
a nothingness that would be the "ambiguity of nothingness and
the unknown." Thanks to this unknown of death, which, in its
ambiguity (in the sense of mystery or an enigma), is combined
with death's nothingness, the pure *question mark* inscribed by
death would be held fast in the annihilation that death undeniably is, in the nothingness that death incontestably opens. Moreover, owing to this question mark, the dimension of nonsense and
absurdity—but also the dimension of emotion—that all death
carries within it would in its turn be inscribed in the neutrality of
nothing.

It is this determination of death as the nothingness *and* the unknown, or the pure question, this determination of death as the
supreme indetermination, that permits Levinas to oppose Kant
to Heidegger. Kant will not deny death or its nothingness, but,
through the demands of practical reason, he will be brought to
postulate the immortality of the soul. Yet we must be cautious:
what we must see here is that this immortality cannot be asserted
—or denied (which would simply be a reverse dogmatism)—but
can only be *hoped*. The hope in question, then, which is like the
excluded term between affirmation and negation, inscribes a *perhaps* into the undeniable nothingness of death. However—and
here we must emphasize what is no doubt one of the most stimu-
lating thoughts suggested by these lectures—this perhaps does not

fill the void of nothingness, nor dull the cutting edge of death. It is all to the contrary. To death in its nothing, the "perhaps" adds a question. It is a question without a response other than "perhaps." Yet the question adds weight to death and restores it to its enigma, or to its mystery, as, we recall, *Time and the Other* put it. It restores it to its ambiguity of annihilation *and* unknowability.

~

On a number of occasions I have said that the 1975–76 lectures belong to the period of *Otherwise than Being*, whose "theme" is the subjectivity of the subject, whereas that of *Totality and Infinity* was the alterity of the other [*l'autre*] or the other person [*autrui*]. It is thus within the horizon of thought opened by this work, and in relation to the subject (in the sense in which his subjectivity is there pondered), that time will itself be able to be thought. Now, what is decisive, and decisively new, in *Otherwise than Being* is that the subject there is no longer "the subject isolated and alone." This Levinas had already attained in the hypostasis thought in the immediate postwar period and encountered above. Neither is this subject the "I" [*Moi*] who is the Same in *Totality and Infinity*, the "I" that is "identity par excellence and the very work of identification" in that it has "identity as its contents."[27] In *Totality and Infinity*, the isolated subject, or "I" qualified by identity, certainly encounters the other [*l'autre*] in the face of another [*autrui*]. And this is a subject or "I" whose isolation and sameness will no doubt be affected, contested, and overturned by that encounter—but only in a second time, following the constitution of the subject or the "I." Here, on the contrary, the subject's identity comes to him from outside; his uniqueness arises from his assignation by the other. And this, in such a way that exteriority or alterity must be understood as *constitutive* of his subjectivity. "The identity of the *same* in the ego [*je*] comes to it despite itself from the outside, as an election or an inspiration, in the form of the uniqueness of someone assigned."[28] Consequently, the deepest layer of the psyche or of the human—the preoriginal subjectivity, as Levinas will say—that can no longer be thought in terms of consciousness, nor described as the Same, but must be thought as the Other-*in*-the-Same. Subjectivity is then this Same already open to the Other, to the Other that—according to the analyses of *Time and the Other*, whose results are preserved here— the Same can neither grasp nor comprehend nor contain, nor even anticipate. Subjectivity is already turned toward him [the other person], but without ever joining him. As the identity "that comes from the outside," the identity of the *sub-jectum*, "under the weight of the universe, responsible for everything,"[29] subjectivity is always already open to the Outside and to the Different, which it will never attain. And it is in this *never* that, according to the lectures, the *forever* of time should be sought. "The always of time would be engendered by that disproportion between desire and what is desired." A time no doubt always liable to be brought back to a synchrony through retention and protention, through memory and anticipation, through history and prevision, it remains a time characterized firstly by its *diachrony*. This "is the disjunction of identity where the same does not rejoin the same,"[30] and, in that sense, it can be understood as another name for the subjectivity just evoked. "Stated as properly as possible (for the ground of the Saying is never properly said), the subject is not *in* time, but is di-achrony itself."[31] We have already understood that this subject al-ways comes *late* to the other that it desires. And, in this lateness, we find a subjectivity as exposure—despite itself—to the other, as patience and, finally, as passivity.

Totality and Infinity, however, had taught us that "the Other [*l'Autre*] par excellence is Another [*Autrui*]."[32] And this lesson is retained as much in *Otherwise than Being* as in these lectures. The subjectivity originally open to the other [*autre*] is consequently a subjectivity susceptible—susceptible but not capable—of a rela-tion of responsibility with another person [*autrui*], with the neigh-bor, whose approach sketches the most severe diachrony. "The more I answer the more I am responsible; the more I approach the neighbor with whom I am charged the further away I am. This debit which increases is infinity as an infinition of the infinite, as glory."[33] Without entering too deeply into the extreme difficulties of this book, we can say that, as in *Time and the Other*, although in different terms, it is in the relationship with another person that time is originally produced.

⁓

In time thus thought, death comes to be twice inscribed. First, as the mortality of another person ("Is the nothingness of death not the very nudity of the neighbor's face," asks the lecture), which would be the concrete modality by which, within the subject, the same does not rejoin the same but offers itself passively and gratuitously to the service of another. It is next inscribed with my own death, the nonsense of which "would guarantee" in some fashion that this passivity will not be inverted into activity, or that this disquiet will not finish by finding rest. "My mortality, my being condemned to death, my time at the point of death, and my death are not the possibility of impossibility but pure being seized; this constitutes this absurdity that makes possible the gratuity of my responsibility for another."[34]

What preceded were but a few notes, aiming not so much to explicate, but to underscore certain essential traits, certain nodal points of a thought whose difficulty we would not seek to mask. Yet in this difficulty, Levinas's thought comes "to think death on the basis of time rather than time on the basis of death, as Heidegger does." Death is no longer nothingness becoming a possibility but the ambiguity of nothingness and the unknown; time is no longer the horizon of being but the intrigue of subjectivity in its relation to another.

God Without Being[35]

"But to hear [*entendre*] a God not contaminated by Being is a human possibility no less important and no less precarious than *to bring Being out of the oblivion* in which it is said to have fallen in metaphysics and in onto-theology."[36] Such is the task that "God and Onto-Theo-Logy" set for itself. Such is the exigency to which it responded in the form of a lecture course. This amounted to reproducing, as it were, the Heideggerian gesture that endeavored to think a being [*un être*] *not contaminated by an entity* [*l'étant*], even if that were the ὄντος ὄν, the *summum ens*, the supreme being—in a word, God, according to the name philosophy had loaned him —and this, although being is and cannot fail to be the being *of* an entity.[37] The intent amounted thus to thinking the *word* "God" *in its own right*, and not such as it is masked in philosophy. In other terms, "to hear the word God as a signifying word."[38] A word that did not have the same status in the history of philosophy as its kindred terms "death" and "time," which were no sooner welcomed than thrust aside as *questions* by philosophy. For, in that philosophy, to borrow the words of the bourgeois, the word "God" enters[39] with all the appearance of the highest glory, to take on straightway, in the superlative, the highest attributes and thereby claim to be uncreated. Consequently, it soon lays claim to being the indubitable foundation of all that *is* and *can* be, only to complete its ascent in becoming *das Absolut* in the sense of the supreme concreteness [*du suprême concret*] (understood according to the etymology of *con-crescere*), and so forgetting its sense (albeit also etymological!) of absolution or the absolute. It thus forgets the sense *of absolvere*, of what escapes or absolves itself of what wanted and will always want to encompass it. An ab-solute that rhymes with the Hebrew first name of the philosophical "God": *kodesh*, which, without distinction, is the *holy* and the *separated*,[40] as though the inscription of holiness inscribed separation by its own gesture, as though the chance coming of God into human language were the original inscription of the *difference*.[41]

Yet the history itself of this word is the reason for which Levinas's meditations require an approach wholly other than that which terms such as "death" or "time" command. To be sure, these words are thrust aside by philosophy at the very moment when they knock at the door of its *logos*. However, they are taken up again (in Hegel and in Heidegger), and, be that as it may, they were never *travestied* in the way that the Name of God had been. Here, the recovery of the meaning of the word can no longer be effected in the pursuit of a dialogue, a *Gespräch*, or—as Levinas dares to translate it in an intangible dialect in these lectures—a *conversation* with the thinkers who inscribed their names in the Table of Contents of the

History of Philosophy. Indeed, the Name of God would never have been "properly said" by philosophy; that was its drama and its wrong—its own excessively triumphant grandeur. Except, perhaps, "during some flashes,"[42] in the breathlessness through which philosophy—the Wisdom of the Nations[43]—hears the ex-ception of the *other* than being. Consequently, we must enter forcibly into the questioning without tarrying "to converse" with a tradition that, from the outset, chose or was compelled to ignore the *proper* Name of God.

Thus the lecture course proceeds as it does—that is, it proceeds as it can, according to the rhythm of a thinking that *knows* that it *must* think *more* than it thinks—taking up tasks from *Otherwise than Being*, tasks from "God and Philosophy,"[44] and tasks from this series of lectures. This is a rhythm that can only be chaotic and jolting as it takes up from week to week and, as it were, from word to word, a single *question*, received or grasped breathlessly in its emergence as a question: how can something (with the exception of the "something in general" from the renowned and necessary, yet tyrannical, *etwas überhaupt*) escape or absolve itself from what seeks and seeks again to grasp it anew [*cherche et recherche à le re-saisir*]? How is an absolute possible, and thinkable? An absolute that, without being confused with the Hegelian *Absolut*, does not founder in the *Schwärmerei* [revelry] "where all the cows are black," but gets taken up again—only to be bogged down, this time, in the unknown that was too quickly taken for the well-known. So true it is that the string that "tries to surround, circumscribe or circumvent, fasten or bind transcendence . . . is assuredly neither too short, nor too frayed."[45] And so true it is that the task of thinking remains to *think* more than it thinks.

In *Otherwise than Being*, in those texts contemporary with it, and in the present lectures, Levinas's entire effort consists, as it were, in giving God back His freedom, which had been seduced by philosophy, or by what Heidegger justly named onto-theo-logy, in the guise of *thought's* own defrauding [*subreption*] by *metaphysics*.

How is this done? That is the sole question of value. We have here attempted merely to give the attentive reader a few keys, permitting him to set the heavy door that opens to this path ajar. The reader should be advised that no commentary could push this heavy and awkward gate further open. For the true name of this threshold is *ambiguity*, where transcendence can only be heard in words that betray it while they endeavor to translate it. We can help the reader only by signaling a few traps on the way, with which we have, ourselves, struggled for twenty years.

Notes

Notes

1. [See Emmanuel Levinas, *Totalité et infini: Essai sur l'extériorité* (The Hague: Martinus Nijhoff, 1961); in English, *Totality and Infinity: An Essay on Exteriority*, trans. Alphonso Lingis (Pittsburgh: Duquesne University Press, 1969). Emmanuel Levinas, *Autrement qu'être, ou au-delà de l'essence* (The Hague: Martinus Nijhoff, 1974; 2d ed., 1978); in English, *Otherwise than Being, or Beyond Essence*, trans. Alphonso Lingis (Dordrecht: Kluwer Academic, 1991). Emmanuel Levinas, *De Dieu qui vient à l'idée* (Paris: Librairie philosophique J. Vrin, 1982; 2d ed., 1986); in English, *Of God Who Comes to Mind*, trans. Bettina Bergo (Stanford, Calif.: Stanford University Press, 1998).—Trans.]

It seems to me [J. Rolland] that the philosophically perspicacious and acute Jacques Derrida, Levinas's first reader in the sense in which Levinas was Husserl's first reader (see the postscript to this volume), was not deceived as to the nature and importance of this "turn" begun just after the publication of *Totality and Infinity*. I would suggest as proof—or at least as a sign—the final words of the first note in the significant "Violence and Metaphysics: Essay on the Thought of Emmanuel Levinas," published first in 1964 in the *Revue de métaphysique et morale* (nos. 3 and 4). Derrida comments: "This essay was written when two important texts of Emmanuel Levinas appeared, 'The Trace of the Other' (*Tijdschrift voor Filosofie*, Sept. 1963) and 'Meaning and Sense' (*Revue de métaphysique et morale*, 1962, no. 2). Unfortunately, we can make only brief allusions to these here." [Derrida's "Violence and Metaphysics" was printed in English in Jacques Derrida, *Writing and Difference,* trans. Alan Bass (Chicago: University of Chicago Press, 1978). Levinas's essay "Meaning and Sense" was revised and republished in English in *Emmanuel Levinas: Basic Philosophical Writings,* ed. and trans. Adriaan Peperzak, Simon Critchley, and Robert Bernasconi (Bloomington: Indiana University Press, 1996).—Trans.]

2. The word *new* is used here in the sense that Levinas used it: that of which the old tradition knew nothing, even by anticipation; that whose idea had not even come to it.

3. The second lecture course poses, with each line, the question of *language [langage],* of which Richard A. Cohen, in his translation of *Time and the Other,* was quite correct in saying that it is the element in which the questioning developed in *Otherwise than Being* was sought. (See Emmanuel Levinas, *"Time and the Other" and Additional Essays,* trans. Richard A. Cohen [Pittsburgh: Duquesne University Press, 1987].) As to the native tongue *[langue]*—without mentioning Hebrew, Russian, or German in Levinas's case—I would simply say that there is a phrase of Merleau-Ponty's, in *Signs,* that always seemed to me, by the way, written as if to name Levinas's relationship to French: "It is as if it (the language) had been made for him (the writer) and he for it; as if the task of speaking, to which he was destined in learning the language, was him more justly than the beating of his own heart; as if the instituted language appealed to the existence, with him, of one of its possibilities." [Maurice Merleau-Ponty, *Signs,* trans. Richard C. McCleary (Evanston, Ill.: Northwestern University Press, 1964), p. 79, translation modified for consistency with Rolland's text.—Trans.] How better to speak of the language of *Otherwise than Being!*

4. [Rolland is referring to Martin Heidegger's *Vorträge und Aufsätze* (Essays and lectures), vols. 1–3 (Pfullingen: Verlag Günther Neske, 1967). Several of these texts were edited and translated into English by David Farrell Krell in *Martin Heidegger: Basic Writings from "Being and Time" (1927) to "The Task of Thinking" (1964),* ed. David Farrell Krell (New York: Harper and Row, 1977).—Trans.]

5. This expression can be found in Levinas, *Autrement qu'être,* 2d ed., p. 10; *Otherwise than Being,* p. 8.

6. [This is an oblique reference to Maurice Blanchot's *L'entretien infini,* which has been published in English as *The Infinite Conversation,* trans. Susan Hanson (Minneapolis: University of Minnesota Press, 1993). The dialogue between Blanchot and Levinas lasted over 40 years.—Trans.]

7. Once again out of concern for "philological probity," to hearken this time to Nietzsche or Gershom Scholem.

8. ["God and Philosophy" was published in English most recently in Levinas, *Of God Who Comes to Mind.*—Trans.]

Initial Questions

1. A French translation of this 1924 text by Heidegger, "The Concept of Time," has since appeared in the issue of the *Cahier de l'Herne* devoted to Heidegger, 1991, no. 45. For the English translation, see Martin Heidegger, *The Concept of Time*, trans. William McNeill (Cambridge, Mass.: Blackwell Publishers, 1996).

2. "[We are writing] ess*a*nce with an *a* to designate the verbal sense of the word 'to be' or 'being': we mean here the effectuation of being, *Sein* as opposed to the *Seiendes.*" Emmanuel Levinas, *De Dieu qui vient à l'idée*, 2d ed. (Paris: Librairie philosophique J. Vrin, 1986), p. 78 n. 1; in English, "From the Carefree Deficiency to the New Meaning," in Emmanuel Levinas, *Of God Who Comes to Mind*, trans. Bettina Bergo (Stanford, Calif.: Stanford University Press, 1998), p. 43 and p. 195 n. 1. The preliminary "Note" to Otherwise than Being was lexically or orthographically less daring, although the thinking was exactly the same: "The dominant tone, necessary to the understanding of this discourse, and even its title, must be emphasized at the threshold of this book, although it may be frequently repeated at the heart of the work, as well: the term *essence* there expresses being [*l'être*] that is different from beings [*l'étant*], the German *Sein*, distinct from *Seiendes*, the Latin *esse* distinct from the Scholastics' *ens*. We have not dared to write *essance* as the history of the language would require, wherein the suffix *-ance*, coming from *antia* or from *entia*, gave rise to abstract nouns for action." (Emmanuel Levinas, *Autrement qu'être, ou au-delà de l'essence*, 2d ed. [The Hague: Martinus Nijhoff, 1978], "Note préliminaire," p. ix; in English, *Otherwise than Being, or Beyond Essence*, trans. Alphonso Lingis [Dordrecht: Kluwer Academic, 1991], "Note," p. xli.) We note, but simply for curiosity's sake, that in that work one finds the term *essance* written out once (ibid., p. 81; Eng., p. 65). This is a matter of mere curiosity, to be sure, because it is clear that this is a typographical error!

3. Vladimir Jankélévitch, *La mort* (Paris: Flammarion, 1966).

4. For these two lectures, all citations from Plato come from Léon Robin's translation, *Platon: Oeuvres complètes* (Paris: Bibliothèque de la

Pléiade, Gallimard, 1950). [I follow Robin's French translation for consistency with the text.—Trans.]

5. [Here at this early point in the French text, Levinas has already begun to use a rhetorical style that is characteristic of him, especially in his works after *Totality and Infinity: An Essay on Exteriority* (1961). The French style combines a wealth of comparatives and superlatives—his "method of emphasis" by which meaning is conveyed otherwise than by ordinary predication—and paratactic constructions from which the verb "to be" is omitted. Combined with the emphasis, the parataxis effectively conveys the excess of meaning of which he will speak throughout this course (see the lecture of May 21, 1976, "To Conclude: Questioning Again"). And the dropping of constructions such as "This is" or "It is" deliberately keeps his listener from setting his claims into an ordinary predicative logic, as though what he is trying to say really could be said simply. It is all to the contrary; what Levinas will attempt to express, especially in the May 14th and May 21st lectures, where he sketches his own philosophy most clearly, is, as he repeats, inexpressible, scarcely thinkable. This unique style is of the greatest significance to a philosophy in which expression and content are one. However, using it consistently in the English would perhaps create more confusion than does using it in the French, where certain grammatical possibilities make such stylistic work somewhat more accessible.—Trans.]

What Do We Know of Death?

1. [*Adieu* expresses the definitive "farewell" in French. But *à Dieu* also connotes a movement toward God, or the conferral of something upon or giving of someone to God.—Trans.]

The Death of the Other ['D'Autrui'] and My Own

1. Michel Henry, *Essence de la manifestation*, 2 vols. (Paris: P.U.F., 1963); in English, *The Essence of Manifestation*, trans. Girard Etzkorn (The Hague: Martinus Nijhoff, 1973).

2. [The state Levinas is characterizing as nonintentional and as a static nonstate is the emotional state being examined in this lecture, not the sensible state posited by the sensualist empiricists.—Trans.]

3. [The French texts reads, "mais inquiétude où s'interroge une interrogation inconvertible en réponse . . . "—Trans.]

4. ["Nearness," or *proximité*, is the mode by which an other concerns

me ethically. Therefore his "nearness" can approach me without being tautological.—Trans.]

5. [Levinas will speak on many occasions of "l'intrigue de . . . " The noun *intrigue* is translated as "plot" in Emmanuel Levinas, *Otherwise than Being, or Beyond Essence*, trans. A. Lingis (Dordrecht: Martinus Nijhoff, 1991); see, for example, p. 48 ("the plot of proximity") and p. 190 n. 34, which explains the sense of "plot" here. Levinas will also speak of the "intrigue of subjectivity," the "intrigue of hope," and the "intrigue of being" in this text. In the sense of a plot or situation, in which forces and elements are brought together and mingled, "intrigue" emphasizes the complexity and multiple elements in these combinations. However, Levinas would also have us be aware of the Latin sense of *intricare*, "to entangle." The intrigue of subjectivity thus denotes both the complex weaving of components of the "I" and also their entangled aspect, making it difficult to speak of something as a definitive principle or predicate in the cases of "intrigues."—Trans.]

6. ["I," which Levinas writes in French as *Moi*, means the personal or intimate "I" as affected by the other without understanding the other. It does not mean the "I" of one's social or cultural system of roles; neither is it strictly the Freudian *Ich*, or Ego.—Trans.]

An Obligatory Passage: Heidegger

1. See Emmanuel Levinas, *Autrement qu'être, ou au-delà de l'essence*, 2d ed. (The Hague: Martinus Nijhoff, 1978), pp. 49–55; in English, *Otherwise than Being, or Beyond Essence*, trans. Alphonso Lingis (Dordrecht: Kluwer Academic, 1991), pp. 38–43.

2. See Emmanuel Levinas, *De Dieu qui vient à l'idée*, 2d ed. (Paris: Librairie philosophique J. Vrin, 1986), pp. 81–82; in English, *Of God Who Comes to Mind*, trans. Bettina Bergo (Stanford, Calif.: Stanford University Press, 1998), pp. 45–46.

3. [See Martin Heidegger, *Letter on Humanism*, trans. Frank A. Capuzzi and J. Glenn Gray, in *Martin Heidegger: Basic Writings from "Being and Time" (1927) to "The Task of Thinking" (1964)*, ed. David Farrell Krell (New York: Harper and Row, 1977), pp. 193–242.—Trans.]

4. [See ibid., pp. 222, 224ff.—Trans.]

5. [*Metaphysics* A, 2, 983a11, states, "We begin by wondering that things are as they are." Aristotle, *Metaphysics*, trans. W. D. Ross (Oxford: Oxford University Press, 1958), 1: 121.—Trans.]

6. [Heidegger's *Ereignis* also plays on the sense of the prefix *er-*, which

intensifies the meaning of a verb to which it is attached, and on the sense of *eignis*, whose verbal form *etwas zu sich eignen* implies an appropriation of something, or an act by which one makes something one's own. In this case, then, the event of being, the event that being as a question "is," is also the act by which the being concerned with the question makes being his own by way of the question.—Trans.]

7. [*Eigentlich* is the adverb denoting the quality of what is most proper to one. It denotes the quality of what is *eigen*, or "own." By extension it could be rendered as "authentic," but this would emphasize a certain truth about or claim to "realness," to the neglect of all connotations of the proper, the ownmost.—Trans.]

8. *Uneigentlich* has been frequently translated as "inauthentic."

9. ["Alongside of" is the mode by which *Dasein* finds itself among the objects of the world. Here "alongside of" is implicit in the expression Levinas gives for being in the world.—Trans.]

10. Levinas is referring to Heidegger's 1924 text "The Concept of Time." See above, note 1 for "Initial Questions," the lecture of November 7, 1975.

11. [Aristotle, *Physics* IV, 11, 219b.—Trans.]

The Analytic of 'Dasein'

1. [Levinas's term *signifiance* is not a word one finds frequently in French. The French term *signification* denotes "what a term means" or the act of signifying that meaning. It is sometimes translated as "significance," but that lends to it the connotation of "importance." Throughout this volume, I have translated *signification* as "signification" to preserve the active dimension of the French term. I translate *signifiance* as "meaningfulness" or, at times, as "significance" to underscore the sense implicit in its nominal cognate *signifiant*.—Trans.]

2. [French differentiates between "*le* geste," which denotes a gesture, a sign, or a movement of the body, and "*la* geste," which refers to the medieval epic poems recounting the exploits or adventures of a single hero, for example *La chanson de Rolland*. I therefore translate *la geste* throughout the text as "the epic" or "the adventure" of being.—Trans.]

3. [Levinas is underscoring the indicative participial quality of be*ing*, or *esse*, by writing not "essence" but "ess*a*nce." For further discussion of his use of the term *essance*, see above, note 2 for the lecture "Initial Questions," November 7, 1975; and below in Part II, the lecture "Being and Meaning," November 14, 1975.—Trans.]

4. [Stéphane Mallarmé, "Le tombeau d'Edgar Poe," in *Mallarmé: The Poems*, trans. Keith Bosley (New York: Penguin, 1977), p. 175. The French verse reads, "Tel qu'en Lui-même l'éternité le change, . . . "—Trans.]

5. Martin Heidegger, *Etre et temps*, trans. Emmanuel Martineau (Paris: Authentica, 1985, privately circulated edition), § 46, p. 176. (The Martineau translation was chosen as the source for French citations throughout the present volume, though it appeared after Levinas's course itself.) In German, *Sein und Zeit* (Tübingen: Max Niemeyer Verlag, 1963), p. 236. The English edition, *Being and Time*, trans. John Maquarrie and Edward Robinson (New York: Harper and Row, 1962), here reads: "The possibility of this entity's Being-a-whole is manifestly inconsistent with the ontological meaning of care, and care is that which forms the totality of Dasein's structural whole" (p. 279).

6. Ibid.

'Dasein' and Death

1. [In logic, the *tiers-exclu* refers to "exclusive disjunction," i.e., either *a* or *b* is true, but not both.—Trans.]

2. [*Epos* denotes the body of poetry composing the tradition of a people.—Trans.]

3. [See my note 6 for "An Obligatory Passage: Heidegger," the lecture for November 28, 1975, above.—Trans.]

4. [Martin Heidegger, "Zeit und Sein," in *Zur Sache des Denkens* (Tübingen: Max Niemeyer Verlag, 1969). In English, *Martin Heidegger on Time and Being*, trans. Joan Stambaugh (New York: Harper and Row, 1972).—Trans.]

5. See Henri Maldiney, *Regard, parole, espace* (Lausanne: L'Age d'homme, 1973). [John Macquarrie and Edward Robinson translate *Vorhanden* and *Vorhandenheit* as "present-at-hand" and "presence-at-hand" respectively. The Maldiney interpretation of *Vorhandenheit* as something on exhibit or display accords well with remarks of Macquarrie and Robinson about the usual usage of these terms. See their note 1 in Heidegger, *Being and Time*, p. 48: "In ordinary German usage it may . . . be applied to the stock of goods which a dealer has 'on hand,' or to the 'extant' works of an author."—Trans.]

6. ["Ipseity" refers, in Levinas, to the precognitive, preconative self that is not taken up in the force of persevering in being, which characterizes "essence." "Ipseity" is the dynamic of the "other-in-the-same" or the "oneself that does not bear its identity as entities . . . thematized and ap-

pear{ing} to consciousness." See Emmanuel Levinas, *Otherwise than Being, or Beyond Essence*, trans. Alphonso Lingis (Dordrecht: Kluwer Academic, 1991), pp. 99–113.—Trans.]

7. [Levinas compare the cases of anxiety and fear more clearly below in "Death, Anxiety, and Fear," the lecture for January 16, 1976.—Trans.]

8. One cannot but recall here the title of an important essay by Levinas, "Énigme et phénomène" (1965), reprinted in Emmanuel Levinas, *En découvrant l'existence avec Husserl et Heidegger*, 2d ed. (Paris: Vrin, 1967). [Translated into English by Alphonso Lingis as "Phenomenon and Enigma," in *Collected Philosophical Papers of Emmanuel Levinas* (Dordrecht: Kluwer Academic, 1993), pp. 61–73. The Lingis translation was revised by Robert Bernasconi and Simon Critchley as "Enigma and Phenomenon," in *Emmanuel Levinas: Basic Philosophical Writings*, ed. and trans. Adriaan T. Peperzak, Simon Critchley, and Robert Bernasconi (Bloomington: Indiana University Press, 1996), pp. 65–77. Also see Emmanuel Levinas, *Discovering Existence with Husserl*, trans. Richard A. Cohen and Michael B. Smith (Evanston, Ill.: Northwestern University Press, 1998).—Trans.]

The Death and Totality of 'Dasein'

1. Martin Heidegger, *Etre et temps*, trans. Emmanuel Martineau (Paris: Authentica, 1985, privately circulated edition), § 47, p. 178. The German text reads: "*No one may take from another his dying.* One may, to be sure, 'go to death for an other,' but this never means more than this: one sacrifices oneself for the other '*in a determinate affair.*' On the other hand, such a dying can never signify that his death might be lifted in the least from the other." Martin Heidegger, *Sein und Zeit* (Tübingen: Max Niemeyer Verlag, 1963), p. 240.

2. [These words are said by Rodrigo in Corneille's *Le Cid*, act 2, scene 2: "La valeur n'attend pas le nombre des années."—Trans.]

3. [Levinas translates *übernehmen* with *saisir*, meaning to seize or to grasp. But *übernehmen* also means to take over, to take possession of, or to accept or assume.—Trans.]

4. Heidegger, *Etre et temps*, § 48, p. 182; *Sein und Zeit*, p. 245. [The English translation, Martin Heidegger, *Being and Time*, trans. John Maquarrie and Edward Robinson (New York: Harper and Row, 1962), reads, "Death is a way to be, which Dasein takes over as soon as it is" (p. 289). I follow the French text.—Trans.]

5. "Der Ackerman aus Böhmen" [The peasant from Bohemia], in Konrad Burdach, *Vom Mittelalter zur Reformation: Forschungen zur Geschichte der deutschen Bildung / im Auftrage der Preussischen Akademie der Wissenschaften* (Berlin: Weidmann, 1912), cited by Heidegger, *Sein und Zeit*, p. 245. [The English translation reads, "As soon as man comes to life, he is at once old enough to die." Heidegger, *Being and Time*, p. 289.—Trans.]

Being-Toward-Death as the Origin of Time

1. [Levinas consistently translates Heidegger's *Sein-zum-Tode* as *être-pour-la-mort*, literally "being-for-death," where *pour* connotes both "toward" and "in favor of." I follow the Maquarrie and Robinson translation, "being-*toward*-death," since the preposition "toward" underscores a dynamic sense of the expression better than would the preposition "for." Martin Heidegger, *Being and Time*, trans. John Maquarrie and Edward Robinson (New York: Harper and Row, 1962).—Trans.]

Death, Anxiety, and Fear

1. [For Heidegger's discussion of the "existentiell-existentiale" distinction, see Martin Heidegger, *Being and Time*, trans. John Maquarrie and Edward Robinson (New York: Harper and Row, 1962), §§ 9–12 (pp. 68–86), where it is considered in light of the meaning of *Dasein* and the ontic-ontological difference, and §§ 27–34 (pp. 163–211), which discusses it in light of concern with and for "others" and *Dasein*'s constitution.—Trans.]

2. [The French translation of *das Man* is *le On*, the "one" of anonymous descriptions and normativity, as in "one says" or "one does something."—Trans.]

3. Martin Heidegger, *Etre et temps*, trans. Emmanuel Martineau (Paris: Authentica, 1985, privately circulated edition), § 51, p. 187; in German, *Sein und Zeit* (Tübingen: Max Niemeyer Verlag, 1963), p. 254. [The English translation reads, "The 'they' does not permit us the courage for anxiety in the face of death" (Heidegger, *Being and Time*, p. 298). Because Levinas translates *Angst* as *angoisse*, rather than *anxiété*, I do not follow his choice and use "anguish," because the usual German terms for "anguish" are *Schmerz* and *Qual*, rather than *Angst*. "Anguish," moreover, does not connote the sentiments of agitation or dread that "anxiety" and *Angst* do.—Trans.]

Time Considered on the Basis of Death

1. Martin Heidegger, *Etre et temps,* trans. Emmanuel Martineau (Paris: Authentica, 1985, privately circulated edition), § 53, p. 192; in German, *Sein und Zeit* (Tübingen: Max Niemeyer Verlag, 1963), p. 262. [The English translation reads, "Death, as possibility, gives Dasein nothing to be 'actualized,' nothing which Dasein, as actual, could itself *be*." Martin Heidegger, *Being and Time,* trans. John Maquarrie and Edward Robinson (New York: Harper and Row, 1962), p. 307).—Trans.]

2. [Levinas's condensed French sentence reads, "Si être, c'est à-être, être, c'est être-pour-la-mort."—Trans.]

Inside Heidegger: Bergson

1. [John Macquarrie and Edward Robinson translate *Zu-sein* as "to be," in Martin Heidegger, *Being and Time* (New York: Harper and Row, 1962).—Trans.]

2. [Recall Levinas's use of Henri Maldiney's translation of *Vorhandenheit*: that which "appears as on exhibit." See above, note 5 for the lecture "*Dasein* and Death," December 12, 1975.—Trans.]

3. Henri Bergson, *Évolution créatrice,* in his *Œuvres* (Paris: P.U.F., 1970), pp. 724–25; in English, *Creative Evolution,* trans. Arthur Mitchell (New York: Random House, 1944), p. 295.

4. [See Henri Bergson, *Two Sources of Morality and Religion,* trans. R. Ashley Audra and C. Brereton (Westport, Conn.: Greenwood, 1974); and Bergson, *Creative Evolution,* pp. 3–108.—Trans.]

The Radical Question: Kant Against Heidegger

1. See Emmanuel Levinas, *Autrement qu'être, ou au-delà de l'essence,* 2d ed. (The Hague: Martinus Nijhoff, 1978), p. x. [In English, *Otherwise than Being, or Beyond Essence,* trans. Alphonso Lingis (Dordrecht: Kluwer Academic, 1991), p. xlii: "But *to hear a God not contaminated by Being* is a human possibility no less important and no less precarious than *to bring Being out of the oblivion* in which it is said to have fallen in metaphysics and in onto-theology."—Trans.]

2. I reread the following lines from *Otherwise than Being* as a counterpoint to this and the following chapter: "If one had the right to retain one trait from a philosophical system and neglect all the details of its ar-

chitecture (even though there are no details in architecture, according to Valéry's profound dictum, which is eminently valid for philosophical construction, where the details alone prevent collapse), we would think here of Kantianism, which finds a meaning to the human without measuring it by ontology and outside of the question, 'What is there here . . . ?' that one would like to take to be preliminary, outside of the immortality and death which ontologies run up against. The fact that immortality and theology could not determine the categorical imperative signifies the novelty of the Copernican revolution: a sense that is not measured by being or not being; but being on the contrary is determined on the basis of sense." Levinas, *Autrement qu'être*, p. 166; *Otherwise than Being*, p. 129.

A Reading of Kant (Continued)

1. See Georg Trakl, *La parole dans l'élément du poème*, cited in Martin Heidegger, *Acheminement vers la parole*, trans. Jean Beaufret, W. Brockmeier, and F. Fédier (Paris: Gallimard, 1976), pp. 39–83. In English, see Martin Heidegger, *On the Way to Language*, trans. Peter D. Hertz and Joan Stambaugh (New York: Harper and Row, 1971).

How to Think Nothingness?

1. See Eugen Fink, *Metaphysik und Tod* (Stuttgart: W. Kohlhammer, 1969), p. 722.

2. [H. Bergson, *Evolution créatrice*, in his *Œuvres* (Paris: P.U.F., 1970), p. 734. In English, *Creative Evolution*, trans. Arthur Mitchell (New York: Random House, 1944), p. 308, translation modified.—Trans.]

3. Edmund Husserl, *Idées directrices pour une phénoménologie*, trans. Paul Ricœur (Paris: Gallimard, 1950), § 117, p. 400. In German, *Ideen zu einer reinen Phänomenologie und phänomenologischen Philosophie* (The Hague: Martinus Nijhoff, 1952), p. 244. In English, *Ideas Pertaining to a Pure Phenomenology and to Phenomenological Philosophy, First Book*, trans. F. Kersten (Dordrecht: Kluwer Academic, 1982), p. 282.

Hegel's Response: The 'Science of Logic'

1. [For a discussion of the word *essance*, see above, note 2 for the lecture "Initial Questions," November 7, 1975; and below in Part II, the lecture "Being and Meaning," November 14, 1975.—Trans.]

2. [See G. W. F. Hegel, *Hegel's Science of Logic*, trans. A. V. Miller (Atlantic Highlands, N.J.: Humanities Press International, 1969), bk. 1, pp. 67–78.—Trans.]

3. [Ibid., p. 73. Rolland cites from the French translation of the 1812 edition by Pierre-Jean Labarrière and G. Jarczyk, G. W. F. Hegel, *Science de la logique* (Paris: Aubier-Montaigne, 1972), p. 45. The original is on p. 12 of the German text, *Wissenschaft der Logik* (1812; Nuremberg: J. L. Schray, 1816).—Trans.]

4. It is Derrida who, as we know, proposed that we translate the untranslatable Hegelian *Aufhebung* by the term *relève*. The verb *relever* connotes the following: to set something upright or put it in good condition, to gather up, to set something in high relief, to orient it toward a height or give it greater value. [The noun *relève* adds the connotation of replacing something or someone with something, etc. The English "relieve" and "raising up" fail to capture such a wealth of meaning. See Jacques Derrida's essays "Différance" and "The Pit and the Pyramid," in *Margins of Philosophy*, trans. Alan Bass (Chicago: University of Chicago Press, 1982), pp. 19–20 n. 23 and p. 88 n. 16 (the French texts were first published in 1972). Bass leaves *relever* untranslated, arguing that the term "sublation," used in J. B. Baillie's translation of Hegel's *Phenomenology of Mind* (2d ed. {New York: Humanities, 1977}) "is misleading," whereas *relever* "*does* take account {of} the effect of *différance* in its double meaning {of conservation and negation}." Also note Derrida's remarks on *Aufhebung* in his essay on Levinas, "Violence and Metaphysics: Essay on the Thought of Emmanuel Levinas," in Jacques Derrida, *Writing and Difference*, trans. Alan Bass (Chicago: University of Chicago Press, 1978), pp. 113–14.—Trans.]

5. G. W. F. Hegel, *Lessons on the History of Philosophy*, trans. J. Sibree (New York: Dover, 1956).

6. Hegel, *Science of Logic*, p. 82. Levinas translates this passage, combining it with the following line, "only this intuiting itself, pure and empty."

7. [This is Levinas's terse commentary on § C, "Becoming," in Hegel's *Science of Logic*, chap. 1. Levinas capitalizes *d'ores et déjà* ("always and already"), which underscores the difference between, on the one hand, Hegel's nothing and becoming, and, on the other hand, Aristotle's nothingness.—Trans.]

8. [Hegel, *Science of Logic*, pp. 82–83; *Wissenschaft der Logik*, p. 23. I have followed the published English translation here rather than Le-

vinas's French translation. The latter introduces no Levinasian idiosyncrasies that would make it deviate significantly from the Miller translation.—Trans.]

9. Eugen Fink, *Metaphysik und Tod* (Stuttgart: W. Kohlhammer, 1969), p. 159.

Reading Hegel's 'Science of Logic' (Continued)

1. G. W. F. Hegel, *Hegel's Science of Logic*, trans. A. V. Miller (Atlantic Highlands, N.J.: Humanities Press International, 1969), p. 83. [In the French translation, *Science de la logique*, trans. Pierre-Jean Labarrière and G. Jarczyk (Paris: Aubier-Montaigne, 1972), the expression is "Leur vérité est donc ce mouvement où les deux sont différents, mais *par le truchement d'*une différence qui s'est dissoute." The bracketed words in the passage just quoted in the text, "the mediation of," thus come from the French that Levinas cites, and they concern the question of mediation, which is of great importance to Levinas's thought.—Trans.]

2. [The French title translates as "The Opposition of Being and Nothingness in Representation." Except in citations from Miller's English translation, I translate *néant* as "nothingness."—Trans.]

3. [The French translation adds, at the end of this sentence, a phrase that is not in the German original: "*nothingness purely in and for itself.*" The italics in the quotation in the text are Rolland's.—Trans.]

4. Hegel, *Science of Logic*, p. 83.

5. Ibid., p. 83; in French, Hegel, *Science de la logique*, p. 60; in German, G. W. F. Hegel, *Wissenschaft der Logik* (1812; Nuremberg: J. L. Schray, 1816), p. 24. [The English text here is quite different, so I follow the French.—Trans.]

6. Ibid., p. 83; German, p. 24. [Levinas adds the italics and the German expression.—Trans.]

7. Ibid., p. 84; German, p. 25.

From the 'Science of Logic' to the 'Phenomenology'

1. [Levinas is citing G. W. F. Hegel, *La phénoménologie de l'esprit*, trans. Jean Hyppolite (Paris: Aubier, 1941), 2: 14ff.; in English, see *Phenomenology of Spirit*, trans. A. V. Miller (Oxford: Clarendon, 1977), pp. 266ff.—Trans.]

2. [See, among Hegel's concluding remarks on Spirit and substance,

the following: "This last becoming of Spirit, *Nature*, is its living immediate Becoming; Nature, the externalized Spirit, is in its existence nothing but this eternal externalization of its *continuing existence* and the
movement which reinstates the *Subject*." Hegel, *Phenomenology of Spirit*,
p. 492.—Trans.]

3. [See ibid., pt. BB, "Spirit," sec. a, "The Ethical World: Human and
Divine Law," pp. 267ff.—Trans.]

4. Hegel, *Phénoménologie de l'esprit*, 2: 23; *Phenomenology of Spirit*,
pp. 272–73.

5. Ibid., p. 18; Eng., p. 269.

6. Ibid., p. 19; Eng., p. 269 [translation modified for fluency with Levinas's text.—Trans.].

7. Ibid., p. 19; Eng., pp. 269–70 [Levinas's italics; translation modified.—Trans.].

Reading Hegel's 'Phenomenology' (Continued)

1. G. W. F. Hegel, *La phénoménologie de l'esprit*, trans. Jean Hyppolite
(Paris: Aubier, 1941), 2: p. 21; in English, *Phenomenology of Spirit*, trans.
A. V. Miller (Oxford: Clarendon, 1977), p. 271. [Levinas italicizes "uni-
versal individuality" and "passive being-for-another."—Trans.]

2. Eugen Fink, *Metaphysik und Tod* (Stuttgart: W. Kohlhammer,
1969), p. 179.

The Scandal of Death: From Hegel to Fink

1. Eugen Fink, *Metaphysik und Tod* (Stuttgart: W. Kohlhammer, 1969),
pp. 179–208.

Another Thinking of Death: Starting from Bloch

1. Ernst Bloch, *Das Prinzip Hoffnung*, in his *Gesamtausgabe*, vol. 5
(Frankfurt am Main: Suhrkamp, 1959), p. 1608. In English, *The Princi-
ple of Hope*, trans. Neville Plaice, Stephen Plaice, and Paul Knight, vol. 3
(Cambridge, Mass.: MIT Press, 1986), p. 1359.

2. [See Michel Henry, *Marx* (Paris: Gallimard, 1976). In English,
Marx: A Philosophy of Human Reality, trans. Kathleen McLaughlin (Bloomington: Indiana University Press, 1983).—Trans.]

3. Levinas deliberately writes *marxien* rather than *marxiste* to avoid
the latter's dogmatic redolence.

4. [Note the way in which Levinas takes up, here and in subsequent lectures, Heidegger's discussion of the relation between thinking and being in responding to J.-P. Sartre. "Thinking," for Heidegger, "is bound to the advent of Being, to Being as advent." In Levinas's rethinking of ontology (principally Heidegger's), the alterity of the future, and of the other human being, will be what arrives or *l'à-venir*. See *Letter on Humanism*, trans. Frank A. Capuzzi and J. Glenn Gray, in *Martin Heidegger: Basic Writings from "Being and Time" (1927) to "The Task of Thinking" (1964)*, ed. David Farrell Krell (New York: Harper and Row, 1977), p. 241.—Trans.]

A Reading of Bloch (Continued)

1. Ernst Bloch, *Das Prinzip Hoffnung*, in his *Gesamtausgabe*, vol. 5 (Frankfurt am Main: Suhrkamp, 1959), p. 1388. In English, *The Principle of Hope*, trans. Neville Plaice, Stephen Plaice, and Paul Knight, vol. 3 (Cambridge, Mass.: M.I.T. Press, 1986), p. 1180.

2. Ernst Bloch, *Spuren* (Frankfurt am Main: Suhrkamp, 1967), pp. 274ff. [Levinas cites from the French translation, *Traces*, trans. H. Hildenbrand and P. Quillet (Paris: Gallimard, 1968), pp. 235–38. Trans.]

A Reading of Bloch: Toward a Conclusion

1. [The term "astonishment" is from the published English translation of Bloch's *Das Prinzip Hoffnung*. Regarding the citation, I modify the English translation to remain close to Levinas's text ("it gives space to the consciousness of a utopian aura in man"). See Ernst Bloch, *Das Prinzip Hoffnung*, in his *Gesamtausgabe*, vol. 5 (Frankfurt am Main: Suhrkamp, 1959), p. 1388. In English, *The Principle of Hope*, trans. Neville Plaice, Stephen Plaice, and Paul Knight, vol. 3 (Cambridge, Mass.: MIT Press, 1986), p. 1180.—Trans.]

2. See Leo Tolstoy, *War and Peace*, bk. 3, pt. 2, chap. 36.

3. [Levinas's French text says *lien*; I read this as a typo for *lieu*, in the phrase *lieu d'habitation humaine*, which I thus translate as "site of human habitation." See the last line of this paragraph.—Trans.]

4. Vladimir Jankélévitch, *La mort* (Paris: Flammarion, 1966), p. 383.

5. Ibid., p. 389.

6. Ibid., pp. 383–84.

7. Eugène Ionesco, *Le roi se meurt* (Paris: Gallimard, 1963), p. 112; cited in Jankélévitch, *La mort*, p. 390. In English, Eugène Ionesco, *Exit the King*, trans. Donald Watson (New York: Grove, 1963), p. 68.

8. Jankélévitch, *La mort*, p. 391. The expression is from Plato, *Symposium*, trans. Alexander Nehamas and Paul Woodruff (Indianapolis: Hackett, 1989), 207a.

To Conclude: Questioning Again

1. [For discussion of the word *essance*, see above, note 2 for the lecture "Initial Questions," November 7, 1975; and below in Part II, the lecture "Being and Meaning," November 14, 1975.—Trans.]

2. [Here, Levinas is explicitly playing on the dual meaning of *à Dieu*, for the "time" he is describing is given over to the Infinite; it is not of the world but of, or, in a sense, unto God. By the same token, it departs from the world to join nothing and is not assimilable to being, so the *à-Dieu* also signifies a "farewell" to being.—Trans.]

3. [Although throughout Levinas's works, his use of *autre* and the object case *autrui* often appears no more consistent than his use of capitalization with these terms, *Autre* refers paradoxically to the concept of what is beyond a concept, the other as transcendence, and *Autrui* tends to refer to the human other, to every other human being. The choice of these two terms is a matter of focus; they are two sides of the same coin. The idea of the infinite arises in the encounter with the human other, and it is the nonphenomenal force of the human other that so overcharges meaning that one conceives a word like "God." See Emmanuel Levinas, *Autrement qu'être, ou au-delà de l'essence*, 2d ed. (The Hague: Martinus Nijhoff, 1978), pp. 181–206; in English, *Otherwise than Being, or Beyond Essence*, trans. Alphonso Lingis (Dordrecht: Kluwer Academic, 1991), pp. 149–62. Also see Emmanuel Levinas, *De Dieu qui vient à l'idée*, 2d ed. (Paris: Librairie philosophique J. Vrin, 1986), pp. 94ff.; in English, *Of God Who Comes to Mind*, trans. Bettina Bergo (Stanford, Calif.: Stanford University Press, 1998), pp. 56ff.—Trans.]

4. [Although I use the indefinite pronoun "it" in reference to "the Other" and "the Same" here, "the other" will sometimes take a masculine pronoun because of Levinas's tendency to speak of the neighbor and the other in the same breath as he speaks of the "other man." Levinas's *Totality and Infinity* refers to the other as the "widow," the "stranger," the "orphan." Levinas does not think of ethical alterity—that of the face—as gender specific. Indeed, the ethical force of the face, as an interruption of the flow of "my" consciousness, is *not* phenomenal; it does not appear in the way that an entity does. Nevertheless, the "feminine" constitutes a

very specific mode of otherness in his work. There has been considerable discussion (too considerable to enumerate here) of this mode, and of the treatment of "the feminine" in Levinas's work. See Emmanuel Levinas, *"Time and the Other" and Additional Essays*, trans. Richard A. Cohen (Pittsburgh: Duquesne University Press, 1987), pp. 84–94 (lectures given 1946–47). Also see Emmanuel Levinas, *Totalité et infini: Essai sur l'extériorité* (The Hague: Martinus Nijhoff, 1961), pp. 232–51; in English, *Totality and Infinity: An Essay on Exteriority*, trans. Alphonso Lingis (Pittsburgh: Duquesne University Press, 1969), pp. 254–74.—Trans.]

5. [*Synopsie*, or "synopsia" in English, is a term found in nineteenth-century psychiatric literature, in which it denoted disorders related to "synesthesia"—the association of sensations of different natures, as when, for example, one hears colors. Levinas here uses "synopsia"—a virtual synonym for "synthesis"—to express the unifying force of consciousness that continually integrates the interruption he calls "diachrony." In this sense, "synopsia" has a strong Kantian resonance. (See Kant's use of "synopsis" in the "Transcendental Deduction," *Critique of Pure Reason* A94–95.) In Levinas, "synopsia" also points to the often-discussed passive synthesis that was Husserl's "ground" of intentionality; see Edmund Husserl, *On the Phenomenology of the Consciousness of Internal Time (1893–1917)*, trans. John Barnett Brough (Dordrecht: Kluwer Academic, 1991). Levinas uses the same term in *De Dieu qui vient à l'esprit*, pp. 100, 107, 214; *Of God Who Comes to Mind*, pp. 60, 64, 139. In this collection, see below in Part II, the lecture of May 14, 1976, "Outside of Experience."—Trans.]

Beginning with Heidegger

1. "Die onto-theo-logische Verfassung der Metaphysik" is the second part of Martin Heidegger, *Identität und Differenz* (Pfullingen: G. Neske, 1957); in English, *Identity and Difference*, trans. Joan Stambaugh (New York: Harper and Row, 1969). The French translation Levinas uses is "La constitution onto-théo-logique de la métaphysique," trans. A. Préau, in Martin Heidegger, *Questions I* (Paris: Gallimard, 1968).

2. See, for example, this remark from the second volume of Heidegger's *Nietzsche*: "The 'today,' calculated neither according to the calendar, nor according to the events of universal history, is determined on the basis of the time proper to the history of metaphysics: it is the metaphysical determination of historial humanity starting from the metaphysics of

Nietzsche." Martin Heidegger, *Nietzsche*, trans. Pierre Klossowski (Paris: Gallimard, 1971), 2: 201–2. In English, see *Nietzsche*, ed. and trans. David Farrell Krell, 4 vols. (New York: Harper and Row, 1979–87), 4: 195.

3. See *Das Ende der Philosophie und die Aufgabe des Denkens*, trans. Jean Beaufret and F. Fédier, in Martin Heidegger, *Questions IV* (Paris: Gallimard, 1976), pp. 112–57. In English, *The End of Philosophy*, trans. Joan Stambaugh, in *Martin Heidegger: Basic Writings from "Being and Time" (1927) to "The Task of Thinking" (1964)*, ed. David Farrell Krell (New York: Harper and Row, 1977), pp. 369–92.

4. "Language is at once the house of being and the home of human beings"—this is one of the first propositions of Martin Heidegger, *Lettre sur l'humanisme*, trans. R. Munier (Paris: Aubier-Montaigne, 1964), pp. 26–27. In English, *Letter on Humanism*, trans. Frank A. Capuzzi and J. Glenn Gray, in *Martin Heidegger: Basic Writings from "Being and Time" (1927) to "The Task of Thinking" (1964)*, ed. David Farrell Krell (New York: Harper and Row, 1977), p. 239.

5. See, in this regard, the illuminating remarks of Heidegger in "Protocole d'un séminaire sur la conférence 'Temps et être,'" trans. J. Lauxerois and C. Roëls, in Heidegger, *Questions IV*, pp. 58–59. In English, "Summary of a Seminar on the Lecture 'Time and Being,'" in *Martin Heidegger on Time and Being*, trans. Joan Stambaugh (New York: Harper and Row, 1972), p. 29–30. [The first printing of the German and French texts was in Martin Heidegger, *L'endurance de la pensée*, trans. F. Fédier (Paris: Plon, 1968).—Trans.]

6. [Regarding *relève*, see above in Part I, Levinas's lecture "Hegel's Response: The *Science of Logic*," of February 27, 1976, and note 4 for that lecture.—Trans.]

7. [See again Heidegger's late seminar, the title of which is itself eloquent: "The *End* of Philosophy and the *Task* of Thinking." The English translation by Joan Stambaugh appears in *Martin Heidegger: Basic Writings*, pp. 369–92.—Trans.]

8. [Levinas frequently plays on the Latin infinitive *esse* ("to be"), to suggest that, for example, a moral disinterestedness or non-egotism is at root the possibility of being uprooted from being, i.e., dis-inter-*esse*, and turned toward the Good. "Essement" here means the inevitable human state of existing within the economy of being.—Trans.]

9. The fact that the ethical, as preoriginal and prelogical, must *account for* onto-theo-logy, which is "less old than it" and which covers the ethical to the point of being forgotten, is one of the fundamental motifs

of *Otherwise than Being*, to which we shall return. But here we may already cite some clarifying sentences from that work:

> The Reduction nowise means to dissipate or explain some "transcendental appearance." The structures with which it begins are ontological. . . . But here the reduction of the Said to the Saying, beyond the *Logos*, beyond being and non-being—beyond essence—beyond the true and the non-true—the reduction to signification, to the one-for-the-other of responsibility (or more precisely of substitution), to the site or non-site, the site and non-site, the utopia of the human dimension; this reduction to restlessness in the literal sense of the term, or in its diachrony, which, despite all its assembled forces, despite all the simultaneous forces in its union, being cannot make eternal. The subjective and its Good could not be comprehended on the basis of ontology. On the contrary, starting from the subjectivity that is the Saying, the signification of the Said will be interpretable. It will be possible to show that it is only a question of the Said and of being because the Saying or responsibility call for justice. In this way alone shall justice be rendered to being; in this way alone shall we comprehend the assertion—which, when taken literally, is strange—that by injustice "all the foundations of the earth are shaken." In this way alone shall truth be rendered to the ground of disinterestedness that permits us to separate truth from ideology.

Emmanuel Levinas, *Autrement qu'être, ou au-delà de l'essence*, 2d ed. (The Hague: Martinus Nijhoff, 1978), pp. 57–58; in English, *Otherwise than Being, or Beyond Essence*, trans. Alphonso Lingis (Dordrecht: Kluwer Academic, 1991), p. 45. [I have modified the translation here to remain closer to the capitalizations and parataxis of the French text, which largely drops the copula "to be" and proceeds as if unsaying a predicative, thematizing discourse.—Trans.]

Being and Meaning

1. See "La constitution onto-théo-logique de la métaphysique," trans. A. Préau, in Martin Heidegger, *Questions I* (Paris: Gallimard, 1968), p. 290; in English, *Identity and Difference*, trans. Joan Stambaugh (New York: Harper and Row, 1969), p. 55. [Translation modified for fluency with the French text.—Trans.]

2. *Otherwise than Being* speaks of what "does not escape the same order, does not escape Order." *Autrement qu'être, ou au-delà de l'essence*, 2d ed. (The Hague: Martinus Nijhoff, 1978), p. 9; in English, *Otherwise than Being, or Beyond Essence*, trans. Alphonso Lingis (Dordrecht: Kluwer Academic, 1991), p. 9.

3. See Plato, *Meno* 82b.

4. [Levinas appears to mean the following: If I speak in a human fashion at all, and even if I speak of a relation with what is beyond being, then in both cases, I must use classical Greek rationality.—Trans.]

5. Such a remark partially explains Levinas's attachment to Michel Henry's research, particularly as it is expressed in Emmanuel Levinas, *Essence de la manifestation*, 2 vols. (Paris: P.U.F., 1963); in English, *Essence of Manifestation*, trans. Girard Etzkorn (The Hague: Martinus Nijhoff, 1973). This work seeks to think of being in its *manifestation*. Levinas devoted a seminar to this book during the academic year 1976–77.

6. [See Immanuel Kant, *Critique of Pure Reason*, trans. Norman Kemp Smith (New York: Saint Martin's, 1963), p. 113.—Trans.]

7. This privilege of Greek, as the language of the universal, and for this reason of the university, is constantly asserted by Levinas. One finds this even outside his philosophical work, in a Talmudic lesson such as "La traduction de l'Écriture," in which he argues that the Torah can be translated only into Greek. The essay is printed in Emmanuel Levinas, *A l'heure des nations* (Paris: Minuit, 1988); in English, *In the Time of the Nations*, trans. Michael B. Smith (Bloomington: Indiana University Press, 1994).

8. "Para-doxical" is to be taken here in the obvious sense of the term, and yet it likewise indicates a way of thinking that contrasts with doxical thinking; it is a Husserlian *terminus technicus* the best explanation for which is no doubt furnished by § 117 of the *Ideas*.

9. This remark of Aristotle's recalls the beginning of "Dieu et la philosophie," in Emmanuel Levinas, *De Dieu qui vient à l'idée*, 2d ed. (Paris: Librairie philosophique J. Vrin, 1986), p. 94; in English, "God and Philosophy," in Emmanuel Levinas, *Of God Who Comes to Mind*, trans. Bettina Bergo (Stanford, Calif.: Stanford University Press, 1998), p. 55.

10. On the word "ess*a*nce," see above in Part I, the lecture "Initial Questions," November 7, 1975.

11. Several texts contemporary with this course have meditated on this repose of the firm ground of the earth as a fundamental fact.

Being and World

1. [The French *explication* is also Jacques Derrida's translation of *Auseinandersetzung*, which is little clarified in English if we translate it as "explanation." Alan Bass translates *Auseinandersetzung* as "coming to terms critically"; see Jacques Derrida, *Margins of Philosophy*, trans. Alan Bass

(Chicago: University of Chicago Press, 1982), p. 37. Given the prolonged, extensive conversation between Levinas and Derrida, there is little doubt that Levinas is thinking here of Derrida's use of *explication* for *Auseinandersetzung*. (I thank Michael Nass for his insight into *explication*.)—Trans.]

2. Plato, *Timæus* 37c.

3. For this meaning of the "interplanetary voyage," see Levinas's essay "Heidegger, Gagarin et nous," in Emmanuel Levinas, *Difficile liberté*, 2d ed. (Paris: Albin Michel, 1976); in English, "Heidegger, Gagarin and Us," in *Difficult Freedom: Essays on Judaism*, trans. Seán Hand (Baltimore: The Johns Hopkins University Press, 1990), pp. 231–34.

4. In this same sense, *Of God Who Comes to Mind* will pose this question. See Emmanuel Levinas, *De Dieu qui vient à l'idée*, 2d ed. (Paris: Librairie philosophique J. Vrin, 1986), p. 164; in English, *Of God Who Comes to Mind*, trans. Bettina Bergo (Stanford, Calif.: Stanford University Press, 1998), p. 104.

5. The notes that I [Rolland] have consulted to draw up this text have written on them: "It is of the essence of repose to show itself, and of the essence of its activity to be synthetic." But we must recall that the preliminary note of *Otherwise than Being*, after specifying the meaning of the word *essence* (see the first lecture in this book, "Initial Questions," November 7, 1975), adds the following: "We shall carefully avoid using the term *essence* and its derivations in their traditional usage. For *essence, essential, essentially*, we will say *eidos*, eidetic, eidetically, or nature, quiddity, fundamental, etc." ("Note préliminaire," in Emmanuel Levinas, *Autrement qu'être, ou au-delà de l'essence*, 2d ed. [The Hague: Martinus Nijhoff, 1978], p. ix; in English, "Note," in *Otherwise than Being, or Beyond Essence*, trans. Alphonso Lingis [Dordrecht: Kluwer Academic, 1991], p. xli.) It is out of faithfulness to that remark that I have here replaced "essence" with "nature." I mean a faithfulness that is neither complacency nor coquetry, for the simple reason that the language of *Otherwise than Being* (which Levinas admits is "barbaric" or deliberately incorrect) is an integrated whole, and that this seminar belongs to the former's philosophical space in sharing that language.

6. We cannot give references here because Levinas has, in a single sentence, run through the entirety of Hegel's *Phenomenology of Spirit*, from the first pages of "Sense Certainty" to the very last pages of the book, devoted to "Absolute Knowledge."

7. This is the entire meaning of Edmond Husserl, *Logique formelle et Logique transcendentale*, trans. Susanne Bachelard (Paris: P.U.F., 1957).

The original German text was first published in 1929. In English, *Formal and Transcendental Logic*, trans. Dorion Cairns (The Hague: Martinus Nijhoff, 1969).

8. In this regard, see Edmund Husserl, *Leçons pour une phénoménologie de la conscience intime du temps*, trans. H. Dussort (Paris: P.U.F., 1964). In English, *On the Phenomenology of the Consciousness of Internal Time (1893–1917)*, trans. John Barnett Brough (Dordrecht: Kluwer Academic, 1991). The original German text was first published in 1928.

To Think God on the Basis of Ethics

1. See Martin Heidegger, *Etre et temps*, trans. Emmanuel Martineau (Paris: Authentica, 1985, privately circulated edition), §§ 52–53, pp. 187–94; in English, Martin Heidegger, *Being and Time*, trans. John Maquarrie and Edward Robinson (New York: Harper and Row, 1962), pp. 299–311.

2. See Pierre Aubenque, *Le problème de l'être chez Aristote: Essai sur la problématique aristotélicienne* [The problem of being in Aristotle] (Paris: P.U.F., 1972), p. 330: "God is the only theologian, or, at least, there is no perfect theology except of him. . . . Now, we know what this doubly divine theology consists in: as the knowledge of God by God, it is knowledge only of God, since it would be unworthy of God to think something other than Himself [*que Soi-même*]."

3. [At the risk of a certain distortion of Levinas's own intention, I have given this sentence a subject-verb structure. The French original reads simply, "Une *transcendance* qui ne reviendrait pas au remplissement d'une visée par une vision?"—Trans.]

4. In light of this, see Emmanuel Levinas, *Autrement qu'être, ou au-delà de l'essence*, 2d ed. (The Hague: Martinus Nijhoff, 1978), p. 109; in English, *Otherwise than Being, or Beyond Essence*, trans. Alphonso Lingis (Dordrecht: Kluwer Academic, 1991), p. 86 [translation modified—Trans.]: "The neighbor as other would not be preceded [*ne se laisse pas précéder*] by any precursor who would describe or announce his silhouette. He does not appear. . . . Absolving himself from all essence, from every genus and every resemblance, the neighbor, *the first come*, concerns me for the first time (even if he were an old acquaintance, an old friend, old love, and long since implicated in the fabric of my social relationships), *in a contingency that excludes the a priori*." (I [Rolland] italicize the last words, which propose to our thinking the excess of a *before the a priori*).

5. Recall that in Latin, "hostage" is said to be *obses*, which designates the hostage as a prisoner of war.

6. This is what Levinas, in the most recent years [late 1980s and early 1990s—Trans.], has called *holiness* [*sainteté*], finding in this notion the only or the ultimate *incontestable*; and this, despite the lessons of "modern anti-humanism" that Levinas discusses in *Autrement qu'être*, p. 164; *Otherwise than Being*, pp. 127–28.

7. To my [Rolland's] mind, it is in this opposition that the difference between Levinas's two great works, *Totality and Infinity* and *Otherwise than Being*, is focused. The first work is a phenomenology of the I [*Moi*], which is I in a world in which it encounters the other who overthrows it and places it in question in its initial innocence. The second work proceeds to the archeology of this I, in order to discover the "me" [*moi*], already altered by alterity. "The infinite does not signal itself to a subjectivity, a unity already formed, by its order to turn toward the neighbor. In its *being* subjectivity undoes *essence* by substituting itself for another." Emmanuel Levinas, *Autrement qu'être, ou au-delà de l'essence*, 2d ed. (The Hague: Martinus Nijhoff, 1978), p. 16; in English, *Otherwise than Being, or Beyond Essence*, trans. Alphonso Lingis (Dordrecht: Kluwer Academic, 1991), p. 13.

8. [Rolland has added the word *battement* here, which I translate as "striking or beating," between brackets. I suggest two words because the other does not "strike" within the same, but a clock does not "beat" the hour. See the following note, by Rolland.—Trans.]

9. See Judges 13:25, in regard to Samson: "Then the spirit of Yahweh began to agitate him, in Mahaneh-dan, between Zorah et Eshtaol." The text uses the verb *pa'am* ("to agitate," "to strike against," or again "to beat" in the sense in which the heart beats), which gives us the noun *po'am* ("beating, pulsation"); and *pa'amon*, which signifies the clock, has the same root. (I [Rolland] thank Ariane Kalfa for indicating this etymology.) Here, and in the following pages, unless otherwise indicated, all citations from the Bible are taken from *La Bible*, ed. É. Dhorme (Paris: Bibliothèque de la Pléiade, 1956). [Except for names, I follow Rolland's citation for consistency with the text.—Trans.]

The Same and the Other

1. [The French term *l'intrigue* has frequently been translated, adequately enough, into English as "the plot." However, because "plot" does not always connote the complexity, even mystery and secrecy, connoted by the French term, I prefer "intrigue" here.—Trans.]

2. It seems to me [Rolland] that, in this notion of the me "escaping its concept," we find one of the marks of Levinas's Rosenzweigian inspi-

ration. I am thinking in particular of a page from the famous *Urzelle* of 1917, which I must cite at length:

> Once it [philosophy,—J. Rolland] has gathered up everything into itself, and has proclaimed its universal existence, man suddenly discovers that he, who has long since completed his philosophical digestion, discovers that he is still there. And he is surely not there as a man carrying the palms of victory . . . but as "I" ["*Je*"], and as an "I who am dust and ashes." I, as the private subject altogether general, I as noun and pronoun, I dust and ashes, I am still there. And I philosophize: that is to say that I have the impudence of passing through the sieve of the dominant universal philosophy that philosophy is. Philosophy did not even make me say [dust and ashes] to myself directly, but only by the intermediary of the man holding the palm in his hand: I, a noun and pronoun, I should be silent, quite simply; but thereupon, the man haloed in his victory, the same man because of whom philosophy had covered me with embarrassment, that man was humiliated by philosophy in his turn, and she [philosophy] shrunk altogether before a few unfortunate ideas, only then to engulf these ideals in the Absolute—and then, suddenly, I come, me, as though nothing had happened, and, like Grabbe (19th century playwright), I illuminate the entirety of the last act. *Individuum ineffabile triomphans.* It is not that he "might do philosophy" that is the astonishing thing, it is simply that he is still there, that he still dares to breathe, that he "does."

From the original core of Franz Rosenzweig, *The Star of Redemption*, trans. J.-L. Schlegel, in Jacques Rolland, ed., *Cahiers de la nuit surveillée*, 1982, no. 11: 101.

3. [By this hyphenation, Levinas underscores the root of the verb "conceive," in Latin *capere*, "to grasp." To conceive is to grasp by forming a concept from disparate or related elements.—Trans.]

4. This "special passivity" is that which, in *Otherwise than Being*, is exasperated to the point of being said to be "more passive," "more passive than any passivity," etc. This amounts neither to a password nor to a *flatus vocis*, but, all to the contrary, has a meaning sufficiently precise to qualify as a veritable *terminus technicus*. As Levinas says in a note, "The passivity of affection is more passive than the radical receptivity Heidegger speaks of in connection with Kant, where the transcendental imagination offers the subject an 'alcove' or 'cavity' [*alvéole*] of nothingness in order to precede the given and assume it" (Emmanuel Levinas, *Autrement qu'être, ou au-delà de l'essence*, 2d ed. [The Hague: Martinus Nijhoff, 1978], p. 111 n. 25, p. 88 in the text; in English, *Otherwise than Being, or Beyond Essence*, trans. Alphonso Lingis [Dordrecht: Kluwer Academic, 1991], p. 192 n. 25 [translation modified—Trans.]). It is clearly to Heidegger's first *Kantbuch* that Levinas is alluding. (See Martin Heidegger, *Kant and the Problem of*

Metaphysics, trans. J. Churchill [Bloomington: Indiana University Press, 1962]. The French translation was published in 1953.) This specification is decisive, for it is precisely in thinking a passivity that *does not take charge* of what it undergoes that Levinas breaks with Western thought, here including Heidegger. This entire course, as well as *Autrement qu'être* and the texts belonging to its manner of expression, cannot be understood unless one takes account of this essential specification.

5. The expression comes from Jean La Fontaine, *Fables* (Paris: Gallimard, 1954), book 2, fable 11, "Le lion et le rat": "Patience et longueur de temps / Font plus que force ni que rage." ["Time for what patience first began, / Is better than embattled strength." *The Fables of La Fontaine*, trans. Marianne Moore (New York: Viking, 1965), p. 45.—Trans.]

The use of these verses is characteristic of a certain use that Levinas makes, not only of poetry, but of what he calls "national literatures," one of whose wonders is to have inscribed in our language a number of formulas, locutions, and expressions that hold a particular authority, as only a proverbial language could do, itself being admired as a mine of resources for the philosopher-writer.

6. This notion of the "fear of God"—which is not firstly a fear of chastisement [*châtiment*] (and in this sense a fear *for oneself,* which is what *both* fear *and* anguish are in Heidegger)—is found in several of Levinas's texts from the beginning of the 1980s. See especially "Du langage religieux et de la crainte de Dieu," in Emmanuel Levinas, *L'au-delà du verset* (Paris: Minuit, 1982); in English, "On Religious Language and the Fear of God," trans. Gary D. Mole, in Emmanuel Levinas, *Beyond the Verse: Talmudic Readings and Lectures* (Bloomington: Indiana University Press, 1994).

7. It is therefore not for nothing that a book (which, at its origin, was a series of talks) could receive for its title, precisely, *Time and the Other.* This book's thinking is found in the course that inaugurates this volume, but evidently not without modifications. On this problem, which is not simple, see the explanations provided in my [Rolland's] Afterword.

8. "The phenomenon of transcendence" is quite evidently an *abuse of language* (which in Levinas is the contrary of a pejorative notion). Transcendence—as an enigma and not a phenomenon, to borrow the title from an essay by Levinas (in Emmanuel Levinas, *En découvrant l'existence avec Husserl et Heidegger* [Paris: Vrin, 1967]; in English, *Discovering Existence with Husserl,* trans. Richard A. Cohen and Michael Smith [Evanston, Ill.: Northwestern University Press, 1998])—contrasts with phenomenality, even if this *contrasting with* itself requires a certain phe-

nomenology, which describes the "phenomenological circumstances" of transcendence. This is remarkably put in the first lines of the foreword of Emmanuel Levinas, *De Dieu qui vient à l'idée*, 2d ed. (Paris: Librairie philosophique J. Vrin, 1986), pp. 7ff.; in English, *Of God Who Comes to Mind*, trans. Bettina Bergo (Stanford, Calif.: Stanford University Press, 1998), p. xi. Transcendence requires a certain phenomenology or a counter-phenomenology, as I [Rolland] tried to show in the chapter devoted to Levinas's "Theology," in Jacques Rolland, *Parcours de l'autrement: Lecture d'Emmanuel Levinas* (Paris: P.U.F., 2000).

9. [Levinas devoted several essays to the authors mentioned, with the exception of Feuerbach. See the following works: Emmanuel Levinas, *Noms propres* (Montpellier: Fata Morgana, 1976); in English, *Proper Names*, trans. Michael B. Smith (Stanford, Calif.: Stanford University Press, 1996). And Emmanuel Levinas, *Hors sujet* (Montpellier: Fata Morgana, 1987); in English, *Outside the Subject*, trans Michael B. Smith (Stanford, Calif.: Stanford University Press, 1994).—Trans.]

10. See Descartes's letter to Friar Mersenne, January 28, 1641, in René Descartes, *Œuvres et lettres* (Paris: Bibliothèque de la Pléiade, Gallimard, 1953), p. 1111: "I have read through Mr. Morin's short book, whose principal fault is that it treats everywhere of the infinite, as though its spirit were above, and it had been able to comprehend the properties of the infinite, which is a fault common to all; one that I attempt to avoid carefully, for I have never treated of the infinite except in order to submit to it, and not to determine what it is, or what it is not." [Cf. "Author's Replies to the Fourth Set of Objections," in *Descartes: Philosophical Letters*, ed. and trans. Anthony Kenny (Minneapolis: University of Minnesota Press, 1981).—Trans.]

11. Amos 3:8.

12. Maurice Blanchot, "Discours sur la patience," *Le nouveau commerce*, nos. 30–31 (1975): 21. This fragment was reprinted with most of the others composing this text in Maurice Blanchot, *L'écriture du désastre* (Paris: Gallimard, 1980); in English, *The Writing of the Disaster*, trans. Anne Smock (Lincoln: University of Nebraska Press, 1995).

The Subject-Object Correlation

1. We must therefore think that the *in* already has the structure of the *in* of the in-finite, at once *within* the finite and, as nonfinite, *outside* the finite. See the subsequent lectures in this work, and "Dieu et la philosophie," in Emmanuel Levinas, *De Dieu qui vient à l'idée*, 2d ed. (Paris: Li-

brairie philosophique J. Vrin, 1986), pp. 106–12; in English, "God and Philosophy," in *Of God Who Comes to Mind*, trans. Bettina Bergo (Stanford, Calif.: Stanford University Press, 1998), pp. 64–67.

2. We can see that subjectivity is here the decisive word and notion for the thinking of *Otherwise than Being*, and of the texts of the same time, among which we find the present two courses. In this regard, note the following initial remarks in *Otherwise than Being*: "Otherwise than being. It is a question of stating the bursting open of a destiny that reigns in essence, and whose fragments and modalities, despite their diversity, belong to each other; that is, they do not escape the same order, as they do not escape Order. . . . It is up to us to think of the possibility of being torn out of essence. . . . We must, *consequently* [*dès lors*], show that the exception of the 'other than being'—beyond the not-being—*signifies subjectivity*, or humanity, the oneself who repels the annexations by essence." Emmanuel Levinas, *Autrement qu'être, ou au-delà de l'essence*, 2d ed. (The Hague: Martinus Nijhoff, 1978), p. 9, Rolland's italics. [I follow the French text here, for consistency with the present note.—Trans.]

3. This remark is clarified in the first paragraph of chapter 5 in Levinas, *Autrement qu'être*, "La signification et la relation objective," pp. 167–78; *Otherwise than Being*, "Signification and the Objective Relation," pp. 131–40.

4. In Levinas's texts from this period, *apparoir* functions as a *terminus technicus* that amounts to "manifestation," a term used by Michel Henry. Levinas admired Henry's way of conceiving the essence of "manifestation"; see above, note 4 for the lecture "Being and Meaning," November 14, 1975.

5. This is a perfectly Heideggerian remark; in this regard, see the last lines of his Thor Seminar in 1969, trans. Jean Beaufret, in Martin Heidegger, *Questions IV* (Paris: Gallimard, 1976), pp. 305–6. In particular, note this sentence: "Being, in order to be opened up, needs man as the There of its manifestation."

6. See Plato, *Phædo* 68b, in particular: "Will he not be glad to make that journey? We must suppose so, my dear boy, that is, if he is a real philosopher, because then he will be of the firm belief that he will never vend wisdom in all its purity in any other place."

The Question of Subjectivity

1. On Kant, see the following lecture, as well as those of February 1976 above in Part I, "Death and Time."

2. Thus, in Hegel, being comprises a subject essential to its course of

being, to the point that Spirit needs a Phenomenology to become what it is: a substance that is a subject knowing itself absolutely. (This note is a remark from the course itself.—Rolland).

3. The word is taken here in the technical sense used by Heidegger after the *Kehre*. [The *Kehre* is the turn toward approaching being, not from Dasein but from Being itself as *Ereignis*, or event.—Trans.]

4. [See above in Part I, note 5 for "To Conclude: Questioning Again," the lecture for May 21, 1976.—Trans.]

5. See again Pierre Aubenque, *Le problème de l'être chez Aristote: Essai sur la problématique aristotélicienne* (Paris: P.U.F., 1972), pp. 335ff.

6. "The essence of communication is not a modality of the essence of manifestation." Emmanuel Levinas, *Autrement qu'être, ou au-delà de l'essence*, 2d ed. (The Hague: Martinus Nijhoff, 1978), p. 62 n. 34; in English, *Otherwise than Being, or Beyond Essence*, trans. Alphonso Lingis (Dordrecht: Kluwer Academic, 1991), p. 190 n. 34.

7. See Martin Heidegger, *Unterwegs zur Sprache* (Frankfurt am Main: V. Klostermann, 1985). In French, *Acheminement vers la parole*, trans. F. Fédier (Paris: Gallimard, 1976), p. 16. In English, *On the Way to Language*, trans. Peter D. Hertz and Joan Stambaugh (New York: Harper and Row, 1971). [The first essay in the German text is omitted from the English edition but may be found in Martin Heidegger, *Poetry, Language, Thought*, trans. Alfred Hofstadter (New York: Harper and Row, 1971).—Trans.]

8. [See Martin Heidegger, *Lettre sur l'humanisme*, trans. R. Munier (Paris: Aubier-Montaigne, 1964), p. 139 n. 1. This note is not in the English translation—*Letter on Humanism*, trans. Frank A. Capuzzi and J. Glenn Gray, in *Martin Heidegger: Basic Writings from "Being and Time" (1927) to "The Task of Thinking" (1964)*, ed. David Farrell Krell (New York: Harper and Row, 1977)—but see p. 239: "Being is the protective heed that . . . houses ek-sistence in language."—Trans.]

9. In making this remark, Levinas cited, *sotto voce*, 1 Kings 19:11–13: "And see that Yahweh passes. A strong wind stirs the mountains and breaks the rocks before Yahweh; but Yahweh is not in the wind. And after the wind, an earthquake, a fire; but Yahweh is not in the fire. And after the fire, the sound of a light breeze. As soon as he heard it, Elijah covered his face with his coat and went out." Regarding the possible biblical influences on the Heideggerian reading of the Greeks, see the work of Marlène Zarader, *La Dette impensée: Heidegger et l'héritage hébraïque* (Paris: Le Seuil, 1990).

10. See Martin Heidegger, *Der Satz vom Grund* (Pfullingen: G. Neske, 1957), p. 160. In English, *The Principle of Reason*, trans. Reginald Lilly (Bloomington: Indiana University Press, 1991), p. 107: "Λέγειν . . . means to gather, to lay one beside the other."

11. And it is in this sense that being requires a *receptivity*, and not the "special passivity" that Levinas is looking for. See, in this regard, the remark from *Of God Who Comes to Mind*: "Our Western 'passivity' is a receptivity that is followed by a taking charge [*assomption*]." Emmanuel Levinas, *De Dieu qui vient à l'idée*, 2d ed. (Paris: Librairie philosophique J. Vrin, 1986), p. 142; in English, *Of God Who Comes to Mind*, trans. Bettina Bergo (Stanford, Calif.: Stanford University Press, 1998), p. 89.

Kant and the Transcendental Ideal

1. Immanuel Kant, *Kritik der reinen Vernunft* (Hamburg: Felix Meiner, 1971), B 76; in English, *Critique of Pure Reason*, trans. Norman Kemp Smith (New York: St. Martin's, 1963), p. 93.

2. Ibid., B 391; Eng., p. 323.

3. Ibid., B 696; in French, Immanuel Kant, *Critique de la raison pure*, trans. A. Tremesaugues and B. Pacaud, 6th ed. (Paris: P.U.F., 1968), p. 467, Rolland's italics. [I follow the French translation here for fluency with the text. Kemp Smith's translation of this section, "The Final Purpose of the Natural Dialectic of Human Reason," (*Critique of Pure Reason*, p. 549), is as follows: "The ideas of pure reason can never be dialectical in themselves; any deceptive illusion to which they give occasion must be due solely to their misemployment. For they arise from the very nature of our reason; and it is impossible that this highest tribunal of all the rights and claims of speculation should itself be the source of deceptions and illusions. Presumably, therefore, the ideas have their own good and appropriate vocation as determined by the natural disposition of our reason."—Trans.]

4. Ibid., B 696; Eng., p. 550, Rolland's italics.

5. Ibid., B 601; French, p. 419. In Kemp Smith's translation see p. 489. The latter reads, "the predicates are not merely compared with one another logically, but the thing itself is compared, in transcendental fashion, with the sum of all possible predicates."

6. Ibid., B 608; French, p. 419. Kemp Smith's English translation, p. 493, is as follows: "Now, if we pursue this idea further and make of it a hypostasis, we will be able to determine the originary being by the con-

cept of supreme reality, as a single, simple being, sufficient to all things, eternal, etc., in a word, we shall determine it in its unconditioned perfection by its predicates. The concept of such a being is that of *God*, conceived in a transcendental sense, and thus the ideal of pure reason is the object of a transcendental *theology*, as I indicated above."

7. Ibid.

Signification as Saying

1. [See Emmanuel Levinas, *Autrement qu'être, ou au-delà de l'essence*, 2d ed. (The Hague: Martinus Nijhoff, 1978), pp. 47ff., 195–206; in English, *Otherwise than Being, or Beyond Essence*, trans. Alphonso Lingis (Dordrecht: Kluwer Academic, 1991), pp. 37ff., 153–62.—Trans.]

2. This is again one of the points of proximity between Levinas and Heidegger: the break with the thinking of foundations; this is at least as radical in the first as it is in the second figure, about whom commentaries have been so insistent and prolix. Let us note, however, that when Levinas breaks with the thinking of foundations, it is still another *rationality* that he is seeking.

3. See the reference to Heidegger, *Being and Time*, § 47, above in Part I, the lecture "Death and Totality of *Dasein*," December 19, 1975, note 1.

4. [The French verb *désappointer* means "disappointed" in the English sense of being discontented or having one's hopes deceived; but it retains the tones of its original meaning of *dés-appointé*, or divested of position or possessions. To preserve that richness of sense, I have hyphenated the word here.—Trans.]

5. In Levinas's first philosophical reflection, published as *De l'évasion* [On evasion, first published in 1935—Trans.], he had already attempted implicitly to find, on the basis of "nausea," a facticity that broke with its Heideggerian concept in that it would not turn immediately back into a project, an *Entwurf.* See my commentary on this work, in Emmanuel Levinas, *De l'évasion*, ed. and annotated by Jacques Rolland (Montpellier: Fata Morgana, 1982), pp. 21ff.

6. [The term *susception* is a *terminus technicus* for Levinas, who coins it from the prefix *sus-*, or "beneath," and *capere*, "to be taken or seized"; *susception* is thus to be in the grasp of responsibility, in a time that no memory discerns, beneath everyday consciousness as intentionality. The term does not belong to a typical French vocabulary, yet its meaning is clear; Alphonso Lingis translates it as "susceptiveness." See Levinas, *Autrement*

qu'être, pp. 157, 174, 176; *Otherwise than Being,* pp. 122, 136, 138, and below, note 4 for the lecture "Freedom and Responsibility," February 27, 1976.—Trans.]

7. As in the case of Jean-Paul Sartre's "authentic Jew," who can and must *choose* the situation that is *made for him,* according to the arguments of his *Réflexions sur la question juive* (Paris: Gallimard, 1985); in English, *Anti-Semite and Jew,* trans. George Becker (New York: Schocken Books, 1995). Again, what Levinas is looking for, this time with our birth, which turns philosophically into the concept of *creaturality,* is a situation of passivity without any taking charge: "The 'creaturality' of the subject cannot become a representation of the creation." See Emmanuel Levinas, *Humanisme de l'autre homme* (Montpellier: Fata Morgana, 1972), p. 108 n. 17.

8. This can be explained by the way in which *sensibility* is conceived in *Otherwise than Being,* which constitutes a veritable subversion of the way in which that notion was thought in Levinas's *Totality and Infinity.* On this point see my analyses in Jacques Rolland and Silvano Petrosino, *La vérité nomade* (Paris: La Découverte, 1984), pp. 44–48.

9. [The reflexive *se* could be translated as "itself" or "himself," giving us "to exile itself," etc. However, such a translation would obscure the passive quality of these circumstances, even though "to be exiled" introduces the verb "to be" where it is least appropriate. See Levinas, *Autrement qu'être,* p. 177; *Otherwise than Being,* p. 138.—Trans.]

10. Simone Weil, *Attente de Dieu* (Paris: Gallimard, 1950), p. 205; in English, *Waiting on God,* trans. Emma Craufurd (London: Routledge and Kegan Paul, 1979); cited in Levinas, *Autrement qu'être,* p. 176 n. 3; *Otherwise than Being,* p. 198 n. 3. Lingis translates this appeal, "father take from me this body. . . . "

Ethical Subjectivity

1. The fundamental thought of the 1962 lecture "Zeit und Sein" ("Temps et être," trans. F. Fédier, in Martin Heidegger, *Questions IV* [Paris: Gallimard, 1976]) is to show that, although being is always the being *of a being* or entity, it must nevertheless be thought *without the entity,* otherwise than as only the *foundation of the entity.*

2. "But to hear a God not contaminated by Being is a human possibility no less important and no less precarious than to bring Being out of the oblivion in which it is said to have fallen in metaphysics and in onto-

theology." This is the last line of the "Note préliminaire" in Emmanuel Levinas, *Autrement qu'être, ou au-delà de l'essence*, 2d ed. (The Hague: Martinus Nijhoff, 1978), p. x; in English, "Note," in *Otherwise than Being, or Beyond Essence*, trans. Alphonso Lingis (Dordrecht: Kluwer Academic, 1991), p. xlii.

3. See Martin Heidegger, *Vorträge und Aufsätze* (Pfullingen: Verlag Günther Neske, 1967). In French, see Martin Heidegger, *Essais et conférences*, trans. A. Préau (Paris: Gallimard, 1969), p. 214. In English, see Martin Heidegger, *Basic Writings: From "Being and Time" (1927) to "The Task of Thinking" (1964)*, ed. David Farrell Krell (New York: Harper and Row, 1977), p. 170.

4. G. W. F. Hegel, *Encyclopédie des sciences philosophiques*, trans. B. Bourgeois (Paris: Vrin, 1970), p. 191.

5. On the way in which Marx and Heidegger can be thought together and as distinct, see above all the work of K. Axelos, *Einführung in ein Künftiges Denken* (Tübingen: Niemeyer, 1966).

6. [Alphonso Lingis translates *en deçà*, as it occurs in *Otherwise than Being*, as "on the hither side." For Levinas's remarks on this concept, see *Autrement qu'être*, p. 138 n. 11; *Otherwise than Being*, p. 195: "On the hither side of {personal freedom}, the I is itself, does not belong to Being or history, is neither an effect at rest nor a cause in movement." —Trans.]

7. With these remarks, we come to a new critical point in Levinas's thought. For a discussion of this point, see the previous course, "Death and Time."

Transcendence, Idolatry, and Secularization

1. Levinas is anything but a thinker of the *sacred*. On the contrary, he opposes this concept to the *holy*, for example in the title of his second collection of five Talmudic readings, *Du sacré au saint* (Paris: Minuit, 1977), the translation of which would be "From the Sacred to the Holy." These readings are combined with an earlier collection of Talmudic interpretations (*Quatre lectures talmudiques* [Paris: Minuit, 1968]) in Emmanuel Levinas, *Nine Talmudic Readings*, trans. Annette Aronowicz (Bloomington: Indiana University Press, 1990).

The Hebrew term for "holy," *kadosh*, has for its etymological sense "the separated." Thus the inscription of the name of God itself would be the original inscription of the difference. Note that we can read Levinas as a thinker of secularization, looking to grasp the opportunity provided to thought by the death of a certain God, tenant of the world-behind-the-world. In this respect, his is a thought that is fundamentally not so far from Jean-Luc Marion's problematic, such as it was explored in Marion's, *L'idole et la distance* (The idol and distance) (Paris: Grasset, 1976), or in his *Dieu sans l'être: Hors-texte* (Paris: Fayard, 1982). The second work has been translated into English as *God Without Being: Hors-Texte*, trans. Thomas A. Carlson (Chicago: University of Chicago Press, 1991).

2. Recalling the etymology of the Latin *re-ligio*: "scrupulous attention" or "veneration."

3. Aristotle, *Metaphysics* A, 2, 983 a13. [The Greek is θαυμάζειν, which W. D. Ross translates as "wonder." See *Aristotle's Metaphysics: A Revised Text with Introduction and Commentary*, trans. W. D. Ross (Oxford: Clarendon, 1958), vol. 1, 983 a13.—Trans.]

4. For the philosophical meaning of economy, recall section 2 of *Totality and Infinity*, "Interiority and Economy," which describes the life of the I [*Moi*] in its world as an *economy*. Emmanuel Levinas, *Totalité et infini: Essai sur l'extériorité* (The Hague: Martinus Nijhoff, 1961), pp. 81–158; in English, *Totality and Infinity: An Essay on Exteriority*, trans. Alphonso Lingis (Pittsburgh: Duquesne University Press, 1969) 109–83.

5. [See Rabelais, "The Fourth Book of the Heroic Deeds and Sayings of the Good Pantagruel," chaps. 57 and 62, in *The Complete Works of François Rabelais*, trans. Donald M. Frame (Berkeley: University of California Press, 1991). Levinas's concept of the universality of the economic is, in brief, that concrete human hunger, as need *and* desire, drives all activities of the economic life that "opens to being." See Levinas, *Totalité et infini*, pp. 82–90; *Totality and Infinity*, pp. 110–17.—Trans.]

6. These remarks should allow us to understand that technology has, in Levinas, a *philosophical* meaning, not simply a technical or instrumental one, and this perhaps may be thought not "according to its essence" but from the point of view of its meaning. Heidegger's attacks upon every technical conception of technology could therefore not touch Levinas. For the development of his discussion of technology, see Emmanuel Levinas, "Sécularisation et faim," in Enrico Castelli, ed., *Herméneutique de la sécularisation: Actes du Colloque organisé par le Centre International d'Études humanistes* (Paris: Aubier, 1976), pp. 101–9. In English, "Secularization and Hunger," trans. Bettina Bergo, *Graduate Faculty Philosophy Journal*, 20, no. 2–21, no. 1 (1998).

Don Quixote: Bewitchment and Hunger

1. This is right in line with Levinas's distinction, which cannot be repeated enough, between receptivity and passivity "more passive than any passivity."

2. Recall, in this respect, that Levinas's *Totality and Infinity* had for its subtitle "An Essay on Exteriority." This is perhaps one of the reasons for the critique of this work that Levinas wrote after its first appearance. Today his internal critique is found in "Préface à l'édition allemande," reprinted in Emmanuel Levinas, *Entre nous: Essais sur le penser-à-l'autre* (Paris: Grasset, 1991); in English, *Entre Nous: Essays on Thinking-of-the-Other*, trans. Michael B. Smith and Barbara Harshav (New York: Columbia University Press, 1998).

3. Miguel de Cervantes, *Don Quixote (The Ormsby Translation)*, ed. J. R. Jones and K. Douglas (New York: W. W. Norton, 1981), chap. 46, p. 365.

4. Ibid.

5. Ibid., p. 366.

6. See chap. 46.

7. No doubt! But the Evil Genius such as Levinas interprets it. See Emmanuel Levinas, *Totalité et Infini: Essai sur l'extériorité* (The Hague: Martinus Nijhoff, 1961), pp. 62–74; in English, *Totality and Infinity: An Essay on Exteriority*, trans. Alphonso Lingis (Pittsburgh: Duquesne University Press, 1969), 90–101.

8. Cervantes, *Don Quixote*, p. 366: They "covered their faces and disguised themselves in one way or another. Thus they would seem to Don Quixote quite unlike the persons he had seen in the castle. . . . When [Don Quixote] awoke with a start, he was unable to move and invariably conjured up before him, taking it into his head that all these shapes were phantoms of the enchanted castle and that he himself was unquestionably enchanted."

9. Ibid., pp. 381–82.

10. According, that is, to Levinas, *Totality and Infinity*, hunger is already taken up in the essential *enjoyment* [*jouissance*] that is eating.

11. See, as a counterpoint, the following lines from Emmanuel Levinas, "The Thought of Martin Buber and Contemporary Judaism." Here, in the form of humor, Levinas's fundamental debate with the author of *I and Thou* comes through: "One may wonder whether dressing those who are naked and feeding those who are hungry do not bring us closer to the neighbor than the ether in which Buber's Encounter some-

times stands. Saying 'Thou' [*'Tu'*] goes through my body here and now, all the way to the hands that give, beyond the organs of the voice. This is in keeping with the tradition of Maine de Biran and conforms to the biblical truths. We must not go empty handed toward the face of God. It is also consistent with the Talmudic texts, which proclaim that 'to give another something to eat' is a great thing, and loving God with all one's heart and all one's life is surpassed again when one loves God with all one's money. Ah! Jewish materialism!" Reprinted in Emmanuel Levinas, *Hors sujet* (Montpellier: Fata Morgana, 1987), pp. 32–33; in English, *Outside the Subject,* trans. Michael B. Smith (Stanford, Calif.: Stanford University Press, 1994), p. 19.

Subjectivity as An-Archy

1. "An-archy" must be understood in two ways: First, as what does not result from an ἀρχή, and thus what *Otherwise than Being* calls the preoriginal. Second, as anarchy and anarchism in the obvious sense, contesting the power of the State; which likewise gives to prophetism another meaning. [See Emmanuel Levinas, *Autrement qu'être, ou au-delà de l'essence,* 2d ed. (The Hague: Martinus Nijhoff, 1978), pp. 151ff., 157ff. 185ff.; in English, *Otherwise than Being, or Beyond Essence,* trans. Alphonso Lingis (Dordrecht: Kluwer Academic, 1991), pp. 118ff., 122ff., 145ff.—Trans.]

2. "Le cœur de Danko," or "Danko's Heart."

3. The notion of substitution is the object of chapter 4 of *Otherwise than Being.* That chapter, as the prefatory "Note" indicates, is the "centerpiece" of the book. See Levinas, *Autrement qu'être,* p. ix; *Otherwise than Being,* p. xli.

4. Shakespeare, *Hamlet,* act 2, scene 4, verses 593–94: "What is Hecuba to him, or he to Hecuba / That he should weep for her?"

5. The Fichtean thesis is explained by the simple consideration that "the I {*Moi*}, like the non-I {*Non-Moi*} is the product of an originary act of the I, and consciousness itself is the product of the first originary act of the I, of the self-positing of the I." Johann Fichte, *Principes de la doctrine de la science,* trans. A. Philonenko, in Fichte's *Œuvres choisies de philosophie première* (Paris: Vrin, 1972), p. 28. [I follow the French text to avoid confusion between Levinas's notion of the "self" and the English use of the term here. In the published English translation, the passage reads: "Both self and not-self are alike products of original acts of the self, and consciousness itself is similarly a product of the self's first original act, its

own positing of itself." Johann Fichte, "Fundamental Principles of the Entire Science of Knowledge," in *J. G. Fichte: The Science of Knowledge with the First and Second Introductions*, trans. Peter Heath and John Lachs (New York: Cambridge University Press, 1982), p. 107.—Trans.]

6. And it is in this sense that "the psyche is already a psychosis." [See Levinas, *Autrement qu'être*, p. 181; *Otherwise than Being*, p. 142: "The psyche, a uniqueness outside of concepts, is a seed of folly, already a psychosis. It is not an ego, but me under assignation."—Trans.]

7. [The French *pâtir* and *passion* share the same root, which refers, through the Latin, to the Greek πάσχειν, "to undergo, to suffer."—Trans.]

8. On this point, see below, the lecture of May 21, 1976, "A God 'Transcendent to the Point of Absence'" (pp. 219–24) and note 10 for that lecture. Also see below, note 3 for the lecture "Outside of Experience," May 14, 1976.

9. Eugen Fink, especially his book *Metaphysik und Tod*, is mentioned often in the first course transcribed in this book, "Death and Time." Yet it is to his work *Le jeu comme symbole du monde* (The game as a symbol of the world), trans. Hans Hildenbrand and Alex Lindenberg (Paris: Minuit, 1966), that Levinas is here referring. The German original is *Spiel als Weltsymbol* (Stuttgart: W. Kohlhammer, 1960). For Jeanne Delhomme, see, above all, the essay that Levinas devotes to her in his *Noms propres* (Montpellier: Fata Morgana, 1976), pp. 57–64; in English, *Proper Names*, trans. Michael B. Smith (Stanford, Calif.: Stanford University Press, 1996), pp. 47–54. For a debate about the two thinkers, see H. Valavanidis-Wybrands's essay "Manière de dire," in *Cahiers de la nuit surveillée*, 1991, no. 4, the issue devoted to Delhomme.

10. It is therefore not for nothing that Dostoyevski entitled one of the chapters of his *The Devils* "The Sins of the Other."

11. This is the response that Cain gives to God in Genesis 4:9. Dostoyevski places it in Ivan's mouth in *The Brothers Karamazov*; see the translation by David McDuff (New York: Penguin, 1993), pt. 2, bk. 5, chap. 3.

12. The prehistory of the "I" is found in Levinas's *Totality and Infinity*, which his *Otherwise than Being* undertook to write at length.

13. "I am you, if I am I." Paul Celan, "Lob der Ferne," in *Gesammelte Schriften*, vol. 1 (Frankfurt am Main: Suhrkamp, 1986), p. 33. Translated into French by Maurice Blanchot in "Le dernier à parler," *Revue des Belles Lettres*, 1972, nos. 2–3: 177. [This passage is also cited by Levinas as the epigraph to chapter 4, "Substitution," in his *Autrement qu'être*, p. 125; *Otherwise than Being*, p. 99.—Trans.]

Freedom and Responsibility

1. We should take this in the oft-repeated sense of "the passivity more passive than receptivity."

2. [See below, notes 1 and 7 for "The Extra-Ordinary Subjectivity of Responsibility," the lecture of March 12, 1976.—Trans.]

3. It is on the basis of *this* election that the election of Israel may be understood; the latter, like the reverence due to a former president, signifies something altogether different from domination and self-certainty.

4. [The term *susception*, which is not in current French usage, could be also translated, awkwardly, as "to sub-ceive," following the Latin *suscipere*, "to take from below, to undergo." It belongs to a collection of critical terms Levinas uses, built upon the root *capere*, "to grasp or to take" (see above in Part II, note 4 for the lecture of December 12, 1975, "The Same and the Other," and note 11 for the lecture of January 9, 1976, "The Question of Subjectivity"). *Susception* expresses a pure vulnerability without agent or object. See above in Part II, note 6 for "Signification as Saying," the lecture of January 23, 1976.—Trans.]

5. *Diachrony* is a *temporality*, originally and in a profoundly anti-Husserlian manner; it is because of this that neither the past nor the future have their origin in a present moment.

6. It is this survival that Levinas admired in Vassily Grossman's *Life and Fate: A Novel* ([New York: Harper and Row, 1986], trans. Robert Chandler), where, in the mind of a man half-mad (Ikonnikov), a "little goodness without ideology" proves stronger than the malignancy of the executioners.

7. We hereby understand the profound anti-Freudianism of Levinas!

8. [Levinas means "declines" in the sense in which one declines a noun or pronoun, here the accusative "me."—Trans.]

9. It is on this question of self-affectivity that Levinas breaks decisively with Michel Henry, while admiring his philosophical work. Moreover, we can understand why there might not be causality here, since we are in the midst of a thinking *without foundations*.

10. See Emmanuel Levinas, *Autrement qu'être, ou au-delà de l'essence*, 2d ed. (The Hague: Martinus Nijhoff, 1978), pp. 156–66; in English, *Otherwise than Being, or Beyond Essence*, trans. Alphonso Lingis (Dordrecht: Kluwer Academic, 1991), pp. 121–30.

11. A redoubtable boredom, according to the last pages of Levinas, *Autrement qu'être*, pp. 207–8; *Otherwise than Being*, pp. 175–76: "But the

imperturbable essence, equal and indifferent to all responsibility which it henceforth encompasses, turns, as in insomnia, from this neutrality and equality into monotony, anonymity, insignificance, into an incessant buzzing that nothing can now stop and which absorbs all signification, *even that of which this bustling about is a modality.* Essence stretching on indefinitely, without any possible halt or interruption . . . is the horrifying *there is* behind all finality proper to the thematizing ego, which cannot sink into the essence it thematizes." [For the notion of the *there is* (*il y a*), see Emmanuel Levinas, *De l'existence à l'existant* (Paris: Vrin, 1947; 2d ed., 1978), and Levinas's remarks in the "Preface to the Second Edition." In English, *Existence and Existents,* trans. Alphonso Lingis (The Hague: Martinus Nijhoff, 1978).—Trans.]

12. This smothering or suffocation is what Levinas, in 1935, had already grasped in his analysis of nausea. See Emmanuel Levinas, *De l'évasion,* ed. and annotated by Jacques Rolland (Montpellier: Fata Morgana, 1982), passim.

The Ethical Relationship as a Departure from Ontology

1. On the Saying as a *terminus technicus,* see, above all, Emmanuel Levinas, *Autrement qu'être, ou au-delà de l'essence,* 2d ed. (The Hague: Martinus Nijhoff, 1978), pp. 167–78; in English, *Otherwise than Being, or Beyond Essence,* trans. Alphonso Lingis (Dordrecht: Kluwer Academic, 1991), pp. 131–40.

2. This reversal is precisely what overturns the reasoning of Levinas's *Totality and Infinity.*

3. [Just as Levinas wants to speak of the lived "me" (*moi*) of responsibility and being for-the-other, in contrast to the *concept* of the I or the capitalized "*Moi,*" he appears to refer, here, to his concept of the Other or "*Autrui.*"—Trans.]

4. This denial of singularity is also a way of ignoring Hegel—while also acknowledging him, as we see in Levinas, *Autrement qu'être,* pp. 223–24; *Otherwise than Being,* pp. 176–78—by thus insisting upon the *particularity* to which Hegel denies all legitimacy. This is, in other words, a way of being Rosenzweigian.

5. In this regard, see the forceful lines of Levinas, *Autrement qu'être,* p. 164; *Otherwise than Being,* pp. 127–28.

6. This society appears with the first *socius,* or social formation, which is called not the other [*autrui*] but the third party [*le tiers*]. This is the

whole reversal that comes about in Levinas, *Autrement qu'être*, starting from page 200 (*Otherwise than Being*, p. 157).

7. [The French term *conscience* denotes at once "consciousness" and "conscience."—Trans.]

8. We must here recall the last page of *Otherwise than Being*, a sentence of which we cite: "In any case nothing less is needed, for the little humanity that adorns the world—even if this were only pure politeness or a pure polish of morals." Levinas, *Autrement qu'être*, p. 233; *Otherwise than Being*, p. 185 [translation modified—Trans.].

9. [That is, a limitation of responsibility that occurs thanks to the third party.—Trans.]

10. See in this regard the lectures of February 1976, in Part I, "Death and Time."

The Extra-Ordinary Subjectivity of Responsibility

1. But we must emphasize that this is the point that is difficult to think: this break—which is *originary*—is the very identification of the me [*moi*] who is not I [*Moi*]; it is the subjectivity of the subject.

2. Or if, as in Heidegger, "ἦθος means abode, dwelling place." See Martin Heidegger, *Letter on Humanism*, trans. Frank A. Capuzzi and J. Glenn Gray, in *Martin Heidegger: Basic Writings from "Being and Time" (1927) to "The Task of Thinking" (1964)*, ed. David Farrell Krell (New York: Harper and Row, 1977), p. 233; in French, *Lettre sur l'humanisme*, trans. R. Munier (Paris: Aubier-Montaigne, 1964), p. 145.

3. This is Levinas's question: how can the *word* "God," how can the Name of God, *take on a meaning*? See the first lines of Emmanuel Levinas, *De Dieu qui vient à l'idée*, 2d ed. (Paris: Librairie philosophique J. Vrin, 1986), pp. 7ff.; in English, *Of God Who Comes to Mind*, trans. Bettina Bergo (Stanford, Calif.: Stanford University Press, 1998), Foreword, pp. xiff.

4. This is so by the very fact of the intentional character of *Erlebnis*, such as Husserl describes it in § 88 of the *Ideen*. See Edmund Husserl, *Idées directrices pour une phénoménologie*, trans. Paul Ricœur (Paris: Gallimard, 1950), pp. 303ff.; in English, *Ideas Pertaining to a Pure Phenomenology and to Phenomenological Philosophy, First Book*, trans. F. Kersten (Dordrecht: Kluwer Academic, 1982), pp. 213–26.

5. [Edmund Husserl, *Recherches logiques*, trans. H. Élie, A.I. Kelkel, and R. Schérer (Paris: P.U.F., 1972), vol. 2, pt. 2, p. 268; in English, *Log-*

ical Investigations, trans. John N. Findlay (London: Routledge and Kegan Paul, 1970), vol. 2, pt. 2, p. 743.—Trans.]

6. See F. Dostoyevski, *The Brothers Karamazov*, trans. David McDuff (New York: Penguin, 1993), pt. 2, bk. 6, chap. 2.

7. "The psyche . . . is . . . already a psychosis," says *Otherwise than Being*, in the same sense. See Emmanuel Levinas, *Autrement qu'être, ou au-delà de l'essence*, 2d ed. (The Hague: Martinus Nijhoff, 1978), p. 181; in English, *Otherwise than Being, or Beyond Essence*, trans. Alphonso Lingis (Dordrecht: Kluwer Academic, 1991), p. 142.

8. In saying *Me voici*, *Autrement qu'être* is recalling the biblical expression *hineni* and referring to Isaiah 6:8: "Here I am, send me," explaining that "here I am" means "send me." See Levinas, *Autrement qu'être*, p. 186 and n. 11; *Otherwise than Being*, p. 146 and p. 199 nn. 11, 17. [Note that "send me" or even "behold me" serves better than "here I am" in preserving the accusative of the French "*me* voici," which originally arises from the components *(tu) me vois ici*, or "(you) see me here."—Trans.]

9. Song of Songs 2:5; 5:8.

10. On the meaning of money, see the last pages of the 1954 essay "Le moi et la totalité," translated as "The I and the Totality," in Emmanuel Levinas, *Entre Nous: Essays on Thinking-of-the-Other*, trans. Michael B. Smith and Barbara Harshav (New York: Columbia University Press, 1998).

11. Nothing would be worse than to interpret Levinas as a "philosopher of dialogue." That represents his entire debate with Buber, to which his texts in the following volumes bear witness: Emmanuel Levinas, *Proper Names*, trans. Michael B. Smith (Stanford, Calif.: Stanford University Press, 1996), and Emmanuel Levinas, *Outside the Subject*, trans. Michael B. Smith (Stanford, Calif.: Stanford University Press, 1994).

The Sincerity of the Saying

1. See above in Part II, the lecture "The Ethical Relationship as a Departure from Ontology," March 5, 1976.

2. [The emphasis here is on the contrast between a passive, unlimited exposition and an *act*, willed or intentional, of exposition. The Saying that turns back on itself and does not make itself into a statement of theme is without agency or substance.—Trans.]

3. [The French text reads, " . . . faire signe de ce dont on fait signe sans se reposer dans sa figure de signe."—Trans.]

4. So, too, there is an iteration of awakening, which must wake up

the sleeplessness or waking [*l'éveil*], as the sole manner by which to keep it from going back to sleep and growing fat or becoming middle-class, according to the expressions of the texts collected in Emmanuel Levinas, *De Dieu qui vient à l'idée*, 2d ed. (Paris: Librairie philosophique J. Vrin, 1986); in English, *Of God Who Comes to Mind*, trans. Bettina Bergo (Stanford, Calif.: Stanford University Press, 1998).

5. [We think here of a line from Blanchot: "I did not want to defame the truth by what is truer than itself." Maurice Blanchot, *Au moment voulu* (Paris: Gallimard, 1951), p. 83; in English, *When the Time Comes*, trans. Lydia Davis (Barrytown, N.Y.: Station Hill, 1985), p. 230.—Trans.]

6. Or, as Levinas proposed one morning in December 1970, never to repeat this audacity in public: it would be a "thinking without reflecting." In other words, it is a thinking that *is not* νόησις precisely because it thinks *more* than itself.

7. It seems to me [Rolland] that here—whether voluntarily or not, it makes no difference!—Levinas confirms the *anarchists'* sense of an-archy. We should not forget, in effect, that "they are without principle" was Stalin's fundamental charge against those situated to his "left."

8. [For a discussion of the *en-deçà* of being, which Lingis translates as the "hither side," see Emmanuel Levinas, *Autrement qu'être, ou au-delà de l'essence*, 2d ed. (The Hague: Martinus Nijhoff, 1978), p. 8 n. 4; in English, *Otherwise than Being, or Beyond Essence*, trans. Alphonso Lingis (Dordrecht: Kluwer Academic, 1991), p. 187 n. 5.—Trans.]

9. Paul Valéry himself also belongs to the "national literatures" noted in Levinas's lecture "The Same and the Other," on December 12, 1975. It is from the "Song of the Columns" ["Cantique des colonnes"] in *Charmes* that the following two verses come: "A deep long since it is, / Never long since enough!" See *Paul Valéry: Poems*, trans. David Paul (Princeton, N.J.: Princeton University Press, 1971), pp. 122–27.

Glory of the Infinite and Witnessing

1. According to the meaning of time as conceived in the first course, "Death and Time."

2. Genesis 3:8–10: "And they heard the sound of the Lord God [*Yahweh Elohim*] walking in the garden in the cool of the day, and the man and his wife hid themselves from the presence of the Lord God among the trees of the garden. But the Lord God called to the man, and said to him, 'Where are you?' And he said, 'I heard the sound of thee in the gar-

den, and I was afraid, because I am naked, and I hid myself." *The New Oxford Annotated Bible with the Apocrypha*, revised standard version, ed. Herbert G. May and Bruce Metzger (New York: Oxford University Press, 1977). [Translation modified to remain consistent with the French translation.—Trans.]

3. In regard to this, see the invaluable pages from chapter 5 of *Otherwise than Being*, which revisit a lecture entitled "Truth of Disclosure and Truth of Testimony." [An English translation of the lecture appears in *Emmanuel Levinas: Basic Philosophical Writings*, ed. and trans. Adriaan T. Peperzak, Simon Critchley, and Robert Bernasconi (Bloomington: Indiana University Press, 1996), pp. 97–107. This lecture is developed in Emmanuel Levinas, *Autrement qu'être, ou au-delà de l'essence*, 2d ed. (The Hague: Martinus Nijhoff, 1978), pp. 167–94; in English, *Otherwise than Being, or Beyond Essence*, trans. Alphonso Lingis (Dordrecht: Kluwer Academic, 1991), chapter 5, "Subjectivity and Infinity," §§ 1 and 2, pp. 131–52. Also see *Otherwise than Being*, p. 188 n. 3: "A discovery of being to itself, truth, which should not take anything from being, also should not add anything. Otherwise being would show itself only to be already altered by the event of the discovery. Truth would prevent truth."—Trans.]

4. According to Kierkegaard's theory of *stages*—which Levinas admired for the way in which Kierkegaard expressed *the ambiguity of transcendence*, but which he criticized for having understood ethics poorly. See the two texts on Kierkegaard in Emmanuel Levinas, *Noms propres*, (Montpellier: Fata Morgana, 1976), pp. 77–87, 88–92. In English, "Kierkegaard: Existence and Ethics" and "A Propos of 'Kierkegaard vivant,'" in Emmanuel Levinas, *Proper Names*, trans. Michael B. Smith (Stanford, Calif.: Stanford University Press, 1996), pp. 66–74, 75–79.

5. Lamentations 3:30, "Let him give his cheek to the smiter, and be filled with insults."

6. Cited in Levinas, *Autrement qu'être*, p. 187; *Otherwise than Being*, p. 147.

Witnessing and Ethics

1. [This lecture closely resembles chapter 5, "Subjectivity and Infinity," §§ b–e, in Emmanuel Levinas, *Autrement qu'être, ou au-delà de l'essence*, 2d ed. (The Hague: Martinus Nijhoff, 1978); in English, *Otherwise than Being, or Beyond Essence*, trans. Alphonso Lingis (Dordrecht: Kluwer Academic, 1991).—Trans.]

2. [There is no simple translation of the pronominal form of (*se*) *passer*, which is used to express a process or event as it unfolds. *Se passer* can also be synonymous for "being" (*être*) in the active, verbal sense where it is comparable to "becoming." Significant here is the emphasis placed on *se*. This refers to Levinas's use of a third-person pronoun for the Infinite, which—like the Latin substantive "Illeity" employed in *Otherwise than Being* to designate the Infinite—here denotes neither a being nor a person or personality. See, for example, Levinas, *Otherwise than Being*, p. 14: "'*Se passer*' . . . is for us a valuable expression in which the *self* (*se*) figures as in a past that bypasses itself, as in aging without 'active synthesis.'" Or again, ibid., p. 12: "Illeity lies outside the 'thou' and the thematization of objects. {It} indicates a way of concerning me without entering into conjunction with me." Also see ibid., p. 16.—Trans.]

3. [This can be said as well for Levinas's expression *à-Dieu.*—Trans.]

4. See above, note 2 for the present lecture.

5. In a few lines, this paragraph gives us the red thread of the reflection in Levinas, *Otherwise than Being*.

6. [Jeremiah 22:15–16, cited from *The New Oxford Annotated Bible with the Apocrypha*, revised standard version, ed. Herbert G. May and Bruce Metzger (New York: Oxford University Press, 1977). The last line in the French passage reads "oracle of Yahweh!"—which remains implicit in the English version.—Trans.]

7. Matthew 25:31–40. [English translation modified for consistency with the French (citing the *Bible de Jérusalem* {Paris: Editions du Cerf, 1986}).—Trans.]

8. On the religious philosophy of Hermann Cohen, see Silvain Zac, *La philosophie religieuse de Hermann Cohen* (Paris: Vrin, 1984).

9. [See Levinas, *Autrement qu'être*, p. 189; *Otherwise than Being*, p. 148: "The possibility of finding, anachronously, the order in the obedience itself, and of receiving the order out of oneself, this reverting of heteronomy into autonomy, is the very way the Infinite passes itself." —Trans.]

10. The decisive remarks in Levinas, *Autrement qu'être*, p. 186 (*Otherwise than Being*, p. 146), are a counterpoint to this.

11. [Plato, *Timæus* 48a. This cause belongs to the second species of causes, that is, not "those which are endowed with mind{, which} are the workers of things fair and good," but "those which are deprived of intelligence and always produce chance effects without order or design" (ibid.

46e). The so-called *cause errante* appears in English as the "variable cause" in Plato's *Timæus* 46e.—Trans.]

12. On this remark, see the first lecture course, "Death and Time."

From Consciousness to Prophetism

1. [See above, in the present course, the lecture of December 5, 1975, "To Think God on the Basis of Ethics," note 9, on the etymology of the Hebrew *pa'am*, "to agitate."—Trans.]

2. *Time* as beating—as the beating of the Other *within* the Same—is precisely what the first course, "Death and Time," was attempting to think.

3. [For a discussion of the accusative in *me voici*, which is lost in "here *I* am," see above in this course, note 8 for the lecture of March 12, 1976, "The Extra-Ordinary Subjectivity of Responsibility."—Trans.]

4. "The word God is an overwhelming semantic event that subdues the subversion worked by illeity. The glory of the Infinite shuts itself up in a word and becomes a being. But it already undoes its dwelling and unsays itself without vanishing into nothingness. . . . A Said unique in its kind, it does not narrowly espouse grammatical categories like a noun (neither proper nor common noun), and does not incline exactly to logical rules, like a meaning (being an excluded middle between being and nothingness)." Emmanuel Levinas, *Autrement qu'être, ou au-delà de l'essence*, 2d ed. (The Hague: Martinus Nijhoff, 1978), p. 193; in English, *Otherwise than Being, or Beyond Essence*, trans. Alphonso Lingis (Dordrecht: Kluwer Academic, 1991), p. 151.

5. [With the noun *entente* and the verb *entendre*, Levinas is playing on three related meanings: an act of hearing (*entendre*), an understanding (*entendre*), and, significantly for the responsibility from which "God is not separable," an alliance (*une entente*).—Trans.]

6. On this point, see Emmanuel Levinas, "La réalité et son ombre," *Les temps modernes*, Nov. 1948, and Levinas, *Autrement qu'être*, p. 191 n. 21; *Otherwise than Being*, p. 199 n. 21. ["La réalité et son ombre" appeared in English as "Reality and Its Shadow," trans. A. Lingis, in *Collected Philosophical Papers of Emmanuel Levinas* (Dordrecht: Kluwer Academic, 1993), pp. 1–13.—Trans.]

7. [It is not clear in the original whether the "word" referred to here is "glory" or "God." From what follows, it appears that it is God; if glory undoes its abode in the word given it, the word "God" would do so emphatically.—Trans.]

8. [For a parallel discussion of the philosophical discourse on God, see "God and Philosophy," in Emmanuel Levinas, *Of God Who Comes to Mind,* trans. Bettina Bergo (Stanford, Calif.: Stanford University Press, 1998), pp. 56ff.—Trans.]

9. See above in this course, the lecture of November 14, 1975, "Being and Meaning": "It is Heidegger who poses the question 'How has God come into philosophy?'"

10. [See Immanuel Kant, *Critique of Practical Reason,* trans. Lewis White Beck (New York: Macmillan, 1993), p. 169.—Trans.]

11. The *opinion* of faith is its δόξα, in the Platonic sense, but also in the Husserlian sense, that is, its *thetic* essence and its nature as a *belief* that *posits* what it believes.

In Praise of Insomnia

1. This is because faith *is* naive in that it is doxic, or cannot keep itself from opining (see above in this course, n. 11 for the lecture "From Consciousness to Prophetism," April 30, 1976). This is, after all, the reason why nothing could be more foreign to Levinas than the Kantian claim that consists in "deny{ing} *knowledge,* in order to obtain a place for *faith.*" Immanuel Kant, "Preface to the Second Edition," *Critique of Pure Reason,* trans. Norman Kemp Smith {New York: Saint Martin's, 1963}, p. 29. The French translation of this Kant passage reads: "abolishing *knowledge* in order to obtain a place for *belief* {*Glauben*}."

2. [For a discussion of this notion of wakefulness, see "From Consciousness to Wakefulness: Starting from Husserl," in Emmanuel Levinas, *Of God Who Comes to Mind,* trans. Bettina Bergo (Stanford, Calif.: Stanford University Press, 1998), pp. 15–32. The essay was first published in French in the Dutch journal *Bijdragen* 35 (1974).—Trans.]

3. We note here that the analysis of insomnia—which Levinas's *Existence and Existents* [first published as a book in 1947; second edition in 1978—Trans.] proposed and which is again attested by the lines from *Otherwise than Being* cited above in Part II, in the lecture of February 27, 1976, "Freedom and Responsibility" (see note 11 for that lecture)—is turned back like a glove. On this point I [Rolland] refer the reader to an older study: Jacques Rolland, "Pour une approche de la question du neutre," *Exercices de la patience,* no. 2 (1931): 37ff.

4. [The concept of wakefulness or vigil, *la veille,* whose verbal form is *veiller,* is here contrasted with waking up, or *le réveil.* Waking up would here be like coming back to everyday, thematizing consciousness. Wake-

fulness precedes waking up, just as it also precedes falling asleep, as a passive openness that neither thematizes nor reflects upon itself. Wakefulness is thus a nonintentional "consciousness." Below, Levinas will use "waking up" as synonymous with the disturbance of the other-in-the-same. In this regard, see Emmanuel Levinas, *Autrement qu'être, ou au-delà de l'essence*, 2d ed. (The Hague: Martinus Nijhoff, 1978), pp. 209ff.; in English, *Otherwise than Being, or Beyond Essence*, trans. Alphonso Lingis (Dordrecht: Kluwer Academic, 1991), pp. 164ff.—Trans.]

5. Song of Songs 5:2.

6. [For a discussion of the event of the enucleation of the subject in insomnia, see Levinas, *Otherwise than Being*, chap. 2, sec. 4, "Saying as Exposure to Another," pp. 49ff.—Trans.]

7. [See ibid.—Trans.]

8. [Or that which is set apart from being among, or close to, entities.—Trans.]

9. [Regarding "synopsia," see above in Part I, note 5 for "To Conclude: Questioning Again," the lecture of May 21, 1976.—Trans.]

10. This conveys exactly the Levinasian reading of Heidegger. "Déformé et mal compris?" {"These lines . . . owe much to Heidegger. Deformed and ill understood?"}, asks note 28 on page 189 of Levinas, *Otherwise than Being*. It thereupon responds: "At least this deformation will not have been a way to deny the debt. Nor this debt a reason to forget."

[For a discussion of *Sammeln*, or gathering, see, for example, Martin Heidegger, *The Principle of Reason*, trans. Reginald Lilly (Bloomington: Indiana University Press, 1991), p. 107: "λέγειν . . . means to gather, to lay one beside the other." Also see Heidegger's "Anaximander Fragment": "The Being of beings is gathered λέγεσθαι in the ultimacy of its destiny. The essence of Being hitherto disappears, its truth still veiled. The history of Being is gathered in this departure. The gathering in this departure, as the gathering λόγος at the outermost point ἔσχατον of its essence . . . is the eschatology of Being." Martin Heidegger, "The Anaximander Fragment," in *Early Greek Thinking: Martin Heidegger*, trans. David Farrell Krell and Frank A. Capuzzi (San Francisco: Harper and Row, 1984), pp. 18ff.

Levinas's debate is with Heidegger's thought, over and above that of Kant. In Heidegger's essay "On the Essence of Truth," we find many of the Heideggerian concepts and terms that Levinas would rethink. Heidegger states: "Being as a whole reveals itself as φυσίς, 'nature,' . . . in the sense of *emerging presence* {*aufgehendes Anwesen*}. History begins only when beings themselves are expressly *drawn up* into their unconcealment and conserved in it. . . . 'Truth' is not a feature of correct propositions which are asserted of an 'object' by a human 'subject' and then 'are valid' somewhere . . . rather, truth is disclosure of beings through which an openness essentially *unfolds* {*west*}." (Martin Heidegger, "On the Essence of Truth," trans. John Sallis, in *Martin Heidegger: Basic Writings from "Being and Time" (1927) to "The Task of Thinking" (1964)*, ed. David Farrell Krell {New York: Harper and Row, 1977}, pp. 129, 131.) For Heidegger, as for Levinas, "experience" is never the last word on consciousness. A level of "being attuned" or "exposedness to beings as a whole" underlies all experience and feeling.—Trans.]

Outside of Experience: The Cartesian Idea of the Infinite

1. This is Rudolf Otto's thesis in his well-known work *The Idea of the Holy: An Inquiry into the Non-rational Factor in the Idea of the Divine and Its Relation to the Rational*, trans. John W. Harvey (New York: Oxford University Press, 1968).

2. Because *intentionality* remains.

3. Of which Pascal said, "it [concupiscence] can diminish every day, but it cannot come to an end." See Blaise Pascal, *Pensées et opuscules* (Paris: Hachette, 1971). In English, *Pensées*, trans. A. J. Krailsheimer (New York: Penguin, 1995).

4. See Martin Heidegger, *Being and Time*, trans. John Maquarrie and Edward Robinson (New York: Harper and Row, 1962), § 69, p. 405, for an approach to *Sein lassen*, or "letting be," that is ontological.

5. Slumber *is* dogmatic, in the same way that dogmatism is a slumber; compare the discussion in the preceding lecture.

6. See René Descartes, *Selected Philosophical Writings*, trans. John Cottingham, Robert Stroothoff, and Dugald Murdoch (New York: Cambridge University Press, 1988), p. 86: "But since the habit of holding on to old opinions cannot be set aside so quickly, I should like to stop here and meditate for some time on this new knowledge I have gained, so as to fix it more deeply in my memory."

7. Ibid., p. 94.

8. This "Socratic scandal" is likewise that upon which Kierkegaard meditates, at least in the second chapter of Søren Kierkegaard, *Philosophical Fragments, or a Fragment of Philosophy*, trans. Howard V. Hong (Princeton, N.J.: Princeton University Press, 1962).

A God "Transcendent to the Point of Absence"

1. René Descartes, *Œuvres et lettres* (Paris: Bibliothèque de la Pléiade, Gallimard, 1953), p. 299: "It [the idea of the infinite] is born and produced with me from the moment at which I was created." [This sentence is from the "Third Meditation" in Descartes's *Meditations on First Philosophy*. The English translation in René Descartes, *Selected Philosophical Writings*, trans. John Cottingham, Robert Stroothoff, and Dugald Murdoch (New York: Cambridge University Press, 1988), p. 97, reads as follows: "The only remaining alternative is that it is innate in me, just as the idea of myself is innate in me."—Trans.]

2. See in this regard a few decisive lines from *Otherwise than Being*:

> The astonishing Saying which is a responsibility of another is against "the winds and tides" of being, is an interruption of essence, a disinterestedness imposed with a good violence. But one has to say that . . . this astonishing Saying comes to light through the very gravity of the questions that assail it. It must spread out and assemble itself into *essence*, posit itself, be hypostatized, become an eon in consciousness and knowledge, let itself be seen, undergo the ascendancy of being. Ethics itself, in its *Saying* which is a responsibility, requires this hold. But it is also necessary that the *Saying* call for philosophy in order that the light that is created [i.e., with the Saying] not congeal into *essence* what is beyond essence, and that the hypostasis of an *eon* not be set up as an idol. Philosophy makes this astonishing adventure—showing and recounting as an essence—intelligible, by loosening this grip of being. The philosopher's effort and his position contra-nature consist, while showing the hither [or in-] side, in immediately reducing the eon which triumphs in the *Said*, and in its showing, and, despite the reduction, retaining an echo of the reduced *Said* in the form of ambiguity, of dia-chronic expression. For the *Saying* is both an affirmation and a retraction of the *Said*. The reduction could not be effected simply by parentheses that are, on the contrary, an effect [*œuvre*] of writing. It is the ethical interruption of essence that energizes the reduction.

Emmanuel Levinas, *Autrement qu'être, ou au-delà de l'essence*, 2d ed. (The Hague: Martinus Nijhoff, 1978), p. 56; in English, *Otherwise than Being, or Beyond Essence*, trans. Alphonso Lingis (Dordrecht: Kluwer Academic, 1991), p. 43 [translation modified for consistency with original—Trans.].

3. [Levinas is playing on the Latin infinitive *mostrare* and the noun *monstrum*—"to show" and "what is shown"—whose French cognates are more frequently used to denote the event of showing than are the English ones.—Trans.]

4. Micah 1:3–4.

5. In the words of *Totality and Infinity*, this is a metaphysical desire that "does not long to return, for it is desire for a land not of our birth." Emmanuel Levinas, *Totalité et infini: Essai sur l'extériorité* (The Hague: Martinus Nijhoff, 1961), pp. 3; in English, *Totality and Infinity: An Essay on Exteriority*, trans. Alphonso Lingis (Pittsburgh: Duquesne University Press, 1969), pp. 33–34.

6. Plato, *The Symposium* 192c–d.

7. Ibid. 193a. [I follow the French to preserve Levinas's meaning. The English translation reads, "when we are longing for and following after that primeval wholeness, we say we are in love."—Trans.]

8. Ibid. 192c–d.

9. Ibid. 201e–203d.

10. This is why, despite the consent he gives to Jean-Luc Marion, Levinas always remained reticent about the term "love." See Levinas's responses to the Christian philosopher Marion, in Emmanuel Levinas, *Autrement que savoir* (Paris: Editions Osiris, 1987). [This work has not been translated into English.—Trans.]

11. See above in this part, the lecture entitled "Transcendence, Idolatry, and Secularization," February 6, 1976, note 1.

12. The undesirable other is the other person received "not in the appeal of his face, but in the nakedness and misery of his flesh!" See "Exigeant Judaisme," in Emmanuel Levinas, *L'au-delà du verset* (Paris: Minuit, 1982); in English, "Demanding Judaism," in Emmanuel Levinas, *Beyond the Verse: Talmudic Readings and Lectures*, trans. Gary D. Mole (Bloomington: Indiana University Press, 1994), p. 6.

13. [Levinas is again playing on the notion of erotic or everyday sensuous ecstasy and the Heideggerian *Ekstase* or "ecstasis," understood as the essence of Dasein's temporality, or the temporality of intentionality; that is, Dasein's "primordial 'outside-of-itself' in and for itself." See Martin Heidegger, *Being and Time*, trans. John Maquarrie and Edward Robinson (New York: Harper and Row, 1962), p. 377.—Trans.]

14. This enormous risk, which transcendence must run in order not to be tied up, no doubt explains Levinas's admiration for Blanchot. In Blanchot, the Neutral expresses the *there is*. We will cite at length an important passage from Blanchot, the final sentence of which refers directly to this risk for transcendence, but whose entirety sheds a different light on many of the themes touched on in this course:

> I think that the work and thought of Maurice Blanchot may be interpreted in two directions. On the one hand, this work announces a loss of meaning, a

dissemination of discourse, as though one found oneself at the extreme point of nihilism, where nothingness itself can no longer be contemplated in tranquillity but becomes equivocal for the ear that listens to it. Meaning, tied to language, and becoming literature in which it was to have accomplished and exalted itself, would bring us back to insignificant repetition [*ressassement insignifiant*]—more deprived of meaning than the wreckage of structures or the elements liable to enter them. We are thus doomed to the inhuman, to this frightening thing that is the Neutral [*à l'effrayant du Neutre*]. That is a first direction. But note here, on the other hand, the world from which Blanchot's literary space is excluded. A world that no human suffering can keep from being ordered, a world that is set up willy nilly (no matter! this does not impede Knowledge but make possible a Knowledge freed of all ideology); a world that is totalized in the indifference of Dostoyevski's "All is permitted," and not because of its atheism but because of its spirituality: the internalization of all laws makes us lose the Difference. . . . In truth nothing is better ordered in its synchronous totality than a world such as this. Nothing better suffices it.

   Of this world, Blanchot recalls that its totality is not total; that the coherent discourse it boasts never catches up with an other discourse that it does not manage to silence, that this other discourse is disturbed by an uninterrupted noise, and that a difference does not let the world sleep, and disturbs the order in which being and non-being are ordered in a dialectic. This Neutral is neither someone nor even something. It is but an excluded *third* term [*tiers* exclu], which, properly speaking, *not* so much as *is*. Yet there is in it more transcendence than that opened up by any world behind the worlds. (Emmanuel Levinas, *Sur Maurice Blanchot* [Montpellier: Fata Morgana, 1975], pp. 50–52)

   15. This is a nobility that "*ignores* what is not noble," in the same way that "certain monotheists do not recognize, while knowing, what is not the highest." Levinas, *Autrement qu'être*, p. 223; *Otherwise than Being*, p. 177.

Postscript

   1. [Emmanuel Levinas, *La mort et le temps* (Paris: Editions de l'Herne, 1991). This work has not yet been translated into English.—Trans.]

   2. See Plato, *Timæus* 37d.

   3. Emmanuel Levinas, *Autrement qu'être, ou au-delà de l'essence*, 2d ed. (The Hague: Martinus Nijhoff, 1978), pp. 131–32; in English, *Otherwise than Being, or Beyond Essence*, trans. Alphonso Lingis (Dordrecht: Kluwer Academic, 1991), pp. 103–4 [translation modified—Trans.].

   4. "Heidegger accustomed us to seek in the history of philosophy the

very history of being. His entire work consists in bringing metaphysics back to the history of being," states the first lecture course. (Let us note here that the pagination of citations from these lectures will not be given, since the lectures immediately precede this postscript.) This remark finds a response in another statement from Levinas: "However radical the destruction of metaphysics may be, in Heidegger's thought of being, it is still Western metaphysics that remains the soil his thought runs over or works." Emmanuel Levinas, *Outside the Subject*, trans. Michael B. Smith (Stanford, Calif.: Stanford University Press, 1994), p. 91. The original French is "De la signification du sens," in Emmanuel Levinas, *Heidegger et la question de Dieu* (Paris: Grasset, 1980), p. 239; reprinted in Emmanuel Levinas, *Hors sujet* (Montpellier: Fata Morgana, 1987), p. 138.

5. See Emmanuel Levinas's dissertation, published under the title *La théorie de l'intuition dans la phénoménologie de Husserl* (1930; reprint, Paris: Vrin, 1963); in English, *The Theory of Intuition in Husserl's Phenomenology*, trans. André Orianne (Evanston, Ill.: Northwestern University Press, 1973). [The other works to which Rolland refers here have been published in the following editions: Emmanuel Levinas, *En découvrant l'existence avec Husserl et Heidegger* (Paris: Vrin, 1949); in English, *Discovering Existence with Husserl*, trans. Richard A. Cohen and Michael B. Smith (Evanston, Ill.: Northwestern University Press, 1998). Finally, Levinas's lengthy introduction to Stéphane Mosès's *Système et révélation: La philosophie de Franz Rosenzweig* (Paris: Editions du Seuil, 1982); in English, Stéphane Mosès, *System and Revelation: The Philosophy of Franz Rosenzweig*, trans. Catherine Tihanyi (Detroit: Wayne State University Press, 1992). The introduction to Mosès's book is one of Levinas's two longest works on Rosenzweig and his thought, the other being "Franz Rosenzweig: Une pensée juive moderne," first published in *Revue de théologie et de philosophie* (Lausanne) 1965; reprinted in *Cahiers de la nuit surveillée*, 1982, no. 1; reprinted again in Levinas, *Hors sujet*. In English, "Franz Rosenzweig: A Modern Jewish Thinker," in Levinas, *Outside the Subject*, pp. 49–56.—Trans.]

6. [Emmanuel Levinas, *Totalité et infini: Essai sur l'extériorité* (The Hague: Martinus Nijhoff, 1961), p. xvi; in English, *Totality and Infinity: An Essay on Exteriority*, trans. Alphonso Lingis (Pittsburgh: Duquesne University Press, 1969), p. 28.—Trans.]

7. Emmanuel Levinas, "Un langage qui nous est familier," *Cahiers de la nuit surveillée*, 1984, no. 3: 327, Rolland's italics.

8. It was in 1961 that Levinas occupied his first position as a professor

at the University of Poitiers. We find, of course, instances of his teaching in the various collections of Talmudic lessons, but there it is evidently not a matter of Levinas's philosophical teaching.

9. "The experience of pure being is at the same time the experience of its internal antagonism and of the evasion necessitated by it. Nevertheless, the way out toward which it pushes us is not death." Emmanuel Levinas, *De l'évasion*, ed. and annotated by Jacques Rolland (Montpellier: Fata Morgana, 1982), p. 90.

10. Published first in the journal *Fontaine* in 1947, this essay was reprinted in two editions by the Librairie philosophique J. Vrin: Emmanuel Levinas, *De l'existence à l'existant* (Paris, 1947; 2d ed., 1978). [The first edition was published in English as *Existence and Existents*, trans. Alphonso Lingis (The Hague: Martinus Nijhoff, 1978).—Trans.]

11. First published in Jean Wahl, ed., *Le choix, le monde, l'existence* (Paris: Arthaud, 1948), the essay was reprinted as a separate work, Emmanuel Levinas, *Le temps et l'autre* (Montpellier: Fata Morgana, 1979). It is the latter that I [Rolland] am using here; see p. 90 in that edition. [The essay was translated into English by Richard A. Cohen in Emmanuel Levinas, *"Time and the Other" and Additional Essays* (Pittsburgh: Duquesne University Press, 1987).—Trans.]

12. Levinas, *Le temps et l'autre*, p. 17; *Time and the Other*, p. 39.

13. Ibid., p. 56; Eng., p. 70. For this notion of light, a few lines from *Existence and Existents* are worth citing here:

> Light, whether it emanates from the sensible or from the intelligible sun, is since Plato said to be a condition for all beings. Thought, volition and sentiment, however far they may be from intellection, are first experience, intuition, clear vision or clarity seeking to come about. . . . Whatever may be the physico-mathematical explanation of the light which fills our universe, phenomenologically it is a condition for phenomena, that is, for meaning. In existing an object exists for someone, is destined for someone, already leans toward an inwardness and, without being absorbed in it, gives itself. What comes from the outside—illuminated—is comprehended, that is, comes from ourselves. Light makes objects into a world, that is, makes them belong to us. Property constitutes the world: through the light the world is given and apprehended. (Levinas, *De l'existence à l'existant*, 2d ed. (1978), pp. 74–75; *Existence and Existents*, pp. 47–48)

14. Levinas, *Le temps et l'autre*, p. 56; *Time and the Other*, p. 70.

15. Ibid., p. 47; Eng., p. 64.

16. Ibid., p. 57; Eng., p. 70.

17. Ibid., p. 63; Eng., p. 74.

18. Ibid., p. 59; Eng., p. 71.

19. Ibid., p. 64; Eng., p. 77 [translation modified for consistency with the text—Trans.].

20. Ibid., p. 68; Eng., p. 79, Rolland's italics.

21. Ibid., p. 67; Eng., p. 78 [translation modified—Trans.].

22. Ibid.; Eng., pp. 78–79 [translation modified—Trans.].

23. Ibid., pp. 68–69, Rolland's italics; Eng., p. 79 [translation modified for consistency with the text—Trans.].

24. See Richard A. Cohen, "La non-in-différence dans la pensée d'Emmanuel Levinas et de Franz Rosenzweig," *Cahier de l'Herne*, 1991, no. 60: 343; reprinted in Catherine Chalier and Miguel Abensour, eds., *Cahier de l'Herne: Emmanuel Levinas* (Paris: Editions de l'Herne, 1991), pp. 380–93; and Levinas, "Franz Rosenzweig," *Cahiers de la nuit surveillée*, 1982, no. 1: 68.

25. The citations from Hegel and Bergson are found in the lectures, with accompanying references.

26. Levinas, *Le temps et l'autre*, p. 58; *Time and the Other*, p. 71.

27. See Levinas, *Totalité et infini*, p. 6; *Totality and Infinity*, p. 36.

28. Levinas, *Autrement qu'être*, p. 67; *Otherwise than Being*, p. 52.

29. Ibid., p. 147; Eng., p. 116.

30. Ibid., p. 67; Eng., p. 52.

31. Ibid., p. 73; Eng., p. 57 [translation modified for consistency with the text—Trans.].

32. Levinas, *Totalité et infini*, p. 9; *Totality and Infinity*, p. 39 [translation modified for consistency with the text—Trans.].

33. Levinas, *Autrement qu'être*, p. 119; *Otherwise than Being*, p. 93.

34. This way for death to signify on the basis of the beating of the Other within the Same—or *as* that beating—was admirably expressed by Dostoyevski in *Crime and Punishment*. More precisely, by way of the structure of the first part of the novel. That part narrates the way in which Raskolnikov advances toward the realization of his project, the assassination of the usurious old landlady, and this advancement is carried out by way of the encounter of the other, infinitely repeated under different figures. Now, it is these encounters that produce Raskolnikov's progression and, in that sense, weave together the time of the narrative. More profoundly, they write the time as such, that is, as the beating of the Other-within-the-Same. They thus write, or signify, temporality and, moreover, inscribe death into the signification of temporality, since the

first part of the novel opens upon the murder surpassing its own intention of being a rational assassination. For all these questions, see Jacques Rolland, *Dostoïevski: La question de l'Autre* (Lagrasse: Verdier, 1983).

35. In homage to Jean-Luc Marion.

36. Levinas, *Autrement qu'être*, p. x; *Otherwise than Being*, p. xlii.

37. See above in Part II, the first note to the lecture of January 30, 1976, "Ethical Subjectivity."

38. See Emmanuel Levinas, *De Dieu qui vient à l'idée*, 2d ed. (Paris: Librairie philosophique J. Vrin, 1986), p. 7; in English, *Of God Who Comes to Mind*, trans. Bettina Bergo (Stanford, Calif.: Stanford University Press, 1998), p. xi.

39. As Heidegger puts it at the very beginning of the lecture "Die onto-theo-logische Verfassung der Metaphysik," in Martin Heidegger, *Identität und Differenz* (Pfullingen: G. Neske, 1957); in English, "The Onto-theological Constitution of Metaphysics," *Identity and Difference*, trans. Joan Stambaugh (New York: Harper and Row, 1969). See above in Part II, Levinas's lecture of November 7, 1975, "Beginning with Heidegger."

40. It is thus legitimate to translate the traditional *kodesh baruch ou*, by which God is named in the rabbinical literature, as "The Holy One, blessed be he."

41. A difference that is non-in-difference, as the lectures teach us.

42. Levinas, *Autrement qu'être*, p. 10; *Otherwise than Being*, p. 8.

43. Levinas, *De l'évasion*.

44. ["God and Philosophy" is published in Levinas, *Of God Who Comes to Mind.*—Trans.]

45. Emmanuel Levinas, *Noms propres* (Montpellier: Fata Morgana, 1976), p. 127; in English, *Proper Names*, trans. Michael B. Smith (Stanford, Calif.: Stanford University Press, 1996), p. 87.

MERIDIAN

Crossing Aesthetics